Learning, Teaching & Development

Learning, Teaching & Development

Strategies for Action

Edited by
Lyn Ashmore & Denise Robinson

Los Angeles | London | New Delhi
Singapore | Washington DC

Los Angeles | London | New Delhi
Singapore | Washington DC

SAGE Publications Ltd
1 Oliver's Yard
55 City Road
London EC1Y 1SP

SAGE Publications Inc.
2455 Teller Road
Thousand Oaks, California 91320

SAGE Publications India Pvt Ltd
B 1/I 1 Mohan Cooperative Industrial Area
Mathura Road
New Delhi 110 044

SAGE Publications Asia-Pacific Pte Ltd
3 Church Street
#10-04 Samsung Hub
Singapore 049483

Editor: James Clark
Assistant editor: Rachael Plant
Production editor: Nicola Marshall
Copyeditor: Gemma Marren
Proofreader: Fabienne Pedroletti-Gray
Indexer: Silvia Benvenuto
Marketing manager: Dilhara Attygalle
Cover design: Wendy Scott
Typeset by: C&M Digitals (P) Ltd, Chennai, India
Printed and bound by
CPI Group (UK) Ltd, Croydon, CR0 4YY

MIX
Paper from responsible sources
FSC® C013604
FSC www.fsc.org

First published 2015

Library of Congress Control Number: 2014933338

British Library Cataloguing in Publication data

A catalogue record for this book is available from the British Library

ISBN 978-1-4462-8211-3
ISBN 978-1-4462-8212-0 (pbk)

CONTENTS

ABOUT THE EDITORS

Lyn Ashmore is a Senior Lecturer and teacher educator at the University of Huddersfield and is course leader for the MA in Learning and Development Management. She has a broad range of experience in human resources and learning and development and has provided consultancy services in staff development and facilitated integration of cultural understanding and improved performance in a number of organizations. Lyn has worked extensively to develop and promote learning and development for socially excluded communities, focusing on empowerment and access in both an educational and employment context. She has a great passion for equality of opportunities and access to higher education and widening participation and strives to enable students from disadvantaged communities to become confident in challenging and confronting some of the myths that surround high education. Lyn has co-authored a book on *The Reflective Practitioner in Professional Education* and has also co-written a chapter in J. Avis, R. Fisher and R. Thompson, *Teaching in Lifelong Learning: A Guide to Theory and Practice*. Her research interests are learning and development, reflective practice, personal and professional development, strategies for developing staff within organizations and methods for evaluating learning strategies. She is a Fellow of the Higher Education Academy and a Fellow of the Institute of Leadership and Management.

Denise Robinson is the Director of the Consortium for Post Compulsory Education and Training, an FE teacher education partnership, and Huddersfield University Distributed Centre for Excellence in Teacher Training (HUDCETT). She works with the 23 partner colleges who deliver the University of Huddersfield's Certificate in Education and postgraduate teacher education courses for the FE and skills sector. Denise worked in FE for 25 years before moving into higher education to focus on FE teacher education. Previously, Denise taught on a variety of courses including access, women's taster, A levels, technician and open learning courses. In her present role she initiates and develops activities to support the education and training of teachers in the sector, as well as the teacher educators themselves. Denise is the editor of the journal, *Teaching in Lifelong Learning* (http://consortium.hud.ac.uk/journal/). She is also on the editorial board of the journal *Research in Post Compulsory Education*. Denise has co-written a number of chapters in J. Avis, R. Fisher and R. Thompson, *Teaching in Lifelong Learning: A Guide to Theory and Practice* as well as co-authoring the chapter 'Professional and personal development' in *FDTL Voices: Drawing from Learning and Teaching Projects*. Denise has worked for LLUK and Ofsted; she is a National Teaching Fellow of the Higher Education Academy.

ABOUT THE CONTRIBUTORS

Shailesh Appukuttan is the Technical Development Manager for the Consortium for PCET at University of Huddersfield. He has been the technical lead and consultant for many national collaborative projects with various Higher and Further Education, Work-Based, and Adult and Community Learning institutions. He has designed, developed and provided training and support for various web based applications and online communities. He has also been an external academic course validator. His areas of research include effective and efficient use of technology in learning, teaching and research, addressing risks and sustainability issues of implementing technical solutions. He is a Certified Member of Association for Learning Technology and a Fellow of the Higher Education Academy.

Wayne Bailey has been a teacher educator for over 10 years and he has delivered on teacher education programmes with both Sheffield Hallam University and the University of Huddersfield. He began his teaching career at a small training provider in 1998, working with the long-term unemployed. From 2000 he worked at a large further education college, teaching on both further and higher education courses, specializing largely in Business Studies and Marketing A level and vocational qualifications. Since 2005 he has worked at the University of Huddersfield where he has developed a keen interest in mentoring and coaching. He currently leads on the University of Huddersfield's teacher development programme, which is aimed at HE lecturers. Wayne is a Fellow of the Higher Education Academy.

Jane Burrows is a freelance consultant with teaching experience in secondary, further, higher and adult education. She has been head of departments of humanities and teacher training in further education and has taught non-vocational adult classes for over 30 years. Jane was a Senior Lecturer in higher education and has conducted many research projects investigating the FE/HE interface. She currently divides her time between working in the UK and China, where she trains Chinese teachers. Jane is interested in active and innovative methods of delivering learning, including e-learning; in particular, the development of materials for VLEs and their application in education.

Alison Iredale is a Director of Learning at the University Campus Oldham. She leads on improvements to teaching and learning, research and scholarship and professional development. Her experience ranges from teaching and training in the further and higher education sector, private training organizations and industry. She has worked with young people and adults on a range of programmes from entry level to postgraduate degree supervision. Alison is actively engaged nationally with developments to teacher standards, holds several external appointments, and is a member or fellow of a range of professional and educational research bodies. In addition to her strategic role she reviews for a number of international journals, and maintains a strong social media presence through Twitter.

Mohammed Karolia is a Senior Lecturer and course leader for the MA in Education at the University of Huddersfield and has over 23 years' experience of teaching on a diverse range of courses allied to teacher training and a range of helping professions. As an experienced lecturer and Fellow of the Higher Education Academy, Mohammed's research interests revolve around identifying strategies which help to engage learners' enthusiasm and interest in their personal and professional development and is currently working towards completing his doctorate which aims to explore and evaluate the use of metaphors as means of enhancing reflective practice.

Kathryn Lavender has worked as an Academic Skills Tutor for Higher Education in the FE sector since 2009. Her role includes teaching academic writing, critical thinking and reflective practice. Along with a colleague, she developed the first academic and study skills facility in the college specifically for HE students. Her experience also includes developing a range of transition and progression activities for students with vocational and non-traditional backgrounds. Kathryn's particular interests in teaching and learning in the FE sector are around teaching HE in FE and adult learning in vocational contexts; she is currently working towards a PhD in this area at the University of Huddersfield.

Louise Mycroft is a teacher educator at the Northern College for Adult and Residential Education in Barnsley, South Yorkshire. A former community health development worker and Jill of all trades, she shares the College's mission of transformational education, developing – via the TeachNorthern Programme – initial teacher training and continuing professional development which focuses on teaching for a social purpose. Louise uses popular social media to sustain a Community of Praxis, which brings together students, graduates, colleagues and critical friends from across the globe. She is interested in reflexion, diversity, democratic education and rhizomatic learning, the concept of community as curriculum.

Kevin Orr is Reader in Work and Learning at the University of Huddersfield where he has been since 2006. Prior to this he was a teacher for 16 years in further education (FE) colleges around Manchester, mainly on ESOL and teacher educator courses. He still maintains a keen interest in FE and his PhD thesis was on the dissemination of ideas about teaching in colleges. Both his teaching and research centre on continuing professional development and he is course leader for the Doctor of Education course. His most recent research focuses on vocational pedagogy.

Cheryl Reynolds is a Senior Lecturer and teacher educator at the University of Huddersfield. Her background is in the teaching of Biology and Sports Science in further education. She currently manages the online delivery of teacher training provision across 28 further and higher education centres across the north of England. Her research interests focus on the way that social media can contribute to education. She recently contributed to the completion of the JISC EBEAM project, which evaluated the benefits of electronic assessment management and she is the winner of the Learning Without Frontiers HE/FE Innovator of the Year, 2012 and a Fellow of the Higher Education Academy.

Glenys Richardson has worked in further education since 1981, starting out as a part-time teacher of General Studies for day-release students. Her teaching experience includes Business, Communications and Education, from Level 1 to Masters level. She has held various management posts including leading on A level and HE development; running a Business Services Unit and as the Head of Division of Professional Studies. In 2010 she returned to teaching and has particularly enjoyed working for Huddersfield University in China on their Vocational Education and Training Programme. Glenys is currently the Programme Leader for Education at North Lindsey College.

Ian Rushton is a Senior Lecturer in the School of Education and Professional Development at the University of Huddersfield. Following 28 years as an engineer in the road haulage industry, he taught a range of motor vehicle and engineering courses in a general FE college for nine years before moving to teacher education, HE in FE and the Advanced Practitioner role in the same college for a further five years before joining the University of Huddersfield in 2008. Ian has co-authored a book on reflective practice in the lifelong learning sector and his research interests lie in the borderlands of critical theory, alternative pedagogies and initial teacher education. Ian is a Fellow of the Higher Education Academy.

Nena Skrbic has been a teacher in the FE and skills sector for 12 years. Her doctorate is in English Language and Literature. She has taught English to ESOL learners and native speakers in an FE environment from 2002 to 2004. Her journey into training other teachers began in 2005. Training other teachers gives her an opportunity to work with practitioners from diverse settings. One of Nena's key research interests is how teacher education curricula can be adapted to meet the wide range of interests, cultural backgrounds and needs that trainees in the FE and skills sector have. Currently, Nena is Curriculum Area Manager for Teacher Education at Leeds City College and teaches on the PGDipE, PGCE, Certificate in Education and BA (Hons) Education and Training programmes.

Anne Temple Clothier (SFHEA) is currently employed as a Teacher Fellow and Senior Lecturer in Education at Leeds Beckett University. With over 20 years' experience in academic continuous professional development spanning both FE and HE, the Teacher Fellowship role was awarded as recognition of her contribution to curriculum design. Current interests include ways in which academic staff are responding to policy changes defining these sectors. Her research is based on the premise that changes in national government and subsequent legislative changes have provoked individual reactions from academic staff, and managing this array of individual responses poses significant challenges to corporate management.

Martyn Walker is a teacher educator and researcher at the University of Huddersfield. He is a member of the Centre for Research in Post-Compulsory Education at the university and a Fellow of the Higher Education Academy. He is a co-author, with Mike Cook and Roy Fisher, of *Teacher Education at Huddersfield 1947 to 2007: From Technical Teacher Training College to University School of Education* published by the University of Huddersfield. Martyn also co-wrote a chapter in J. Avis,

R. Fisher and R. Thompson, *Teaching in Lifelong Learning: A Guide to Theory and Practice*. His work has been widely published in scholarly journals.

Jane Weatherby has worked in a variety of non-traditional teaching and learning contexts, including a women's refuge, a centre for deaf people and a community media organization. After several years devising and teaching courses around women's studies, the media, community regeneration and social inequalities, at an adult residential college, she is now a tutor and HE co-ordinator for the college's teacher education team. She has a particular interest in gender issues, in exploring new ways of teaching and learning, and in how education impacts upon individuals to change the world.

Jane Wormald is Senior Lecturer in Education at the University of Huddersfield. Experienced in teaching in FE (contemporary dance studies, performing arts) and HE (education, learning difficulties and disabilities), she currently working closely with HE courses in FE institutions teaching teachers, trainers, community and youth workers and learning support practitioners. Her current role includes liaising with FE colleges in delivering HE courses in education and learning support. Research and teaching interests are in social learning, blended course designs, access to HE and critical education.

ACKNOWLEDGEMENTS

Our thanks go out to many people who have directly or indirectly participated in the development of this book, *Learning, Teaching and Development: Strategies for Action*. We would like to thank all the authors who have contributed to the writing of chapters. All your contributions have brought the subject to life in a way that we may not have achieved. We would also like to thank all the other people who contributed their thoughts and ideas. Thanks also go to Elaine Eastwood who has helped with administrative work and to Shailesh Appukuttan who generously offered technical help in times of need.

CHAPTER 1

INTRODUCTION

Lyn Ashmore and Denise Robinson

Learning outcomes

After reading this chapter, the reader should be able to:

- Understand how work-based learning (WBL) and adult and community learning have changed.
- Understand how the current trends in learning and development have shaped our practice.
- Appreciate ways in which the 'what's in it for me?' factor impacts on progress.
- Understand the themes and arguments covered in each chapter.

In this book we tend to use the word practitioner, which includes teacher, trainer, tutor, facilitator, lecturer and organizational developer. Whatever your role within learning and development you will be involved in providing a valuable service to your learners, the organization in which you work and the organizations in which your learners work. We will use the term further education and skills to incorporate

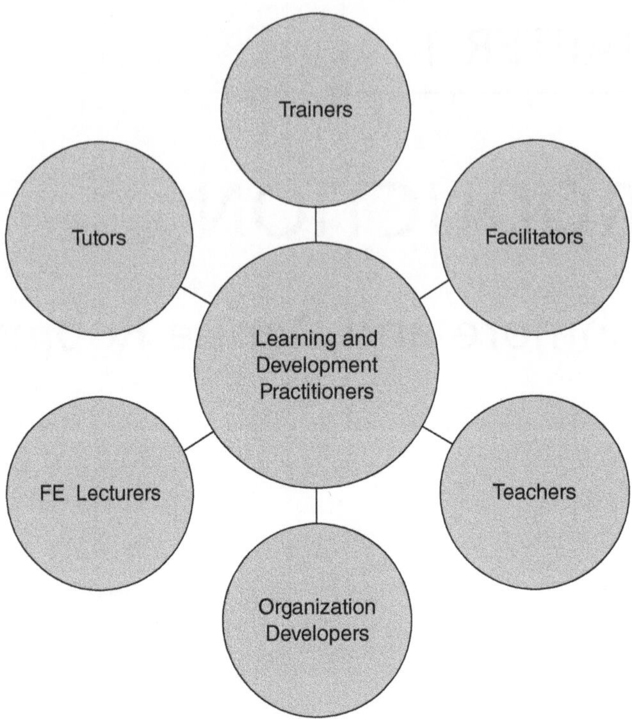

Figure 1.1 Practitioners in further education, skills and organizational learning

providers in the public and private sector (further education colleges, WBL providers, adult and community learning) as well as organizational learning. The terms used to describe this sector have varied over the years. The term further education was regarded as too limited and was replaced by lifelong learning to ensure that it reflected other elements of the sector: vocational, work-based learning and adult education and training. Since the election of the coalition government the term further education and skills has been used to reflect the growing emphasis on the education and training of skills, as well as other aspects of the life-long learning sector. This may apply to private and public sector organizations. We will also use the term learning and development to equate to the array of approaches and institutions in the sector.

1.1 Introduction

This book is uniquely structured, drawing on evolving knowledge and grounded in a problem-based focus, challenging you to find solutions to real problems in your teaching and training practice. In recent years interest in the application of teaching, training, learning and development has seen unprecedented growth, separately emphasizing theory and practice. For experienced and developing practitioners, this then requires a combination of different models of delivery to enable the development of theory alongside the development of practice. With this in mind, this book is designed to provide the underpinning theory alongside its application to practice. Chapters 2 to 10 will include practical examples, such as case studies and discussion questions, to help stimulate the essential link between theory and practice with 'signposts' or 'scaffolding' to additional references that you can use to explore elements of the work elsewhere. We aim to provide a basis for improving understanding as well as providing employers with the assurance that their staff (as learners) will be striving towards a balance between practice and its underpinning theory.

Methods of organizational learning are continually changing, as organizations continue to look for and employ practitioners who are knowledgeable and inspiring in their approach to developing people. Hence staff development is seen as an essential component to real business as well as professional growth. With this in mind practitioners need to be able to introduce new approaches to support employees as learners and in turn benefit employers as well as the learners themselves. All aspects of this book are important to consider when examining your role as a learning and development practitioner and the organization's role; the concept of learning and development cannot be considered in isolation from other aspects of the practitioner's or learner's role, and requires an all-inclusive and collaborative approach.

It is without doubt that learning and development functions in organizations are fundamental to achieving success, because these functions are central to developing organizational needs and for practitioners to do their jobs well. Evidence shows that true learning organizations rely heavily on their learning and development practitioners to support business strategy and this means practitioners need to develop new ways of designing, delivering and evaluating learning (Harrison, 2009; Noe, 2010). This may be clear in training and educational organizations but is also true in business organizations. Practitioners need to ensure that the learning and development functions are efficient and effective in doing their job well, in addition to making learning delivery lively and energetic; in other words a dynamic and enthusiastic approach is required in order to encourage and engage self-motivated learners with the aim of achieving organizational as well as their own personal or professional goals.

Given its incorporation of organizational teaching and training approaches, this book will be useful in relation to a wide range of development activities. For instance, it will satisfy those involved in WBL and adult and community learning who often complain that courses and their resources are focused too much on staff in further education (FE) colleges, rather than the learning and skills sector as a whole, and will also satisfy those operating in the training industry and commerce, both in the private and public sectors. As a consequence this book aims to keep a distinctive feature of providing a focus and stimulus for action alongside theoretical coverage.

Although this book seeks to demonstrate the importance of a structured approach to learning and development as well as the key elements for delivery and professionalism, it also seeks to highlight the various concepts of learning and development as widely diversified terms used within the sector covering teaching, training and facilitating. Throughout, the various chapters explore what you as a learner practitioner can do to create an environment where you can improve upon what you already know as well as what you can do to increase and enhance learning and practice. Each chapter guides you through the actions you will need to take to develop and enhance your skills. Teacher or trainer practitioners, and anyone presenting or facilitating a training session, for classroom or group activity, can keep up to date by pro-actively learning, understanding and applying theory to a practical situation. Furthermore, you will be able to put to use a range of simple but effective techniques to create a productive and conducive learning environment for all. Chapters incorporate recent interest in the possibilities of learning and development as well as pitfalls in delivering learning and development sessions. We have included a range of suggested activities and case studies for readers to carry out and use, in teaching and training. The intention is to involve readers actively at all stages throughout the book.

Finally, the book is intended to be practical and dynamic and is not intended to be read in the same way as a theoretical textbook from cover to cover, but rather it should be used as a resource that can be tapped into at varying times and at various points in your teaching or training.

1.2 Equality and diversity

Although equality and diversity principles and practicalities are often regarded as challenging, and can be interpreted in different and sometimes contradictory ways according to your understanding or even sensitivity (Ashmore et al., 2009), nonetheless they have long been important dimensions in teaching, training and development for practitioners, the organization and especially so for learners. Meeting the needs of a diverse group of learners is about ensuring equality of access and learning opportunities for all and, for example, promotional materials should represent a diverse focus. Equally importantly, active equality and diversity practices enable you, the practitioner, to appreciate what effective implementation really looks like, as well as enabling you to provide a rich environment that is conducive to all learners. That is a favourable atmosphere that successfully provides a positive learning experience for all. Even so, one of the most challenging features is promoting a culture of tolerance and understanding and making sure that no learners are prejudicially excluded because of their difference. Although equality and diversity are not included as a separate chapter in this book, they are embedded throughout all chapters through the examples; one of the overarching aims of the book is to ensure that learning develops the best for all individuals (see for example Chapter 7, section 7.5).

1.3 The intended audience for this book

While it continues the coverage of learning and development delivery, this book will be suited to practitioners across a range of organizations and learners on various courses; for instance, Certificate in Education, Training the Trainers and other contexts in the learning and development sector. It will play an important role in further defining the field of learning, teaching, training and development as well as good practice in delivering sessions. Although the book does not have as its primary focus the learning and training cycle, the issues considered in the chapters are relevant and, significantly, the order of the chapters is akin to the aspects of a practitioner's development. Thus the book maintains the practitioner focus, while reflecting a critical coverage so as to appeal to both learners (especially those undertaking courses or modules and learning, teaching, training and development practitioners in FE, WBL, adult and community and training organizations) as well as continuing professional development (CPD) training in public and private institutions.

1.4 What's new about this book and why is it needed?

This book is different in that it presents a number of different perspectives and practices in learning and development. But our purpose is to move beyond current practices and introduce more creative ways of working in learning and development, consequently offering suggestions for implementation and practice. In the field of teacher and trainer education and training, the range of books extend from those which provide a commentary on theory or practice (or both combined) to those which focus mainly on practice for specific courses or aspects of teaching and training. Increased tuition fees since 2010 and the end to government support (significantly for part-time courses which have typically attracted adult learners), along with learners searching for relevance of their learning to their present and potential employment prospects, have resulted in learners becoming more forthright in asking the question 'what's in it for me?' (WIIFM). As a result, work-based learning in organizations, including educational institutions, has had to change the way learning takes place as well as how practitioners deliver learning.

All contributors to this book are experienced learning and development practitioners from a diverse range of subject specialisms but are deeply concerned with the learning, teaching and development of learners and continuous development for practitioners. Thus given the diverse range of experiences, the different chapters are written in the authors' own style and perspective, which adds to its uniqueness. We hope this book will be relevant for all those concerned with ongoing learning and development of people in both educational and workplace contexts.

1.5 Current state of learning and development and why it needs to change

A number of writers have argued that education is a vehicle for the reproduction of social and economic structures rather than for social mobility (Fisher and Thompson, 2009). 'Education and training' was once used to describe a number of learning and development initiatives, but since the beginning of 2000 the traditional distinction between education and training has become interchangeable with the focus on learning (Armitage et al., 2007). Now 'learning' or 'learning and development' have become the 'buzzword' in place of education and training. This is because we now live in a 'learning society' where continuous learning and skills development has become the norm, replacing what was once considered to be a lifelong job or 'job for life' with not much learning and development, which was the standard pattern in the middle of the twentieth century. The term learning and skills suggests that learners will become more motivated to learn by knowing more about themselves; for example, their own strengths and weaknesses as learners. For this reason, if practitioners can respond to individual learners' strengths and weaknesses, it is possible that learner retention and achievement will improve, hence the skills of 'learning to learn' may possibly provide a firm basis for the term 'learning and skills' (Coffield et al., 2004; Coffield, 2008).

Now the term training may be regarded as somewhat antiquated and not inclusive, though some have argued that by adopting the term 'learning and development' there is a danger that what is gained in scope is lost in generalization (Harrison, 2009). Nonetheless, Harrison notes: 'A very different way of understanding "learning and development" is to perceive it as driven by the individual's curiosity, intelligence and desires and fundamentally shaped by their social interactions in the workplace' (2009: 8). Such a definition focuses on the integration of work and learning as a major route to change, and to learning facilitation rather than training as the key requirement.

As mentioned earlier, most organizations aspire to make the best use of their employees and invest in learning and development through a number of means such as knowledge and talent management, and career management, and need effective, efficient as well as dynamic learning and development functions to achieve that goal (CIPD, 2007; Noe, 2010). The impact of change has been wide-ranging; in 2013, further education colleges, learning providers and other adult and community providers have seen a number of changes governing teaching, training and the initial qualification and CPD of their teachers; for example, the introduction of full-cost fees for adults and the deregulation of the requirement for teaching qualifications. Furthermore, for some time colleges and training providers have found themselves competing with each other because previous and present governments believe that competition is healthy in raising standards for both practitioners and learners. However, as Wallace points out: 'This ideology is the economic equivalent of Darwin's survival of the fittest' (2013: 21); yet, the claim is that those providing the best service and at an affordable cost will continue to exist.

1.6 The benefits of change: the 'what's in it for me?' (WIIFM) factor for learners

For a long time learning has become an important catalyst for change and even more so in the current economic climate. We often fail to accept change because over and over again emotions cloud our perspective and beliefs get overshadowed with doubts, but embracing change is an important part of development; a necessary component in providing the power to frame or alter thoughts, opinions, feelings and behaviours. So how we change as learners and practitioners, especially in turbulent times where political conditions can change the way things are done, is vital to our continued success in terms of our own development and how we support our learners. There is evidence (Gravells and Wallace, 2013) to suggest that highly engaged practitioners not only work harder, but take the initiative and innovate more often, respond to change better and take less time off work, provide better service, will draw on optimism and generally are much better at coping with complex challenges and ideas. There needs to be preparation for change in an attempt to teach, train or facilitate better, and to support 'best practice'. Even though some have argued that there can be no such thing as 'best practice' which can be universally applied in classrooms, training rooms or in other learning contexts, the cultural approach stresses the complexity of all learning which in turn affects the differing social, ethnic, disability and gender positions of learners and practitioners (Coffield, 2008). Still many have argued that any practitioner dependency (where learners are reliant on practitioners) needs to change in order to provide a logically structured method in which to encourage learners' development, both for knowledge, confidence, self-esteem and employability.

Often we make changes in our professional life that are deliberate, whereas other changes take place as a result of innately occurring development in life. We believe that change is about instilling new attitudes which can have a positive influence on behaviour, beliefs and values (what is desirable or undesirable, good or bad) which help to develop a clearer understanding within yourself, and that support new ways of learning and doing things: for example, the way you work as a practitioner or learner and the way you overcome resistance to change. Another dimension to change is the increased attention paid to feedback from learners, and the ways that quality assurance processes and systems make use of this feedback (Race, 2010). A further dimension to change in learning and development is evaluation, which must be a significant part of the change process as it considers the standards and the moral and social worth of what has taken place. Thus it is argued that effective and critical evaluation is an important dimension of professional practice and the change process (Fisher et al., 2009).

Over time colleges in the further education and skills sector together with organizational learning, including practitioners and learners, have realized the importance of ensuring that learning is connected to the application of work. Learning a subject or skill without being able to apply the new knowledge to practical circumstances, as in work related situations, has very little value and becomes meaningless. Yet learning is having the mindset to change behaviour, thoughts and attitudes, which in turn can have implications for practitioners, learners and for the organization in which you work. It is argued that the principal outcome of any component of learning and change is that of gradually learning to become a better learner. As a result, improving teaching and training is more than making learning 'happen', it is also about making learners better at learning, learning to change themselves through self-reflection and in turn becoming more self-assured (Race and Pickford, 2007).

1.6.1 The 'what's in it for me?' factor

A considerable amount of learning takes place outside of the classroom or training room without any directed teaching, training, tutoring, mentoring or coaching. But for this learning to have any impact a process of reflective practice needs to take place and which is encouraged so as to enable this learning or indeed any learning to have the desired results. But before practitioners and learners begin to think of 'what's in it for me', there needs to be a certain amount of self-confidence, optimism and positive attitude that the learning taking place is the right one. Therefore it is fundamental for learners to understand what they need and should learn. What is more, learners need to be able to find their own ways of learning, how best they learn and importantly develop a sense of responsibility for their own learning.

It cannot be denied that the WIIFM factor is a question that is uppermost not only in learners' minds but in your mind as practitioners and consequently can drive almost every decision made. Sometime this can be a subconscious tune that plays rather quietly in the back of learners' heads and appears whenever there are new challenges with which to contend. In order to strive to become more knowledgeable about learning and development, it is normal as a practitioner to engage with and deliver your specialist or vocational subject, and at the same time see yourself not just as a teacher, tutor, trainer or facilitator, but also as an educator who systematically works to improve learners' understanding of the subject. Even so, this view is very much debatable as teaching and training are seen more and more as practical activities in which experience (as in practical ability) is valued over theoretical (academic) knowledge (Armitage et al., 2012: 266).

Sometimes it is easier for learners to reject change rather than try to embrace it, especially when they are working full time or even part time in busy and diverse organizations. Yet it is important to stay focused on the value of change, and remember that change forces us to explore new territory, ideas and behaviours, as opposed to experiencing resistance to change, which can make us feel left out and even uncomfortable. However, increasingly many learners may be tactically

positioning themselves by asking how can they do well or how can they do better through their learning journey, while at the same time intentionally asking that one important question – WIIFM. Though many learners see learning as a developmental journey and not just an immediate here and now, the WIIFM factor may encourage them to do so. However, the fact that they are seeking ways of completing their learning satisfactorily and with minimum effort – that is, not wanting to do more than is necessary to fulfill the requirements to be able to get through the learning (Race and Pickford, 2007) – may be a consequence of this approach. However, the WIIFM factor is not always about what we will get from a particular learning or work situation but it is often about how we will feel as a result of having done it.

We are often inspired to learn and develop for the innate feelings of pride, sharing, safety, security, thrill and even excitement. Still, despite the WIIFM syndrome, if individuals are really serious about gaining or retaining skills, it is vital that they continually engage in learning and development. It is often said that for some people, knowledge is synonymous with power and control; on the other hand, it can be regarded as the sharing of knowledge across the entire organization and creating a healthy learning environment. It is increasingly important to be constantly vigilant in looking for opportunities to develop personal and professional growth, by advancing your skills so as to become more effective and persuasive in what you do which, in turn, makes a difference in the lives of your learners. As is often said, one of the most powerful ways we learn is to contrast and compare what we are doing with what we could be doing (Tracy, 2013). Because the WIIFM factor can consist of multiple questions it should help in making available your best possible teaching, training and facilitating skills, within your area of expertise, to achieve maximum benefit.

1.7 Latest developments in learning and development practice

At times it may appear difficult to overcome the constant build-up and publicity that surrounds learning, education and development. However, thanks mainly to technology, the way we learn has changed over the last decade. Time commitments associated with teaching and training are shifting and often changeable. Learners expect that practitioners are available 24 hours a day, particularly through asynchronous electronic communication; demands for better grades or achievement may develop into a continuous round of informal feedback which results in the assignment reflecting more of the tutor's ideas than those of the learner. So although there is a need to provide structures of intellectual, social and emotional support to help learners to move forward and develop in their learning, there is also a need to ensure that these supports are removed, appropriately and in a timely fashion, so as to make learners more autonomous; though getting this balance right is a matter of continuous examination of the processes of learning.

The focus of how we learn has shifted dramatically over the last ten years, moving from a monological style, characterized by a tutor or trainer lecturing or presenting what they know to learners without an exchange of ideas, towards a more dialogical approach, where learning has become a continually interactive and communicative process at all levels. This is demonstrated by a consideration of a report from the Training and Enterprise Council (TEC, 1993), which revealed that only a small proportion of managers gave their employees training, regarding it as an avoidable cost rather than a crucial investment. Research carried out in 2008, shows that organizations need to put more emphasis on training and developing their staff to get the best out of them (CIPD, 2008; Harrison, 2009). Likewise there is a shift from the traditional classroom learning to approaches that can suit most learners which may include technology-based learning, coaching, mentoring, large group work and/or action learning sets. Learning and development has become more participative, experiential and hands-on; furthermore reflective practice has become a significant part of development and is, in itself, experiential, although at times for some, the idea of reflecting on practice after it has taken place can seem perplexing and problematic. In spite of this, Harrison (2009) and Megginson and Whitaker (2003) explained that reflecting on practice is another way of learning (see Chapter 10) and suggest that learning, training and development can empower people and stimulate them to achieve their occupational aspirations.

Over time the principle of vocational and apprenticeship training and education has remained the same: learners learn best by doing (practice) and do best by learning as part of an integrated approach including employers and educators (Dolphin and Lanning, 2011). In 2008 the National Apprenticeship Service (NAS) was introduced to bring about a growth in the number of employers offering apprenticeships (apprenticeships.org.uk, 2012), and more recently, apprenticeships and how they are delivered have enjoyed a revival (Dolphin and Lanning, 2011), with the number of new starts increasing by over 50 per cent in 2011. Employers have always insisted that young people must have the necessary skills to get into work and demanded that employability skills must be a top education priority for any government.

Learning in academic organizations has long been the norm for most learners, but for economic development businesses are keen for people to also consider vocational courses, thereby capturing application as well as knowledge and understanding. However, Twining (1993) pointed out that training was provided in skill centres in the 1970s but by the late 1980s these were either closed or privatized, and while 'education' was undertaken in schools, colleges and universities, it was seen as something quite separate from the vocational (skills) training.

Back in 1990, Summerfield and Evans reported that one of the contributing factors of the unsatisfactory economic performance of the UK has been its inadequate technical education. A lack of attention by government and the reduction in the number of employers willing to support vocational education has resulted in an erosion of the take-up and status of vocational courses over the years. Various governments have tried to address this and, latterly, new forms of support have been introduced. Recent policy has introduced a range of institutions such as University Technical Colleges (UTCs) sponsored by local universities and local employers. These have been created to specifically focus on providing technical education with the intention of developing vocational skills such as engineering, manufacturing, construction, and information and communication technology (ICT) to prepare learners for a range of careers and continuing education at the age of 19 that meets the needs of 'modern' employers (DfE, 2013a). In addition, the government also instigated a number of what is termed 'studio schools' that offer vocational and academic qualifications, combined with work placements at local and national level with employers (DfE, 2013b). It is believed that these institutions, in addition to developing vocational skills, will also encourage learners to develop those soft skills like punctuality, reliability, team-working and better communication, which are often lacking in young people. These new schools are part of the government's drive to ensure the education system responds to demands from employers for the skills they need to grow and prosper (DfE, 2013b). At the time of writing, a further 13 studio schools have been approved for September 2014. With these in mind, Williams and Hanson (2012) reported that the UK will have an increased knowledge and service-based economy, with vocational skills and qualifications playing a greater role in its competitiveness, not only in its national market, but significantly in global markets. Yet, it is argued, the UTCs and studio schools will lead to a greater division between academic and vocation learning. When the first diplomas started in 2005 it was thought that they would become the new flagship qualification connecting the vocational component as well as the academic element, and were heralded as a major breakthrough.

This led the then Children, Schools and Families Secretary, Ed Balls, in 2007 to say: 'If Diplomas are successfully introduced and are delivering the mix that employers and universities value, they could become the qualification of choice for young people' (BBC News, 2008). However, the opportunity for combining the synergy of vocational and academic learning was lost when it was announced that the diplomas, which genuinely brought academic and vocational learning together, would be discontinued (TES, 2010). As the diplomas had made little headway and achievement rates had been low (TES, 2011), the coalition government announced the scrapping of the diplomas to ensure existing qualifications are recognised as challenging and rigorous enough to prepare young people for further study and work.

1.8 Future vision for learning and development

As practitioners you are likely to sometimes think that your subject or vocation is in some way independent of outside influence or what is happening more widely in society. Yet different approaches to learning and development will have an impact on the way that government policy directs practice, and there will often be a gap between the actions you intend to pursue as a practitioner or as a learner and the outcomes you are expected to achieve (Armitage et al., 2012). All organizations are experiencing huge and ongoing change due to the economic culture and the pervasive nature of new technologies. It is said that the manner in which learning institutions marketed learning resources in the 1990s is good justification for change in how it is now marketed, as well as providing much wider access to courses while cutting the cost of delivering courses (Cole, 2000).

Since 2000, the use of technology has, to a greater or lesser extent, changed how we teach in the classroom, the way we train in a training centre or the workplace and, some would argue, the way we learn. Technology continues to have a large impact on all sectors of the economy and learning and development is no exception; the way we learn, communicate, play and even plan our lives has been reshaped with the use of technology (Noe, 2010). It is now recognized that delivering learning through the use of technology can provide effective, efficient and timely access to excellent quality learning materials (Anderson and Elloumi, 2004), and many report that the use of technology offers the potential to take learning to a different level (Bach and Haynes, 2007). A balanced approach to the use of technology can be a tremendous advantage to practitioners and learners (Bennett et al., 2009). Furthermore,

Harrison (2009) believes that all organizations now need to put in place an adequate amount of technological tools to encourage not just knowledge management but also a strong, well-communicated, fair and equitable approach to allow for creativity and the building of knowledge. With advances in technology, along with reduced purchasing costs, organizations are in a better position to equip computer labs with the latest technological resources and also provide staff with computers, thus changing the way organizations and practitioners deliver courses, sessions and training, and the way learners learn.

Kozma (2001) and Bennett et al. (2009) argue that there are many attributes in using technology in learning, for instance it is beneficial to the learner as well as the organization because it can be used to bring real-life examples to the learner. However, any technological approach must be aligned to organizational goals, while at the same time offering tangible benefit to practitioners and learners. There are a number of terminologies commonly used to describe the incorporation of technology with teaching and learning: for instance e-learning, virtual learning, distance learning, blended learning and others; but regardless of the term used, it involves using technology to move the focus from the classroom or training room and the tutor or trainer, towards interaction and the sharing of ideas with the tutor or trainer. This can include other learners who are part of the class group taking part in discussions and providing peer feedback. As the use of technology has intensified, practitioners must ensure that learning materials that are produced for online learning, or indeed any form of learning, should be designed to promote equality, and effectively engage the learner in participating, and to promote learning. Thus it is said that working with technological tools, while remaining curious about their educational value, means that judgement about their effectiveness requires understanding of their application (Bennett et al., 2009). Furthermore, as Bach and Haynes (2007) and Simmons (2002) have identified, organizations including colleges have looked at ways of adopting online learning as the main delivery method to train and develop employees in the workplace. See Chapter 9 on using technology in learning and Chapter 11 on the impact on CPD for the practitioner.

1.9 Summary of the book's contents

Wenger strongly argued that what differentiates learning from doing is that 'whatever form learning takes it changes who we are, by changing our ability to participate, to belong and to negotiate meaning' (1998: 226). To conclude, we would argue that as a learning and development practitioner you must have sound professional knowledge if you are to play a significant role and have an active part in your own professional development as well as the development of learners. Beevers and Rea (2010: 18) point out: 'As learning and development practitioners your knowledge is your product, if you are not knowledgeable in your subject area or do not know how to support and facilitate learning, then how can you help others or contribute to your organization.'

When reading through the chapters, you will find that the actions, case studies and activities listed throughout the various chapters enhance and embrace each other; a number of these activities can be applied when required. Throughout there are web links and references to additional sources so as to enable you to follow up ideas and issues raised.

The following ten chapters explore issues and ideas related to learning and development, metaphors, reflection and CPD. Each chapter is structured with a chapter outline, learning outcomes and underpinning theory, ending with a summary, case studies and activities. The case studies are lucid, practical and powerful and can be used in small groups in the form of action learning sets (ALS). An ideal ALS should be no more than four learners who are committed to working rigorously and supportively by giving each member of the group an opportunity to question, share ideas and reflect, and undertake action planning on a real scenario so as to complete the task. As McGill and Brockbank (2003) point out, the primary purpose of action learning is that it supports achieving improvement and transformation in professional training and educational contexts.

Chapter 1, which you are currently reading, provides an outline and overview, setting out a practical approach to learning and development, what the book is about and how to use it. Chapter 2 addresses learning needs. It is intended to remind you of the importance of identifying that different people learn in different ways. Effective practitioners are aware that they need to take account of what learners (and especially adult learners) need to know and what they know already (Coffield, 2008), so it is expected to get you thinking about the various methods that can be used in identifying your learners' needs and the fact that the range of learning needs has never been greater than it is at present. Chapter 3 deals with developing learning objectives, it includes a detailed discussion of learning objectives and their importance in learning, while Chapter 4 considers how to select appropriate and relevant learning content.

Although Chapter 5 looks closely at metaphors, it recognises that many learning and development practitioners maybe limited in such an approach. Metaphors, often defined as 'describing one thing as another', have been used for centuries, but are becoming more and more popular as a teaching and learning tool to help explain concepts, ideas, models and hypotheses to learners and can act as a scaffold on which to build and expand new knowledge. Hence having an understanding of how to more effectively use metaphors to aid learning, practitioners can draw upon this often used, though somewhat misunderstood, cost-effective learning resource as a way of enhancing teaching and training practice.

Chapter 6 focuses on designing learning delivery sessions for learning and giving ideas and suggestions on how teaching and training sessions can be designed and developed to include different ability learners. Helping your learners to make sense of what they are learning is one of the most important dimensions of effective teaching and/or training. Chapter 7 explores how to make the delivery of learning most effective. It considers the growing range of delivery skills and styles and looks at a range of aspects of delivering sessions, tutorials and guidance, helping learners to learn with and from each other and giving feedback. It is well reported that feedback is a fundamental part in learning; in particular, feed-forward or feed-ahead so that learners can continuously fine-tune their learning-by-doing using feedback (Race and Pickford, 2007; Race, 2010).

Chapter 8 looks at evaluating learning. It aims to make sure that evaluation is taken seriously and that your teaching or training is working well by having the desired effect on learning. Effective evaluation and reviewing of teaching and training helps to identify and address any emerging barriers. In addition, it also helps to motivate and engage learners, while ensuring learners have a very clear understanding of the knowledge and skills to be achieved. It focuses on the need to make sure that evaluation is not just seen as a paper exercise but rather it must be reliable, so as to provide correct results, valid measures of learners' performance, and be transparent. Chapter 9 considers ways in which learning and development practitioners can use technology to enhance learning. It explores the fast developing area of e-learning and examines the pros and cons relating to the use of contemporary technologies to enhance the learning process.

The first part of Chapter 10 is about CPD. It is essential that CPD is appropriate to the individual learner; therefore this section is designed to encourage learners (and practitioners themselves) to reflect on their development and how CPD can be used to enhance and improve performance. A CPD record framework provides an opportunity for you to reflect on approaches used in your teaching and training, how successful you have been and what improvement is needed to further enhance your development. The second part of Chapter 10 deals with reflection and practice, seeking a common element between theory and practice so as to gain a more coherent understanding of the importance of developing as a reflective practitioner. Many have pointed out that increasingly it has become essential to use the power and potency of reflection to help identify, develop and intensify what you 'can do', and not just what you think you cannot do (Ghaye, 2011: 2).

Finally, Chapter 11 is particularly important in light of workforce development and policy issues. It looks at the different approaches to professionalism and how they relate to the role of teachers, trainers and learners. It proposes future changes to learning and development and considers how these might impact on practitioners, ending with a final summary.

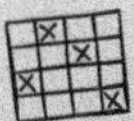

1.9.1 Activity

Reflect on your practice and try and answer these three questions as honestly as you can.

- What does being a learning and development practitioner mean to you?
- What area(s) of your practice would you like to change?
- In undertaking new learning or activities in your professional role, how significant is the WIIFM to you?

As you work your way through this book think of how you can make this change.

References

Anderson, T. and Elloumi, F. (2004) *Theory and Practice of Online Learning*. Athabasca: Athabasca University Press.

Apprenticeships (2012) *Apprenticeships History and News*. www.apprenticeships.org.uk (accessed 2 October 2013).

Armitage, A., Bryant, R., Dunnill, R., Flanagan, K., Hayes, D., Hudson, A., Kent, J., Lawes, S. and Renwick, M. (2007) *Teaching and Training in Post-Compulsory Education*. Buckingham: Open University Press.

Armitage, A., Bryant, R., Evershed, J., Dunnill, R., Flanagan, K., Hayes, D., Hudson, A., Kent, J., Poma, S. and Lawes, S. (2012) *Teaching and Training in Lifelong Learning*. Maidenhead: Open University Press.

Ashmore, L., Dalton, J., Noel, P., Rennie, S., Salter, E., Swindells, D. and Thomas, P. (2009) 'Equality and diversity', in J. Avis, R. Fisher and R. Thompson (eds), *Teaching in Lifelong Learning: A Guide to Theory and Practice*. Maidenhead: Open University Press/McGraw-Hill Education, pp. 59–75.

Bach, S. and Haynes, P. (2007) *Online Learning and Teaching in Higher Education*. Maidenhead: Open University Press.

BBC News (2008) 'Diplomas in England', 7 March. www.news.bbc.co.uk/1/hi/education/6505997.stm (accessed 5 October 2013).

Beevers, K. and Rea, A. (2010) *Learning and Development Practice*. London: CIPD.

Bennett, L., Iredale, A. and Reynolds, C. (2009) 'Teaching with technology', in J. Avis, R. Fisher and R. Thompson (eds), *Teaching in Lifelong Learning: A Guide to Theory and Practice*. Maidenhead: Open University Press/McGraw-Hill Education, pp. 144–152.

CIPD (Chartered Institute for Personnel and Development) (2007) *Latest Trends in Learning and Development: Reflections on the 2007 Learning and Development Survey*. London: CIPD.

CIPD (Chartered Institute for Personnel and Development) (2008) *Promoting Learning and Development in Small Business*. www.cipd.co.uk (accessed 2 October 2013).

Coffield, F. (2008) *Just Suppose Teaching and Learning Became the First Priority*. London: Learning and Skills Network.

Coffield, F., Moseley, D., Hall, E. and Ecclestone, K. (2004) *Should We Be Using Learning Styles? What Research Has to Say to Practice*. London: Learning and Skills Research Centre.

Cole, R. A. (2000) *Issues in Web-based Pedagogy: A Critical Primer*. Westport, CT: Greenwood Press.

DfE (2013a) *What Are University Technical Colleges (UTCs)?* www.education.gov.uk/schools/leadership/typesofschools/technical/a00198954/utcs (accessed 5 October 2013).

DfE (2013b) *What Are Studio Schools?* www.education.gov.uk/schools/leadership/typesofschools/technical/a0077819/about (accessed 2 September 2013).

Dolphin, T. and Lanning, T. (eds) (2011) *Rethinking Apprenticeships*. London: IPPR.

Fisher, R., Iredale, A., Ollin, R. and Robinson, D. (2009) 'Evaluation and quality assurance', in J. Avis, R. Fisher and R. Thompson (eds), *Teaching in Lifelong Learning: A Guide to Theory and Practice*. Maidenhead: Open University Press/McGraw-Hill Education, pp. 238–245.

Fisher, R. and Thompson, R. (2009) 'Introduction to the lifelong learning sector', in J. Avis, R. Fisher and R. Thompson (eds), *Teaching in Lifelong Learning: A Guide to Theory and Practice*. Maidenhead: Open University Press/McGraw-Hill Education, pp. 3–6.

Ghaye, T. (2011) *Teaching and Learning through Reflective Practice: A Practical Guide for Positive Action*. London: Routledge.

Gravells, J. and Wallace, S. (2013) *The A–Z Guide to Working in Further Education*. Northwich: Critical Publishing.

Harrison, R. (2009) *Learning and Development*. London: CIPD.

Kozma, R. B. (2001) 'Counterpoint theory of "learning with media"', in R. E. Clark (ed.), *Learning from Media: Arguments, Analysis, and Evidence*. Greenwich, CT: Information Age Publishing Inc., pp. 137–178.

McGill, I. and Brockbank, A. (2003) *The Action Learning Handbook: Powerful Techniques for Education, Professional Development and Training*. London: Routledge Falmer.

Megginson, D, and Whitaker, V. (2003) *Continuing Professional Development*. London: CIPD.

Noe, R. A. (2010) *Employee Training and Development*. New York: McGraw-Hill.

Race, P. (2010) *Making Learning Happen. A Guide for Post-Compulsory Education*. London: Sage.

Race, P. and Pickford, R. (2007) *Making Teaching Work: 'Teaching Smarter' in Post-Compulsory Education*. London: Sage.

Simmons, D. E. (2002) 'The forum report: e-learning adoption rates and barriers', in A. Rossett (ed.), *The ASTD e-learning Handbook*. New York: McGraw-Hill, pp. 19–23.

Summerfield, P. and Evans, E. J. (eds) (1990) *Technical Education and the State Since 1850: Historical and Contemporary Perspectives*. Manchester: Manchester University Press.

TEC (1993) *North Nottinghamshire Local Economic Review*. Mansfield: North Nottinghamshire Training and Enterprise Council.

TES (2010) 'Diploma rule lifted', *TES*, 25 June.

TES (2011) '"Nobody really wanted it": the diploma meets its doom', *TES*, 13 November.

Tomlinson, M. (2004) *14–19 Curriculum and Qualifications Reform: Final Report of the Working Group on 14–19 Reform*. London: DfES.

Tracy, B. (2013) *Negotiation: The Brian Tracy Success Library*. New York: AMACOM.

Twining, J. (1993) *Vocational Education and Training in the United Kingdom*. Berlin: European Centre for the Development of Vocational Training.

Wallace, S. (2013) *Understanding the Further Education Sector: A Critical Guide to Policies and Practice*. Northwich: Critical Publishing.

Wenger, E. (1998) *Communities of Practice: Learning, Meaning, and Identity*. Cambridge: Cambridge University Press.

Williams, C. and Hanson, W. (2012) *Higher Apprenticeships and Professional Bodies*. www.parnglobal.com (accessed 3 October 2013).

CHAPTER 2

IDENTIFYING LEARNING NEEDS

Ian Rushton and Martyn Walker

Learning outcomes

After reading this chapter, the reader should be able to:

- Gain an appreciation of what learners bring to the table.
- Explore some ideas as to how to work with learners to optimize learning.
- Identify strategies for differentiating learning in classes.
- Identify strategies for making learners work harder than the teacher.

Chapter outline

This chapter considers some of the many components of our teaching and training roles, which are equally important considerations for all practitioners, curriculum and departmental leaders, as they relate to the planning and evaluation of learning. While this sounds simple enough, it is contested terrain and we encourage you to take this chapter as a set of ideas that invite enquiry and experimentation, rather than accept them as a set of truths that are set in stone. From the outset, we make no apology for placing the emphasis on learning rather than teaching and training for a number of reasons including:

- The learners are in our classes in order to learn – they are not there in order for us to teach or train them or for some other teacher or trainer based purpose.
- Performative, target-driven and instrumental systems at work in our context, for example Ofsted, are more interested in the learning that takes place in our classes, rather than the teaching.
- There is a growing body of literature that suggests that learners learn more when they have some influence or control in what and how they learn, as opposed to 'being taught' through the practitioner's preferred style.
- In the same way that you, the teaching or training practitioner, are the person best placed to identify your own continuing professional development (CPD) needs, so the learner may have a very good idea of what they need in order to learn that which is important for their development.

2.1 Underpinning theory

The underpinning theories in this chapter draw on a rich tradition of practitioners and researchers who sought to find alternatives to the traditional didactic approaches which the current education policymakers advocate and which Kelly (2009: 56) identifies (in the first of three ideologies) as, 'Curriculum as content and education as transmission'. The 2010 coalition government's *one-size-fits-all* educational philosophy is one of the legacies of New Labour's approach to education that has been heavily contested by impartial and persistent commentators such as Coffield (2007, 2008, 2009, 2010; Coffield and Williamson, 2011) who argue for a more individualized, learner-centred approach to pedagogy. Yet, education policymakers would have us believe that they already embrace learner-centredness in their use of elastic language, for example, *equality*, *inclusiveness*, *widening participation* and the notion of *responsiveness*.

From this outset, bearing in mind that we are thinking of identifying learning needs, we are immediately concerned with the old underlying question, 'What is the purpose of education?' and which echoes the historic sentiments of many from Lester-Smith (1957), through the Black Papers (Cox and Dyson, 1971) and the Great Debate (Callaghan, 1976) to Coffield (2010) and Pring (2010). Such a literature does not invoke a nostalgia whereby education was previously somehow better than now, but repeats the same unanswered question which Biesta (2007: 20) usefully and linguistically turned into: 'Education professionals need to make decisions about what is educationally desirable'. The subject specialist teaching and training practitioner usually knows, from experience, what is needed. Government seem unable to appreciate this and so practitioners in the further education and skills sector are expected to pay homage to a dominant business model that portrays education as a commodity and learners as consumers, in other words, a tokenistic ideology singularly at odds with the reality of the sector and the needs of many learners. Here, managerialism and performativity serve only to routinize and stifle teacher creativity from the outset (Murphy et al., 2009; Orr and Simmons, 2009) and exemplifies Kelly's (2009: 56) second ideology of, 'Curriculum as product and education as instrumental'.

However, there are those practitioners in our sector who co-modify their existence (pay effective lip service to *the system*, keep the boxes ticked but concentrate mostly on what really matters, effective learning and development). Thus, the learner-centred approach seems to sit well with Kelly's (2009: 56) third ideology of, 'Curriculum as process and education as development'. This shift away from didactic approaches began with the critical works of Dewey and Mead (Scheffler, 2011) at the Frankfurt School in Chicago in the 1930s and might (we cannot know) have been the springboard for Rogers' (1965: 389) seminal belief, becoming popular in the 1960s, that, 'I know I cannot teach anyone anything, I can only provide an environment in which he [sic] can learn'. His humanistic notions concerning the learner developed through a progressive movement in the 1970s, for example Knowles' (1978) work on the adult learner (see Chapter 4), through a transformative phase (Mezirow, 1981) and into a socio-cultural stage where researchers and practitioners found, not surprisingly, that learners learn best when they: have their needs met; work with their peers to discover that which they need or want to know; are helped to learn, as opposed to being taught; and are valued for what they bring to the table, regardless of how unappealing it might seem initially.

Alongside this shift, which ran parallel to policymakers' recurring line that learners should be taught, was an emancipatory literature that makes interesting reading. Here, Trifonas (2000) urges that education is avowedly political and should be challenged like any other politics; Rancière (Bingham and Biesta, 2010) believes that there cannot be any form of equality (despite the ubiquitous organizational *Quality Handbook* and *Equality and Diversity Policy*) where there is teaching, because the education system as we know it in the West, including and especially the further education and skills sector, is not set up to treat learners as equals; and Freire (2005) trusts implicitly in culture and context holding the key to unlocking learners' potential as an emancipatory endeavour.

What these diverse and alternative learner-centred learning ideologies have in common is that they: rely on the teaching or training practitioner knowing the learners and their needs (this is not to be confused with dishing out learning styles questionnaires); offer the learner a voice, albeit a low one in a small space, very often; engage learners with activities and resources that are of interest to them (and creatively so in order to develop attitudes, skills and knowledge that are needed to exist effectively in society, and to pass the exam); and develop deep, rather than surface, learning.

Almost as a postscript here, there is a research-informed literature that argues strongly for deep, as opposed to surface, learning (Smith and Colby, 2007) across a range of disciplines and subject specialisms. For example, the use of video (Mitra et al., 2010), collaborative reading in the humanities (Parrot and Cherry, 2011) and managing institutional change (Wheeler, 2007) and many others, all of which make a robust collective case to suggest that learning is more effective, embedded and reinforced when learning needs and outcomes are clearly identified and articulated.

2.2 Key principles of learner-centred learning (LCL)

The authors of this and some other chapters adopt a particular learner-centred approach when working with, and developing, vocational teachers which we term the learner-centred learning (LCL) model or framework, as follows.

There are ten key principles associated with learner-centred learning and tutors should take these into account when designing a learning session. Implementing such sessions into teaching and learning often requires blended learning such as teacher input and, ideally, facilitated in flexible learning spaces, which are supportive of small group working.

1. The practitioner acts as a facilitator of learning rather than a teacher of knowledge.
2. Learners' prior knowledge and experiences are taken into account.
3. Learners' needs and learning preferences are identified.
4. Activities and resources are used to motivate and support.
5. Learners are actively participating and reflecting in the learning process.
6. Learners are encouraged to become autonomous.

7. Learners are inspired to develop their own ideas and problem-solving skills.
8. Ensure formative, peer, and self-assessments support learning.
9. Learners participate in planning, implementation and evaluation.
10. Learners develop key employability skills.

The first three of these principles, because they are primarily needs related, are discussed next in more detail.

1. The practitioner acts as a facilitator of learning rather than a teacher of knowledge.

Terminology is crucial in the processes of learner-centred learning and the tutor should, early on in the session or programme, explain that their role is as a facilitator and supporter of learning in this context and not a teacher in a traditional sense.

2. Learners' prior knowledge and experiences are taken into account.

It is good practice to know what courses and experiences learners have had prior to enrolling and following a course of study. As in the case of formal or didactic teaching, it is important to know the learners in planning the session, particularly if learner-centred learning is being used very early on in the year. Many teachers, for example, act as facilitator during induction week when learners are being instructed onto a programme through small group and paired activities. In the United Kingdom many younger learners may well have experienced learner-centred learning but in some parts of the world it is still a new way of learning.

3. Learners' needs and learning preferences are identified.

While there is much debate about how helpful learning styles questionnaires are in supporting learners' preferred ways of learning (Coffield et al., 2004), learner-centred learning involves a variety of experiences, presentations, decision-making, collaborative or social working and carrying out research both on their own and in groups. See Chapter 6 for a more detailed discussion about learning styles. Learner-centred learning involves the practitioner seemingly having less control than in more formal situations such as lectures, structured discussion and demonstration. As he or she has more of a facilitator's role, seminars, practical sessions, group work, unstructured discussion (and the value of peer-to-peer dialogue is particularly high), presentations and distance learning are identified as examples where there is less control than in a formal setting.

Least control is associated with discovery projects, own research and real-life experiences.

2.3 Identifying the needs of your audience including differentiation of learning

As we write this chapter we are working with a few assumptions. For example, we assume that you (the reader) have your own individual needs (one of which is your purpose for choosing this chapter and this book) and that you sometimes learn by reading. Other assumptions could be that: you may need to cite a theory or academic source for a written assignment and you think there could be something useful here (that is, you might be reading because you have to rather than because you want to); or that you do not always prefer to learn by reading (it might often depend on what it is you need to discover – for example, the best way to learn how to change the spare wheel on your car might not be to read about it but to attempt it). More fragile assumptions could include the idea that you could be studying for a teaching or training qualification or that you only have 'reading time' on certain evenings of the week. While these assumptions could be understandable, they might also be wrong and they begin to highlight one of the basic mistakes that teaching professionals make – we think that we know the learner.

So, rather than make sweeping assumptions about learners' attitudes, skills and knowledge (ASK) while trying to create the best environment for learning, it may be useful to unpick some of the language and requirements that practitioners are expected to work with in order to make sense of them. Such terminology includes the following four, which are common throughout the further education and skills sector: inclusiveness, initial assessment, learning goals and differentiation.

2.3.1 Inclusiveness (also known as inclusivity)

Inclusiveness is generally taken to mean making your learners feel part of the learning process, treating them all fairly, equally and not excluding them from learning taking place and is based on mutual respect and trust. The term was defined in the Tomlinson report (1996: 27) as requiring a match at three levels, one being at the classroom level, 'by using pedagogy and materials to match the individual's approach to learning and enable them to achieve their learning goals'.

As we will suggest later, this involves both the institution (Tomlinson's second level) and the teacher adapting to the learners' diverse needs rather than expecting the learners to adapt to practitioners; furthermore, expecting the learners to adapt to practitioners may result in disaffected learners' inappropriate behaviour. It is important that you know in advance what learners' needs are and these are not necessarily identified through induction or initial assessment.

2.3.2 Initial assessment

Initial assessment is the process that the teacher or trainer and learners go through at the induction stage of a programme and can be loaded with tension. For example: learners might be uncertain of what can be said; some learners may not fully know what their needs are; others might feel that one of their basic needs is to sleep until lunchtime, regardless of the 9.00 am start; and so on. Yet we suggest that there may be tensions in initial assessment that are even more deep-seated. For example: can we ever really know someone 'well enough'? To what extent can initial assessment results be relied upon to give a sense of being 'near enough' or a good starting point, especially when institutions have their own methods and assessments? The fact that most educational and training institutions have their own unique systems of initial assessment may suggest that there is not a single reliable way of assessing learners' needs. Yet, it is crucial for the teacher to find out what makes each learner 'tick' and this may be difficult in situations where the practitioner does not have the opportunity to build a long-term relationship with the learner. For those practitioners in the position of running short or one day programmes, introductory activities can elicit a wealth of information regarding learners' needs. For example, a one day CPD session concerned with familiarizing staff with a revised programme (or policy or shift in legislation) could use the following:

- Arrange yourselves into three equal sized groups, ideally with others you have not met or worked with before.
- Use the four coloured marker pens and flip chart to briefly outline your group's thoughts on the following aspects:
    - (Black): Aspects of the revised programme that you are certain of (be brief).
    - (Blue): Aspects that you need clarifying.
    - (Red): Aspects that are either unknown or cause concern.
    - (Green): Suggestions or ideas for the programme team.

This activity works very well as an ice breaker to identify learning needs; to identify what is already known (and saves repetition); to suggest where misconceptions might lie; to give participants a voice in determining the outcomes of the day; to gather feedback and specialist input from peers; and as a highly effective concluding resource for participants to revisit at the end of the session when they use the black pen to cross out each blue and red comment.

Initial assessment procedures may be like the piece-of-string analogy and depend on the time and resources allocated to initial assessment by the organization. These tend to include: assessment of any disability or support need; the learning styles questionnaire (Fleming, 1995), although these are sometimes contested (Coffield et al., 2004); and personal pre-enrolment interview where the CV and portfolio of past achievements are considered, if only superficially. More rigorous initial assessment can include all manner of questionnaires and inventories including: processing preferences (similar to the learning styles questionnaire but concerned with what the brain does with new information); personality styles (Honey and Mumford, 1992) (for example, activist or reflector); team-working questionnaire (Belbin, 2009) and others. While some of these will be familiar to practitioners in some contexts, different organizations have their own methods and there is no definitive list of how to identify learning needs (see more on learning styles in Chapter 6). Such methods fail to adequately capture the learner in the same way that the instrumental systems that require us to collect such data fail to capture what teaching and learning are really like.

2.3.3 Learning goals

Learning goals are points of ASK development that are negotiated and agreed between teacher and learner and can be as diverse as the learners themselves. These learning goals are recorded on each individual learning plan (ILP), learning contract or learning record and Ofsted, awarding bodies and other stakeholders are interested in them. During an inspection, it is common for an inspector to pick a learner's name at random and ask the teacher or trainers how that learner's needs were initially assessed, recorded, monitored and are to be catered for specifically in the session that is underway. While Ofsted does not yet have a remit to inspect every branch of the wider further education and skills sector, it is prudent for managers in other organizations where training takes place to be able to evidence learning goals for specific audit purposes.

2.3.4 Differentiation

Differentiation, as the name suggests, involves a variety of approaches and resources to meet the needs of both individuals and whole groups. Groups of learners are not at the same level of ability and do not have the same prior knowledge and experience. Learner-centred learning provides an opportunity for small group work where learners are involved in the same activities but will have different approaches to problem solving. As you get to know your learners, you can mix the groups so that outcomes of the session are supported with different levels of ability, past experiences and current knowledge. At its simplest, differentiation is the name given to the process of task or objective setting, given each learner's known levels of ASK performance. In practice, this has sometimes been interpreted to mean the level and type of additional learning support (ALS) put in place to help particular learners' progress – commonly those who struggle to keep up with the majority of learners in a group. In many organizations, trainers and teachers tend to rely on accommodating all the main preferred learning styles, visual, auditory, kinaesthetic and read/write (Fleming, 1995), in each session as a sweeping and unchallengeable demonstration of differentiation. In contrast, more enlightened organizations and practitioners seek to differentiate according to the level of stretch or challenge for learners in each session, based on a range of individual preferences and resources (Chapter 6 also explores issues around differentiation).

Some examples of what constitutes differentiation include:

- Setting three levels of learning outcomes for a session where, for example:
    - The less able will identify three causes of ...
    - Most learners will explain why three causes of ...
    - More able learners will distinguish between three causes of ...
- Encouraging learners to exploit or generate their own resources, for example:
    - When studying the two main types of plastics in a science or engineering group, having the learners empty their pockets and bags and categorize their own plastic belongings.
    - Encouraging learners to maintain reflective diaries or logs through audio recordings, mind maps, other visual organizers or video diaries rather than linear word documents which many learners are reluctant to use. Such reluctance, we suggest, is understandable since we do not tend to naturally think or reflect in a linear way, therefore the product or outcome of reflection is somewhat inauthentic.
- Locating the learning alongside contexts, materials, activities or resources that learners can relate to from their own cultural or industrial experience, for example:

- Having construction learners comment on how the theory of Health and Safety at Work legislation sits with their experiences on building sites. Such contributions tend to draw out rich information that can link to other themes through critical questioning, for example, 'That's something that we often see – but who else would be liable to prosecution in such a scenario?' or 'Remind me what the penalties are for that', and so on.
- Having learners in the social sciences relate a session's key concepts to current affairs, how commentators contribute to debate and how they are reported. For example, 'This was raised on BBC's *Question Time* last night. Your self-study for this week is to review that programme and complete this question sheet, then we will peer assess them at the start of the next session'.

2.4 A comment on differentiation

Since it became a focus for teacher effectiveness and one of the performative terms used in auditing and inspection regimes, differentiation has perhaps become over-theorized and misunderstood. Notwithstanding this, the regulatory performative system in the sector may be regarded as placing unrealistic responsibilities on practitioners, with the assumption that teaching and training, 'accommodates the particular needs of all their learners whose strengths and weaknesses they know intimately' (Ofsted, 2004: 9). Many of us do not know our *own* strengths and weaknesses intimately, while those of us who think that we do might be reluctant to share all of them. The only way to know all learners' strengths and weaknesses intimately is to adopt an invasive desire to know the *other* in which we have neither the ethical right nor the time for. We suggest that a professional interest in the learners' needs, rather than knowing them intimately, is more appropriate.

2.5 Know your audience: all learning and development has to start with the learner

As briefly discussed in section 2.1, key principles two and three of the LCL model provide a firm foundation in support of establishing learning and development. All programmes need an induction and, depending on whether the course is part-time, full-time or a one-off event, the induction may be over a week for full-time programmes and longer if one day or evening a week. Whichever induction model is used, it is crucial to both the learner and the teacher. In the case of learners, they are often coming together for the first time and they need to feel they are in a safe learning environment, both physically and emotionally. Careful skills are required in planning the types of activities used at induction. Activities should rarely, if ever, focus on the individual but involve group activities so no one person feels 'on show'. Group ice-breakers are helpful and the whole class or group contributing to ground rules, and signing up to them, will support behaviour, trust and respect.

These activities usually take place after the formal induction involving staff introductions, timetable, overview of the session or programme, objectives and assessment as well as institutional policies including health and safety. From such activities both learners and teachers will be able to get to know each other and establish trust.

2.6 Getting the right information

It is, of course, of paramount importance that learners access and receive the right information as part of their learning. Information and communication technology (ICT) has revolutionized teaching and learning. Classrooms have been replaced with learning environments including, in some cases, flexible learning spaces and this has been made possible through ICT. Such environments have computers with access to learner spaces for work and also internet access. Interactive whiteboards provide the opportunity for connecting with online learning programmes and access to knowledge outside the institution. Online discussions, video conferencing, e-portfolios and e-assessment are easily accessible and convenient ways of measuring progress with learning. Many flexible learning spaces have a variety of media embedded within them and provide access to many different forms of communication. The learners and teachers are still at the heart of the learning process through groups and individual discussion with presentations and seminars supported with ICT. Most learners now carry with them the latest smartphones or tablet computers which also have access to the internet and email. Within a few seconds, it is possible to receive information which previously would only be available through published work. Some institutions have their own virtual learning environment (VLE), which provides all learners with online documentation, activities and assessment put on by staff in the institution (see Chapter 9 on using technology to enhance learning).

2.7 Assessing current performance

Assessment is an important way of measuring how much learning has taken place, as well as ultimately (in some cases) providing nationally recognized benchmarks for qualifications. It provides the opportunity for learners to be given feedback as to how far they are meeting the required skills and knowledge at a particular stage of the session or programme. There are various types of assessment that can be embedded into the learning plans and provide feedback for both teachers and learners. This can involve giving feedback on what has been achieved at various stages in the programme, identifying areas for further development and planning future learning goals. Assessment can be formal, for example assessing written work or evidence submitted on portfolio-type programmes such as those associated with vocational education. Informal assessment might include question and answer, observations of presentations and group work and in some cases peer assessment, all of which provide feedback on progress and we point the reader to Chapter 8 for further discussion on this.

Regarding assessing learners' needs, LCL approaches encourage learners to be involved in their own assessment, known as 'Assessment for Learning' (NIACE, 2011) as opposed to 'Assessment of Learning', and to identify what it is that they need to know. Likewise, learners also benefit from being given some autonomy in how they are assessed (as in the earlier example of finding different media and formats for maintaining a reflective log) although this can be difficult in tightly structured accredited programmes.

2.8 Specifying the learning gap

Review of progress is informed through assessment activities which highlight gaps in knowledge or performance. This gives the teacher or trainer the opportunity to discuss with the learner their progress to date and additional support strategies where further development is required. Again, for best results, this ought not to be a provocative analysis but a further chance to give the learner a voice. Usually, records of discussion and agreed targets are kept by both the practitioner and the learner so that progress can be monitored since the last tutorial, in much the same way as appraisal records are maintained in many organizations. On some programmes, there is an opportunity for learners to reflect formally though their portfolio-building on their progress and identify areas for improvement and development to be discussed at their next tutorial or meeting.

2.9 Summary, case studies, discussion questions and learning activities

In this chapter we have tried to give teaching and training practitioners a sense of a number of issues related to the business of identifying the needs of learners in the sector. In short, these amount to: giving the learner a voice in making important decisions regarding how they learn best and how they are assessed; providing opportunities for learners to identify their own needs, learning goals, progress and development; and co-modifying the ways in which practitioners can move towards learner-centred approaches while taking a pragmatic view of regulatory systems at work in this diverse, difficult and frequently misunderstood sector. Smith et al. (2003: 6) condense this well in their belief that, 'it is what the learner says and does that creates learning and not what the teacher says and does'. These issues will be developed in subsequent chapters of the book.

The following two case studies are in two parts: first, an example of what a particular approach or perspective might typically look like; and second, a self-study activity in a similar vein for the reader or team to consider. The third case study is a single activity based on a YouTube video.

2.9.1 Case study The graffiti wall

Sal is a specialist in customer service and has taught on various NVQ and apprentice programmes, from Levels 1 to 4, for a private training provider for the last 10 years. In recent years, Sal has begun to question both her organization's role and her own role within it. Having recently read Coffield and Williamson's (2011) piece on 'exam factories', she began to suggest that she does, indeed, work in one. At the core of Sal's reservations is the growing notion that learners or candidates in her charge have unmet needs, specifically the need to be equipped with softer skills required for industry and employment than the competence-based qualifications she delivers can either provide or adequately measure. Sal's critical interest in her work has been articulated a number of times in modular work for the BA in Education and Professional Development which she is currently studying as a major component of her CPD. Here, Sal was intrigued recently by her tutor's story of how he uses tiled floor and wall areas as graffiti boards, spreadsheets, graph paper and blank tables when teaching large groups of vocational teachers in China. It gave Sal an idea.

At the induction session with her new Level 2 customer service candidates, Sal broke with her traditional and safe (because she thought it always worked well enough) teaching approach, and instead gave each candidate a dry-wipe pen and took them and a cleaning cloth outside. The gable end of the teaching block was entirely clad in weatherproof sheet metal and she instructed them to use it as a graffiti wall. She began by writing the question 'What is the purpose of customer service?' circling it and putting a few legs off it as in a spider diagram. She then left them to write their own 'first thoughts' in no more than five minutes, stood back and observed their interactions. Initially, Sal saw what she thought might be: the natural leaders emerging while others, who may need encouragement, taking a step back; interesting dialogue where there was very early debate concerning whether the question related to the customer or the provider (perhaps they might value more regular debating topics); and different styles of writing (one used 'bubble' writing while others wrote too small for her to read – she wondered whether some might have more creative ways of recording evidence rather than writing lengthy linear reports). When five minutes had passed, Sal stepped forward to read their offerings and noticed: some learners had not contributed anything, either in writing or discussion, and made a mental note of them – a quiet conversation later to see how they felt; there were plenty of competing views and it would, she thought, be interesting to see which perspective the quiet ones inclined towards; and there were errors in punctuation and grammar, for example, 'It's were you provide what the customer wants' and 'The customer is' always write'. Sal was thankful for the functional skills materials she had produced over the summer. The most interesting feature of the activity was the body language of the learners which indicated that they had enjoyed working outside and doing something in a different way.

In summary, Sal thought she had identified a number of learning needs including: literacy support, encouragement for some reluctant learners, the need to further embrace learning activities that accommodated competing views, and the need to explore creative ways of engaging learners with the programme content.

Activity

- Repeat the graffiti wall activity with a question related to your subject specialism. Try to use it as a method for identifying learning needs, both in the gaps in learners' existing skills and in identifying their learning preferences.

2.9.2 Case study The pensive adult returner

Tom is programme leader for a Foundation degree in mental health, validated by a higher education institution (HEI), at a general FE college. Having taught the psychology module for the first time at the start of last year, Tom is aware that the next cohort of learners may represent a much wider and diverse range of learning needs than he is used to in his core A-level psychology programme. In particular, he does not want a repeat of last year when five mature learners withdrew from the programme by the first half term, having seemingly suffered in silence, because they felt that the programme content, delivery and knowledge of their peers were far removed from their own previous learning experiences. Their leaving, in contrast to their enthusiasm at returning to study after many years of bringing up children, had shocked him and he felt that he had let them down badly. He also knew that trying to coax them back was not an option because it did not work last year and, anyway, he should look to remedy anything that was wrong before things deteriorated. The subsequent poor retention figures accounted for, he thought, his increasingly difficult position in the college.

Tom's initial focus in fixing this before it went wrong again was to review the interview, induction and initial assessment processes for the programme against the question, 'What is missing here?' When he thought about the systems in place, fairly acceptable as they were, from the withdrawn learners' point of view he realized:

- We don't find out if they can write at this level.
- We don't ask them to estimate their available home study hours per week.
- We don't even check whether they can read at this level.
- We don't give them a voice to tell us what they need beyond disclosing a perceived disability support need.
- We do nothing to prepare them for the academic demands of the course or their lives as learners in this place.

In short, we assume far too much.

Tom's strategy for overcoming these deficiencies was to initiate a full-day interview process to replace the hurried 'splash-and-go' affair that served only to check their qualifications and get them enrolled. The new interview day was held near to the end of the current teaching year so that the BTEC Level 3 Childcare group could run a crèche to take care of any pre-school children the interviewees had. He did some negotiating with his line manager, called in a few favours and put together the following interview programme which he posted to the interviewees.

Table 2.1 Example interviewing programme

Date:

Agenda

9.30	Registration (meet at main reception, collect temporary college passes and lunch vouchers, leave children at crèche, fire drill and toilets)
9.45	Introductions (icebreaker bingo over coffee – get to know your peers)
10.00	Staff introductions (your tutors will introduce themselves and share their experiences of studying and how they overcame their greatest concerns or difficulties)
10.15	Expectations activity #1 (poster-making, share expectations and/or concerns, opportunities for private discussions with tutors)
11.00	Break and quick check on crèche
11.15	The learner experience (two learners from the same programme last year share their top tips of how to make the most of your time on the programme)
11.30	Campus and library treasure hunt (in groups of three complete the investigation sheet while your tutors check your qualifications)
12.15	Plenary
12.30	Lunch (in refectory) and quick check on crèche
1.30	Expectations activity #2 (review poster from activity #1 and edit/amend if necessary)
1.45	Course requirements (investigation of the course learning outcomes and assessments)
2.15	Plenary
2.30	Break and quick check on crèche
2.45	Academic reading and writing (short exercise: read a short extract from a psychology journal, identify three key points and write a summary of them)
3.30	Plenary (discuss findings with a group of four peers)
3.45	Expectations activity #3 (review poster from activity #2 and edit/amend if necessary)
4.00	Next steps (plan some directed study into the summer schedule; make arrangements to keep in touch with peers/establish home study groups)
4.15	Final thoughts
4.30	Close of session/collect from crèche

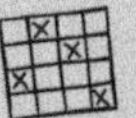

Activity

With regard to a programme or cohort of learners of your choice:

- Identify the features that Tom missed or failed to take account of.
- Replicate Tom's approach, amended with the things he missed, to identifying the gaps in the interview, enrolment and induction procedures.
- Consider how these can be rectified before the learners enrol.
- Suggest strategies for maintaining a needs-focus throughout the duration of the programme.

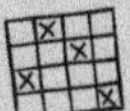

2.9.3 Activity Diverse needs

The following link, correct at the time of writing, is for a 15-minute video of Steve Ritz making a conference presentation as part of the TED (Technology, Entertainment, Design) series:

www.ted.com/talks/stephen_ritz_a_teacher_growing_green_in_the_south_bronx.html

Step 1: Watch the video in one sitting.
Step 2: Take a sheet of A4 paper and divide it into two vertical columns. Head the left-hand column *Needs* and the right-hand column *Solutions.*
Step 3: Watch the video again while listing every learning need that you see or hear evidence of in the left column. Against each perceived need, list Ritz's solution or learner provision.
Step 4: Watch the video again (expect to see something new each time).
Step 5: Borrow a dog and a tennis ball (getting out in the fresh air, away from new technologies and thinking – recommended as a strategy for reflective practice) and spend one hour thinking of your own learners' needs and how you might accommodate them.

References

Belbin, R. M. (2009) *The Belbin Guide to Succeeding at Work.* London: A and C Black.

Biesta, G. (2007) 'Why "what works" won't work: evidence-based practice and the democratic deficit in educational research', *Educational Theory*, 57 (1): 1–22.

Bingham, C. and Biesta, G. (2010) *Jacques Rancière: Education, Truth, Emancipation*. London: Continuum.

Callaghan, J. (1976) 'The Great Debate', speech at Ruskin College, Oxford, October.

Coffield, F. (2007) 'Foreword', in D. James, and G. Biesta (eds), *Improving Learning Cultures in Further Education*. Abingdon: Routledge, pp. xiii–xiv.

Coffield, F. (2008) *Just Suppose Teaching and Learning Became the First Priority*. London: Learning and Skills Network.

Coffield, F. (2009) *All You Ever Wanted to Know about Learning and Teaching But Were Too Cool to Ask*. London: Learning and Skills Network.

Coffield, F. (2010) 'Prioritising teaching and learning in an age of austerity', PCET Conference key note lecture, 8 July 2010, University of Huddersfield, Huddersfield.

Coffield, F., Moseley, D., Hall, E. and Ecclestone, K. (2004) *Learning Styles and Pedagogy in Post-16 Learning: A Systematic and Critical Review*. London: Learning and Skills Research Centre.

Coffield, F. and Williamson, B. (2011) *From Exam Factories to Communities of Discovery: The Democratic Route* (Bedford Way papers). London: University of London.

Cox, C. B. and Dyson, A. E. (eds) (1971) *The Black Papers on Education*. London: Davis-Poynter.

Fleming, N. (1995) *VARK: A Guide to Learning Styles* www.varklearn.com/english/index.asp (accessed 7 October 2013).

Freire, P. (2005) *Teachers as Cultural Workers*. Cambridge, MA: Westview.

Honey, P. and Mumford, A. (1992) *The Manual of Learning Styles* (3rd edn). Maidenhead: Peter Honey.

Kelly, A. V. (2009) *The Curriculum: Theory and Practice* (6th edn). London: Sage.

Knowles, M. (1978) *The Adult Learner: A Neglected Species*. Houston, TX: Gulf.

Lester-Smith, W. O. (1957) *Education: An Introductory Survey*. Harmondsworth: Penguin.

Mezirow, J. (1981) 'A critical theory of adult education and learning', *Adult Education*, 32 (1): 3–24.

Mitra, B., Lewin-Jones, J., Barrett, H. and Williamson, S. (2010) 'The use of video to enable deep learning', *Research in Post-Compulsory Education*, 15 (4): 405–414.

Murphy, L., Mufti, E. and Kassem, D. (2009) *Education Studies*. Maidenhead: Open University Press.

NIACE (2011) *Recognising and Recording Progress and Achievement*. Leicester: National Institute of Adult Continuing Education.

Ofsted (2004) *Why Colleges Fail*. London: Office for Standards in Education.

Orr, K. and Simmons, R. A. (2009) 'Dual identities: the in-service trainee teacher experience in the English further education sector', paper presented at the *Journal of Vocational Education and Training* 8th International Conference, 3–5 July 2009, Worcester College, Oxford.

Parrot, H. M. and Cherry, E. (2011) 'Using structured reading groups to facilitate deep learning, *Teaching Sociology*, 39 (4): 354–370.

Pring, R. (2010) 'The aims of education and the need for a wider vision of learning?', public lecture, 23 June 2010, University of Huddersfield, Huddersfield.

Rogers, C. R. (1965) *Client-centred Therapy*. New York: Houghton-Mifflin.

Scheffler, I. (2011) *Four Pragmatists: A Critical Introduction to Peirce, James, Mead and Dewey*. Oxon: Routledge.

Smith, A., Lovatt, M. and Wise, D. (2003) *Accelerated Learning: A User's Guide*. Stafford: Network Educational Press.

Smith, T. W. and Colby, S. A. (2007) 'Teaching for deep learning', *The Clearing House*, 80, (5): 205–210.

Tomlinson, J. (1996) *Inclusive Learning: Report of the Learning Difficulties and/or Disabilities Committee* (Tomlinson Report). London: HMSO.

Trifonas, P. P. (2000) *Revolutionary Pedagogies: Cultural Politics, Instituting Education, and the Discourse of Theory*. London: Routledge Falmer.

Wheeler, K. A. (2007) 'Learning for deep change', *Journal of Education for Sustainable Development*, 1 (1): 45–50.

CHAPTER 3

SPECIFYING LEARNING OBJECTIVES

Nena Skrbic and Jane Burrows

Learning outcomes

After reading this chapter, the reader should be able to:

- Define and distinguish between aims and objectives.
- Describe the historical development of objectives.
- Appraise approaches to devising and writing objectives.
- Formulate educational objectives that are appropriate to their individual situation.

Chapter outline

As educators and learning and development practitioners we can all relate to that small moment of triumph when we sense that an objective has been achieved. It is that moment perhaps that gives us legitimacy. Objectives, outcomes or goals (we use the terms interchangeably, even though there is some debate regarding whether this should be the case) serve to simplify the complexity of the learning process. They minimize the dangers of leaving our intentions unexpressed, our goals in a state of semi-completion and our overarching plans undone. As Anderson and Krathwohl (2001: 3) explain: 'Objectives are especially important in teaching because teaching is an *intentional* and *reasoned* act'.

The debate about learning outcomes dates back more than 50 years and has become a contemporary obsession. The first part of this chapter will take a generalized view and give a historical account of this debate. Since any discussion about learning objectives necessitates some reflection on the theoretical foundations of learning design, links will be made to learning theory. The characteristics of a well-defined, SMART (specific, measurable, attainable, realistic or relevant and time-bound) and assessable learning objective that has clearly observable results will be shared in section 3.3. Section 3.4 deals with the development of objectives within learning domains. Assessing achievement of learning objectives is addressed in section 3.5 and section 3.6 includes summary comments, discussion questions and learning activities. The chapter will be contextualized in current pedagogy and will make reference to the education and training environments within which courses or sessions are designed.

3.1 Underpinning theory

There is an entire industry devoted to learning objectives and Benjamin Bloom, whose *Taxonomy of Educational Objectives* was originally published in 1956 (Marzano and Kendall, 2007), has become its figurehead. Bloom's ideas have been extensively discussed and elaborated on by numerous writers. His original taxonomy of the cognitive domain, identified below, has a hierarchical structure:

1. knowledge
2. comprehension
3. application
4. analysis
5. synthesis
6. evaluation.

This list is based on a simple rule of precedence and, rather like a series of pedagogical hurdles, outlines a learner's anticipated trajectory of improvement, through the acquisition of factual knowledge and beyond. Domain-specific procedure-related verbs are used at each level and describe the mental processes that will achieve the hoped-for educational ends.

The taxonomy has benefits. To begin with, it has the merit of simplicity. Each stage reflects a certain ability to process information, so it works well with any criteria-based course, examination syllabus or curriculum specification. It is a practical and coherent model that can be used when planning differentiated outcomes. The taxonomy can help the practitioner to explain, categorize and define their educational goals and find alternate wording for their outcomes (Marzano, 2009). The choice of verbs necessitates some degree of conscious selection also. Careful application of the taxonomy can facilitate differentiation so that a learner can progress towards the higher level objectives. These benefits might explain the model's successful application in many education or training contexts.

Colder argued that the taxonomy is 'built on false premises and shifting muddy definitions' (1983: 300). He confidently asserted that: 'The influence of the *Bloom Taxonomy* is set to wane over the next 25 years' (Colder, 1983: 300). However, time has not diminished its importance. The fact that initial teacher training courses, for example, still address Bloom in their schemes (arguably) serves as sufficient validation of its usefulness. For practitioners, the taxonomy has the undoubted appeal of providing a basic step-by-step guide for the formulation of objectives.

It could be argued that the taxonomy presents an overly simplistic view of human learning and that there are more nuances to the process than Bloom is presenting. For instance, supporters of inductive learning or problem-based approaches would argue that 'application' should come before the introduction of a concept or idea. It could also be claimed that the taxonomy is based on the ideal learner. The taxonomic layers are like a jigsaw; assemble them correctly and a picture of the perfect learner forms. Besides, knowledge is not necessarily the default setting for a new group of learners, nor will all learners follow the same trajectory; many will have different starting points, and an infinite distance might separate one learner from another.

Furthermore, the very idea of a taxonomic approach is out of step with the prevailing views of much twenty-first century thought about teaching and training and the psychology of learning, which has abandoned a predominantly linear way of thinking about the learning process. In the contemporary literature of educational philosophy and theory it is routinely assumed that 'a successful course of education serves purposes that cannot be completely stated in advance' (Harđarson, 2012: 223).

Considering the fact that a learning environment's dynamic is always fluid, how can a taxonomy take account of the large number of variables that go into teaching, training and learning? Are such models a reliable indicator of the actual capacities of the learner? What about unforeseen outcomes or the 'non-instrumentally valuable' aspects of learning (Carr, 2003: 209)? Considering that the process of learning is never linear, does setting pre-determined behavioural objectives take into account the 'random and incalculable way' (Wringe, 1988: 12) in which learning often takes place?

As a consequence of such questions, Bloom's taxonomy has been subject to continued development and refinement. In 2001, Anderson and Krathwohl revised the taxonomy of the cognitive domain. This is represented in Table 3.1.

In their book *A Taxonomy for Learning, Teaching and Assessing,* Anderson and Krathwohl (2001: xxii) state that the changes made to Bloom's model in the Revised Taxonomy are meant to be 'consistent with current psychological and educational thinking'. Broadly speaking, the changes itemized below are in line with cognitive approaches to learning (such as remembering and problem solving).

The lowest level of the original taxonomy, 'knowledge', was renamed and became 'remember'. This is an important shift because it recognises the importance of any pre-existing knowledge.

Cognitivists argue that knowledge is the outcome of interaction between the learner and the environment, so the use of active verbs rather than abstract nouns (for example 'apply' rather than 'application') in the Revised Taxonomy is important. They indicate the learner's active involvement in the acquisition of knowledge.

'Comprehension' and 'synthesis' were re-titled 'understanding' and 'creating'. The addition of the verb 'create' reflects the fact that the process of gaining knowledge is just as important as the product.

'Synthesis' and 'evaluation' are inverted. The ability to evaluate comes before the learner's ability to synthesize or create.

The 'evaluation' stage becomes 'creating'.

Ultimately, greater emphasis is placed on transfer in the Revised Taxonomy. As Mayer says, one of the goals of instruction is to promote transfer, so 'objectives should include the cognitive processes associated with Understand, Apply, Analyze, Evaluate, and Create' (2002: 232). He continues: 'The Revised Taxonomy is based on a broader vision of learning that includes not only acquiring knowledge but also being able to use knowledge in a variety of new situations' (2002: 232).

Despite the perceived usefulness of learning taxonomies, some educators view the specification of objectives as an unnecessary burden or 'fearsome constraint' (Laurillard, 1993: 183). Of course we know what we want our learners to learn. Why do we need to specify it? It is a

Table 3.1 Adapted from Anderson and Krathwohl's (2001) Revised Taxonomy

The Cognitive Process Dimension					
Remember	Understand	Apply	Analyse	Evaluate	Create
1.1 Recognizing	2.1 Interpreting	3.1 Executing	4.1 Differentiating	5.1 Checking	6.1 Generating
1.2 Recollecting	2.2 Exemplifying	3.2 Implementing	4.2 Classifying	5.2 Critiquing	6.2 Planning
	2.3 Classifying		4.3 Attributing		6.3 Producing
	2.4 Summarizing				
	2.5 Inferring				
	2.6 Comparing				
	2.7 Explaining				
Retention	Transfer →				

contentious issue; perhaps because it is indirectly linked to debates surrounding the philosophy of teaching, or the purpose of education.

Supporters of process-orientated models of teaching and learning promote the incidental nature of learning. As O'Houle (2009: 180) acknowledges: 'Any learning activity is ... a force field in which many other purposes than the professed goals are in operation'.

The growth of technology mediated learning (TML) is significant in this chapter and raises supplementary questions about the construction of learning objectives. On the one hand, the abundance of e-learning products necessitates the formulation of purpose-oriented and assessable e-learning outcomes. Equally, though, the new competencies that digital literacy requires necessitate a certain amount of expressive flexibility.

The behavioural objective can be linked to certain approaches to pedagogy and linked to a specific time period. Today, as Palliam (2012) observes below, the focus of attention has shifted much further to the learner's inner processes, which constitutes a challenge for the modern educator:

> Traditionally learning outcomes were easily stated and observed in behavioural terms. However, with the onslaught of e-learning the challenge is to equate learning outcomes with artificial intelligence. This brings one to the issue: how does one measure inquiry and analysis, critical and creative thinking, written and oral communication; quantitative literacy; information literacy; teamwork and finally problem solving. (2012: 37–38)

Clearly, the criteria integral to the traditional objective have widened in scope; in addition, e-learning takes us beyond what can be objectively observed. See Chapter 9 for more on e-learning. This being the case, some commentators argue that the learning objective should become more and more a medium for the expression of what cannot be measured.

3.2 Aligning learning objectives to courses, business, departmental and team strategies

We all confront the business of planning and writing objectives in different ways. Decisions can be made on different bases; for example, assessment criteria, professional requirements, module specifications or organizational demands. Indeed, many factors need to be considered when developing objectives in order to avoid 'producing impractical and/or irrelevant projected outcomes' (Caffarella, 2001: 59).

If a course plays an integral part in training people to occupy specific roles, then it makes absolute sense for any outcomes to be linked to workforce and organizational development priorities. Rosemary Harrison's itemization of the eight stages involved in facilitating planned learning events reproduced in the list below is especially useful here:

1. Establish needs.
2. Agree on purpose and objectives for the learning event.
3. Identify profile of intended learning population.
4. Agree on strategy and delivery of the learning event.
5. Select learner cohort and produce detailed specification for the learning event.
6. Finalize strategy and design the learning event.
7. Deliver the learning event.
8. Monitor and evaluate the learning event. (2005: 133)

As we can see from this list, objectives must be formulated quite early on and must fit in with the organization's strategic goals, often referred to as Key Performance Indicators (KPIs) or Educational Key Performance Indicators (EKPIs). The growing popularity of KPIs in educational learning has emerged from employers' demands for more vocational education and training (VET). The growing audit culture has also necessitated the preparation of clearly expressed and assessable learning objectives that have evidentiary value. Thus, learning objectives rely increasingly on demonstration and links to assessment.

Harrison (2009) states that good design is achieved by specifying the performance of the learner at various points in a learning session. Therefore, objectives provide a clear focus and link the session to its purpose. Objectives must have contextual relevance and take account of the conditions in which learners will have to perform once the learning session has ended.

We will use the development of a set of core knowledge learning objectives for a teacher training course as an example of this.

Example

A new curriculum leader in a further education college has been appointed to run the off-site Level 3 Award in Education and Training for a Fire and Rescue Service (FRS). All units in the Level 3 Award in Education and Training are available on the Qualifications and Credit

Framework (QCF) website. The first unit in the Award is Understanding Roles, Responsibilities and Relationships in Education and Training. Units are expressed in terms of learning outcomes and assessment criteria. The first learning outcome is to understand the teaching roles and responsibilities in education and training. The assessment criteria for this learning outcome are as follows:

1. Explain the teaching role and responsibilities in education and training.
2. Summarize key aspects of legislation, regulatory requirements and codes of practice relating to own role and responsibilities.
3. Explain ways to promote equality and diversity.
4. Explain why it is important to identify and meet individual learner needs.

The organization has conducted a gap analysis to determine the training need within the organization and the personal development needs of the participants. This has helped the workforce development team to establish the outcomes, or global objectives, of the programme. The goals of the programme are to: (1) improve the job performance of current staff; (2) to advance or enable employees to change their work roles and functions; and (3) to assist the overall organization to adapt to changing ways of operating. However, the previous scheme of work has not taken into account the FRS's Key Performance Indicators for education and training as defined in the organization's Training and Development Strategy and itemized in Table 3.2. As a result, they have failed to reconcile the outcomes with the workforce and organizational development priorities. In preparation for a meeting with the Head of Training and Development at the FRS, the curriculum leader needs to rework the first few sessions (which deal with Learning Outcome 1) utilizing the KPIs.

Comments

It is apparent that some re-configuration of the unit assessment criteria has to occur to meet the identified training and development needs associated with the EKPIs set by the organization. The first task is to determine operationally focused session outcomes based on the identified priority areas and aligned with the institution's strategic vision.

Alignment with the EKPIs will be enhanced by: (1) liaising with the FRS to ensure a course that is relevant to learners' specific needs; (2) accessing and using non-confidential data and documents from learners' workplaces;

Table 3.2 FRS's Key Performance Indicators for Education and Training

Key Performance Indicators
KPI 1 To prepare all staff sufficiently to carry out their roles effectively
KPI 2 Embed the principles of the Integrated Personal Development System (IPDS) into all training and development activities
KPI 3 To ensure that the Fire and Rescue Service has appropriately skilled and experienced personnel to undertake the wide range of community services that it is required to provide
KPI 4 To address issues identified from a Training Needs Analysis (TNA) to meet the Fire and Rescue Authority's legal duties and responsibilities
KPI 5 Maintain National Occupational Standards and demonstrate Personal Qualities and Attributes (PQAs) and core values of the Service
KPI 6 Effective performance management through the use of annual Professional Development Reviews (PDRs) aligned to organizational and individual objectives

and (3) making full use of the variety of experience of work and life that learners bring to the programme. For example, the FRS's Assurance of Competence Cycle might be included in the first session.

Since the course is designed to give participants an understanding of the skills needed for their specific vocational sector, transfer emerges as a significant concern. Learning outcomes must place emphasis on practical application and foreground opportunities for transfer, which according to Perkins and Salomon, 'occurs when learning in one context or with one set of materials impacts on performance in another context or with related materials' (1992: 422).

3.2.1 Planning your objectives

Robert Mager's typology of the ideal objective, proposed in his seminal work entitled *Preparing Instructional Objectives* (1984), is a helpful framework for the teacher to use when planning their objectives. An objective should meet the following components:

> Component 1: behaviour – 'identify and name the overall behaviour act (terminal behaviour)'.
> Component 2: conditions – 'define the important conditions under which the behaviour is to occur (givens and/or restrictions and limitations)'.
> Component 3: standards – 'define the criterion of acceptable performance'.

Mager pioneered the importance of translating 'knowledge' or 'information' into objectives that can be observed, monitored and controlled. This is a key aim when aligning course objectives to an institution's EKPIs. In our example, participants are not only expected to acquire the skills and knowledge associated with the course, but also must apply what they have learned in the work environment at a certain level of proficiency. In order to achieve this, the outcomes must be mapped to observable performance criteria and be designed to reinforce appropriate behaviours.

Essentially, the predominance of outcome-based education (OBE) or outcome-based learning (OBL) has resulted in the growing popularity of KPIs in education. Broadly speaking, OBE is an approach to education in which curriculum decisions are guided by exit learning outcomes that are based on observable performance criteria. Ross (2012: 141) defines OBE as:

> ...embodying the philosophy that the best way to learn is to first determine what needs to be achieved. Once the desired results or 'exit outcomes' have been determined, the strategies, processes, techniques and means are put in place to achieve the predetermined goals. It is in essence a working-backwards with learners as the centre of the learning–teaching milieu.

It could be said that OBE rests ultimately on economic (namely neoliberalist) principles, which characterize the current political milieu and education and training landscape. In this outcome-focused context, learning outcomes data plays a key role in evaluating programme success. Douglass et al. (2012: 317) make a perfectly reasonable point in this regard: 'The potential to accurately measure learning gains is also a diagnostic tool for institutional self-improvement'.

3.3 Creating SMART learning objectives

3.3.1 Learning aims and learning objectives

Content depends on specifications. Those specifications inform the planning process for learning and teaching. Content of lessons will be specified in a scheme of work and the practitioner must formulate the learning objectives for each session. The first stage is to clarify the general aim for a lesson, from which the learning objectives ensue. An aim is different from an objective, it is a general statement of intent for a learning session or long-term goal.

Examples of learning aims:

- To encourage learners to understand the significance of maintaining good health and physical fitness.
- To develop interests and skills so that leisure time may be used purposefully.
- To introduce the world's major religions.

These are aims because each is a general statement of intent that can be broken down into specific objectives.

An objective is a specific learning result or short-term goal, it expresses what a learner is expected to know, be able to do or understand at the end of a learning session (Donnelly and Fitzmaurice, 2005). A learning objective starts with the statement, 'By the end of the session, the learner will be able to ...'.

Table 3.3 Examples of learning objectives

Examples of learning objectives	
By the end of the session, the learner will be able to:	• Translate 10 infinitives indicating various mental states into appropriate behavioural terms
	• Analyse the various parts of a popular daily newspaper by presenting the material in tabular form
	• Measure alkali levels using a series of experiments

A learning objective is not about what the practitioner is going to do. It does not describe the teaching or training process or the subject matter that is to be learned; rather, a learning objective should:

- State what the learner is expected to learn.
- Describe how the learner will demonstrate what they have learned.

SMART learning objectives

Only after formulating precise learning objectives can planning for learning take place. Therefore, it is imperative that objectives are SMART, an acronym which breaks down as follows:

Specific:

When writing learning objectives, remember the word specific. Objectives are specific to the lesson and must be specifically stated. Avoid using verbs that are vague and cannot be observed, such as appreciate, know, believe. Stick to clear and observable verbs; for example, identify, choose, explain, analyse, solve. Therefore, it is not sufficient to state as a learning objective:

- By the end of the session, the learner will be able to study Darwin's theory of evolution.

A clear objective must specify how the learners will demonstrate their learning. For example:

- By the end of the session, the learner will be able to cite examples in support of Darwin's theory of evolution.

Measurable:

A learning objective not only describes what a learner will do, but also the conditions under which the learning will occur, so that it can be observed and evaluated. The following objective is not measurable:

- By the end of the session, the learner will know the causes of the First World War.

How will the practitioner measure what the learners know? A better formulation would be:

- By the end of the session, the learner will be able to produce a timeline of the events leading up to the outbreak of the First World War.

The completeness and accuracy of the timeline would enable the practitioner to measure the learner's level of knowledge.

Achievable:

To set unachievable objectives is self-defeating for both practitioner and learner. For example:

- By the end of the session, the learner will be able to research the European Union.

A learning objective such as this could not be accomplished in one session of learning, covering, as it does, a highly complex organization that is opaque to many people at the best of times. It is a general aim rather than a specific learning objective and would be better broken down into specifics. For example:

- By the end of the session, the learner will be able to: list member states of the EU; complete a diagram of the organization of the EU; describe the advantages and disadvantages of membership of the EU.

Relevant:

All objectives should be relevant to the learning session. The practice is for teachers and trainers to share their intended learning objectives with learners at the beginning of each session. The latter tend to be far more inclined towards learning when they see the relevance of what they are being asked to do. If the lesson is about nuclear energy, then all learning objectives should be focused on the subject, making learning relevant and ensuring clarity about what the learners are being asked to do, and will be assessed on, within the overall context of their learning for the session.

Time-bound:

A learning session is a finite period of time, objectives must be achievable within the time frame available. An objective that covers entire subjects would not be possible within a given lesson, for example:

- By the end of the session, the learner will be able to understand the philosophy of Plato.

Again, this is more an aim than a specific objective, and needs to be broken down into objectives that are achievable in the time allowed.

3.4 Domains of learning and learning objectives

Learning objectives can be formulated in three domains: cognitive domain, psychomotor domain and affective domain, although it is important to remember that many learning objectives do not purely belong to one domain.

3.4.1 The cognitive domain

The cognitive domain is demonstrated by knowledge recall and the intellectual skills. It is predominant in the majority of study programmes. Bloom identified six levels within the taxonomy of the cognitive domain.

1. Knowledge: the learner remembers previous learned material. The first step in the taxonomy represents baseline competence. It focuses on the ability of the learner to recount facts, if only to show that they have learnt them. Procedure-related verbs are chosen to determine factual accuracy and learning objectives may include verbs such as 'recall', 'reproduce', 'label' or 'recite'. At this level, the learner is on the precipice of understanding, which is the next step.
2. Comprehension: the learner understands the meaning of the material. In this step of the taxonomy, the learner is required to explain the facts that they have learnt. Gaps in knowledge and experience or information imperfectly understood at this stage can result in later misunderstandings and mistakes. Verbs used at this stage might be 'explain', 'describe', 'paraphrase', 'predict' or 'discuss', among many others.
3. Application: the learner uses the material in a new situation. This level determines the ability of the learner to apply the knowledge that has been learnt. This may be evidenced in simulations, projects or demonstrations. Key verbs might be 'use', 'illustrate' or 'operate'.
4. Analysis: the learner deconstructs and analyses the learning, discovers links. This is the point at which the learner is expected to make sense of the knowledge acquired. Procedure-related verbs will focus on the ability to look for patterns and offer analysis, to 'compare', 'contrast', 'differentiate between' and 'examine' information. This is the stage before learners are required to demonstrate that they have formed opinions on the subject matter.
5. Synthesis: the learner re-assembles information and concepts to form new patterns or arguments. At this penultimate stage, learners are expected to be able to 'argue', 'defend', 'support' and 'evaluate' their opinions on the information acquired. Learners might be asked to 'reconstruct', 'conceive' or 'modify' information and are expected to show some critical insight into the process. This level depends on something more nuanced than the simple restatement of knowledge.
6. Evaluation: the learner makes judgements about learning, identifies strengths and weaknesses. At this final stage of their intellectual endeavour, the learner has reached a meta-level of understanding and might be asked to 'appraise', 'argue' and 'criticise' the information acquired. This demands a higher level of self-awareness and, perhaps,

an ability to cope with the ambiguous and uncertain. The moral considerations of an idea might be discussed or ethical or theological objections to a proposed idea might be examined.

The tasks at the lower levels are the mastery tasks, those which are easier, not dependent on prior learning and can be attained in a short time. As the learner moves up the taxonomy, the higher levels contain the developmental tasks, which are more difficult, dependent on prior learning and create deep and transferable learning.

We have already learned that it is important to be specific when identifying learning objectives for a lesson. They must describe the learning that will take place and must be observable and measurable. They must also reflect the appropriate levels of the domain, or domains.

3.4.2 Writing objectives in the cognitive domain

It is important to choose appropriate verbs for each of the taxonomic levels and Bloom initially provided a list, which has been supplemented and extended by various scholars over the years. These lists are not exhaustive, but are reasonably comprehensive. Below are some examples:

Knowledge: arrange, define, duplicate, label, list, memorize, name, order, recall, repeat.

For example: By the end of the session, the learner will be able to:

- Recall genetics terminology; e.g. genotype, chromosome, phenotype.
- List the five Ks of Sikhism.

Comprehension: classify, describe, discuss, explain, express, identify, locate, report, select.

For example: By the end of the session, the learner will be able to:

- Classify reactions as exothermic and endothermic.
- Describe Kolb's experiential learning cycle.

Application: apply, choose, construct, demonstrate, illustrate, operate, practise, select, use.

For example: By the end of the session, the learner will be able to:

- Construct a timeline of events leading up to the outbreak of the First World War.
- Select appropriate techniques for stemming blood loss.

Analysis: analyse, appraise, calculate, compare, contrast, differentiate, discriminate, distinguish, question.

For example: By the end of the session, the learner will be able to:

- Analyse two retail business models.
- Calculate gradient from maps in metres, kilometres, per cent and ratio.

Synthesis: arrange, assemble, compose, construct, create, design, develop, formulate, manage, organize, plan, propose, summarize.

For example: By the end of the session, the learner will be able to:

- Develop a care programme for one in-patient.
- Summarize the causes of the Russian Revolution of March 1917.

Evaluation: appraise, argue, assess, attach, choose, compare, defend, estimate, judge, predict, rate, select, evaluate.

For example: By the end of the session, the learner will be able to:

- Assess the contribution of Faraday to the field of electromagnetic induction.
- Compare the education policies of Gladstone and Disraeli.

Worked example

Table 3.4 Topic – Plato's Analogy of the Cave in 'The Republic' Book VII (AS Level Religious Studies)

	The learner will be able to:
Knowledge	Recall the story of the cave
Comprehension	Explain the meanings within the analogy
Application	Apply the analogy of the cave to an excerpt from *The Matrix*
Analysis	Compare the analogy of the cave with the analogy in an extract from C. S. Lewis' *The Last Battle*
Synthesis	Plan an essay on the analogy of the cave
Evaluation	Assess the merits of the analogy of the cave as an explanation for man's understanding of reality

Activities that can be included in learning objectives at each of taxonomic levels are:

- Knowledge: describe, state the facts, define key terms.
- Comprehension: interpret material, reorganize material, classify knowledge.
- Application: use material to answer a question, choose the most appropriate material in a situation.
- Analysis: categorize, deduce, give reasons, compare.
- Synthesis: solve a problem, write a report or essay, design a leaflet or poster, give a presentation.
- Evaluation: judge or critically appraise, advantages and disadvantages, compare and contrast, consider evidence.

3.4.3 The psychomotor domain

The psychomotor domain is demonstrated by physical skills such as co-ordination, dexterity and manipulation. In the psychomotor domain, the learner demonstrates fine motor skills such as use of precision instruments or tools, or actions that evidence gross motor skills such as the use of the body in dance or athletic performance. Bloom did not develop detailed work on this domain, citing lack of experience in teaching these skills; however, Dave (1970), proposed the following hierarchy:

1. Imitation: the learner observes and copies skills. The learner is introduced to a skill or procedure, they observe and pattern their behaviour after someone else. Performance may be of low quality. Key verbs might be 'repeat', 'mimic', 'copy'.
2. Manipulation: the learner performs a skill. At this level, performance could be accomplished by following instructions, or it could be done from memory. Procedure-related verbs could be 'grasp', 'handle', 'operate', 'assemble'.
3. Precision: the learner accurately reproduces a skill independently. At this stage, the learner becomes more exact, refines their performance and is able to perform with a high degree of precision. The learner has reached a stage where they are able to 'balance', 'calibrate' or 'measure'. Proficiency is indicated by a quick, accurate and highly co-ordinated performance.
4. Articulation: the learner combines more than one skill in sequence. At this penultimate stage, the learner co-ordinates and adapts a series of actions to achieve consistency in their performance. Key verbs at this stage could be 'perform' (skilfully), 'choreograph', 'combine'. It is

at this stage that the learner can modify patterns to fit special requirements or circumstances.

5. Naturalization: the learner performs one or more skills. At the final stage, the learner combines and sequences skills, performing them consistently and naturally. It becomes second nature to perform at a high level, without needing to think too much about their actions. They could be required to 'adapt', 'adjust', 'refine'. Learning objectives emphasize creativity based on highly developed skills.

3.4.4 Writing objectives in the psychomotor domain

As with the cognitive domain, it is important to choose appropriate verbs for each stage, as careful selection of these enable the practitioner to assess the performance of their learners.

Imitation: copy, follow, mimic, repeat, replicate, reproduce, trace.

For example: By the end of the session the learner will be able to:

- Repeat a sequence of dance steps.
- Replicate the procedure for administering an intra-muscular injection using an orange.

Manipulation: act, assemble, bend, build, differentiate (by touch), dismantle, execute, grasp, handle, manipulate, operate, perform.

For example: By the end of the session the learner will be able to:

- Build a 3D model following instructions.
- Perform simple suturing under supervision.

Precision: balance, calibrate, demonstrate, manoeuvre, measure, dissect, master.

For example: By the end of the session the learner will be able to:

- Demonstrate how to lay one course of bricks.
- Manoeuvre a car into a parallel parking place.

Articulation: administer, choreograph, combine, construct, create, modify, organize, perform (skilfully).

For example: By the end of the session the learner will be able to:

- Administer CPR on a patient.
- Modify instructions to meet the needs of different learners.

Naturalization: adapt, adjust, design, develop, mend, refine.

For example: By the end of the session the learner will be able to:

- Adjust the height of the forks on a forklift truck for a range of pallet sizes.
- Design a new gymnastic routine.

Worked example

Table 3.5 Topic – Administering intra-muscular injections

	The learner will be able to:
Imitation	Replicate the procedure for an intra-muscular injection using an orange
Manipulation	Perform an intra-muscular injection under supervision
Precision	Demonstrate how to provide an intra-muscular injection efficiently
Articulation	Administer an intra-muscular injection independently
Naturalization	Adjust the administration of an intra-muscular injection dependent on patient need

Activities that can be included in learning objectives at each of taxonomic levels:

- Imitation: observe, respond to instructions, learn a pattern.
- Manipulation: build a model, operate a machine, perform a procedure, repair.
- Precision: measure the effects, dissect an organ, demonstrate to a beginner.
- Articulation: play in a sports game, perform a role, solve a problem.
- Naturalization: develop a programme, construct a theory, use advanced series of integrated movements, combine a series of skills or activities to meet new requirements.

It is worth noting that Simpson (1972) developed a more detailed hierarchy comprising seven levels:

1. Perception: using observation to guide physical activity.
2. Mindset: willingness to follow a course of action.
3. Guided response: practise to acquire physical skills.

4. Mechanism: learned responses become more habitual, physical skills become more confident and proficient.
5. Complex overt responses: responses are automatic; skills are performed accurately and with good co-ordination.
6. Adaptation: skills are well developed; learner can modify performance dependent on situation.
7. Origination: the learner can utilize highly developed skills in an innovative or creative way.

Other taxonomies in the psychomotor domain have been developed by Guilbert (1987), Dawson (1998) and Ferris and Aziz (2005), the latter specifically for engineering learners.

3.4.5 The affective domain

The affective domain relates to attitudes, values and emotions and was developed by Krathwohl, Bloom and Masia (1964). It concerns behaviours indicating attitudes of awareness, interest, attention, concern and responsibility. It is about listening and responding appropriately, interacting with others and demonstrating values and characteristics that are appropriate to a situation.

1. Receiving: the learner attends passively, is aware of and is willing to receive information. Learning outcomes may emphasize compliance in responding, willingness to respond or satisfaction in responding (motivation). Key verbs would be 'accept', 'listen', 'ask'.
2. Responding: the learner attends or reacts. At this stage, the learner participates in learning and demonstrates interest in the subject. Procedure-related verbs could be 'answer', 'comply', 'join'. The learner questions ideas, concepts and models in an attempt to understand fully.
3. Valuing: the learner displays consistent behaviour and commitment. This can range from simple acceptance to a more complex state of commitment. The learner's values are expressed in their behaviour and can be identified. The learner is able to 'conform', 'justify' or 'share' and is beginning to internalize the values.
4. Organizing: the learner organizes values into priorities. At this stage, the learner brings together different values, resolves conflict and internalizes values. They can 'challenge', 'integrate', 'judge', 'resolve'.
5. Characterizing: the learner behaves in accordance with accepted values. The learner's behaviour is predictable and characteristic of them. Learning objectives are concerned with the learner's personal,

social and emotional patterns of adjustment. At this final stage, learners could 'demonstrate a belief in', 'solve' and 'influence'. There is a higher level of self-awareness and an ability to apply values consistently.

3.4.6 Writing objectives in the affective domain

Krathwohl et al. (1964) provided an initial list of verbs applicable to each stage in the domain. This has, as with the other domains, been added to over the years. The examples of verbs useful in the affective domain given below are not exhaustive.

Receiving: accept, ask, follow, identify, discuss, listen, locate, name, read, use, watch.

For example: By the end of the session the learner will be able to:

- Discuss the arguments about the need for professional ethical standards.
- Locate at least five Neolithic archaeological sites on a map.

Responding: ask, answer, assist, comply, consent, co-operate, follow, help, join, participate, practise, request, share.

For example: By the end of the session the learner will be able to:

- Answer questions posed by their peers.
- Participate in discussions with peers and trainer.

Valuing: adopt, approve, commit, conform, differentiate, display, embrace, endorse, initiate, justify, prefer.

For example: By the end of the session the learner will be able to:

- Justify reasons for company greeting protocol.
- Demonstrate conformity to industry safety standards by completing a risk analysis.

Organizing: arrange, challenge, complete, defend, dispute, establish, integrate, judge, prioritize, propose, question, resolve, synthesize.

For example: By the end of the session the learner will be able to:

- Prioritize time effectively to meet the needs of the organization, family and self.
- Propose amendments to departmental schemes of work.

Characterizing: adhere, advocate, behave, characterize, continue, demonstrate a belief in, exemplify, follow, influence, incorporate, practise, qualify, revise, solve, support, value.

For example: By the end of the session the learner will be able to:

- Practise the Health and Safety regulations in their workplace.
- Revise assessment criteria.

Worked example

Table 3.6 Topic – Equality and diversity awareness training

	The learner will be able to:
Receiving	Identify main points of organization equality and diversity policy
Responding	Share workplace equality and diversity challenges
Valuing	Differentiate between types of discrimination (positive, direct, indirect)
Organizing	Integrate equality and diversity awareness into working practices
Characterizing	Revise current practice to ensure adherence to equality and diversity policy

Activities that can be included in learning objectives at each of taxonomic levels:

- Receiving: question and answer, reading, lecture, note taking, video.
- Responding: discussion, preparing and giving presentations, question and answer, role play, helping or coaching others.
- Valuing: problem solving, planning projects.
- Organizing: debate, decision making, compare and contrast, SWOT analysis.
- Characterizing: group and teamwork, revision, problem solving, active listening.

3.5 Learning objectives and differentiation

One issue in teaching and learning that can cause practitioners difficulty is that of differentiation. Learners are not all the same, do not have the same abilities and capabilities and addressing individual needs is a demanding task. However, formulating appropriate learning objectives can aid this task. Many organizations now provide lesson plan proformas that stimulate the practitioner to consider differentiating their learning objectives thus:

- By the end of the session, all learners will be able to …
- By the end of the session, some learners will be able to …
- By the end of the session, a few learners will be able to …

Formulating objectives in this way enables the practitioner to determine the baseline knowledge or competency that is to be achieved in a learning session, but then allows them to consider what else some learners may be able to achieve in the session, given appropriate support in terms of strategies and resources.

For example:

- By the end of the session all learners will be able to classify reactions as exothermic or endothermic.
- By the end of the session some learners will be able to compare and contrast exothermic and endothermic reactions
- By the end of the session a few learners will be able to assess the energy level differences of exothermic and endothermic reactions

The formulation of learning objectives in this way can greatly help the practitioner. For example, if all learners can compare and contrast exothermic and endothermic reactions by the end of the session, expectations will have been exceeded and the practitioner must question whether the learning objectives they set were challenging enough to begin with. If no learners can assess the energy level differences of the two reactions, was this a realistic objective, even for a few of the learners in the session? If the practitioner believes that a few of the learners could certainly have assessed the energy levels, what prevented them from doing so? What was lacking in the session that prevented the achievement of this objective?

So, formulating learning objectives in this way can improve practice as a whole, assisting as it does the planning, facilitating and assessing of learning.

3.6 Testing achievement of learning objectives

Learning objectives must be written in such a way that they can be assessed. An objective uses an action verb; therefore, the key element is *do*, what do learners need to be able to do by the end of a learning session? How are they going to be assessed?

The challenge here is to align learning objectives, teaching methods and assessment techniques and criteria. A learning objective must state what the learner is going to do to demonstrate that they have met a specific learning objective. For example, consider a learning objective that states:

- By the end of the session, the learner will know the rules for correct punctuation.

This does not detail what a learner is going to do and how they will be assessed by the practitioner.

A better formulation is:

- By the end of the session, the learner will be able to correct punctuation in a given passage.

By doing the task, the learner will demonstrate they know the rules of punctuation and the practitioner can assess that knowledge.

As Ramsden (2003) points out, for learners, assessment defines the curriculum. They are fixated on what they have to do to achieve their qualification. This could be examinations, assignments, building a portfolio, conducting experiments, performance assessment, projects, reflective journals. Therefore, it is important that learning, and the learning objectives formulated by practitioners, also have this focus. Clearly demonstrating the connections between learning objectives, teaching and assessment helps learners make sense of the overall learning experience, making it transparent for the learners who, after all, are the ones who undertake the assessment.

Developing the links between learning objectives, teaching and assessment, and making these links clear to learners, is challenging for a practitioner. The curriculum should be designed so that teaching activities, learning activities and assessment tasks are aligned with the learning objectives. Biggs (2003) calls this 'constructive alignment', where all elements are co-ordinated to support learning.

There are three basic things that the practitioner must do:

1. Formulate clearly defined learning objectives.
2. Select appropriate learning and teaching methods that will support the achievement of the learning objectives.
3. Select appropriate assessment strategies that will enable the practitioner to assess achievement of the learning objectives.

Assessment of the achievement of learning objectives should occur throughout a learning session (formative) and also at the end of a learning session (summative).

A useful strategy to employ to ensure that learners understand the learning objectives for the session and that they can self-assess is to ask them to consider the learning objectives for that session and formulate two or three lesson targets for themselves – these are re-visited at the end of the session for the learners to self-assess their achievement.

3.7 Summary, case studies, discussion questions and learning activities

A lesson is rather like an episode of your favourite drama: even when you think you know where the plot is heading, another twist proves you wrong. A set of clear objectives can give practitioners the security of knowing that things are moving in a very definite direction. As O'Houle (2009: 229) suggests, the educator must exert a degree of 'purposeful effort' to maintain this path and thereby secure their objectives. If learning objectives are written within too narrow a framework, learners will be limited and learning will lack challenge. Similarly, if they are vague and unfocused, both learners and practitioners will easily become confused about exactly what is to be learnt and demonstrated. It could also lead to a situation where the clarity and quality of learning is subsumed into an assessment-driven curriculum. However, when learning objectives are developed appropriately, they provide distinct advantages for the learning process.

Learners will:

- Understand better what they are expected to do.
- Know what they are expected to learn.
- Learn more effectively.

Practitioners will:

- Use appropriate learning and teaching strategies.
- Select appropriate learning materials.
- Assess learners' achievement effectively.

In summary therefore, SMART learning objectives can prevent 'fuzzy and tentative statements of purpose' (Giroux, 1988: 44), as they are intended to provide a clear framework in which everyone involved in the learning process knows what they have to do, how to do it and how it will be assessed.

3.7.1 Case study 1 Mentoring new tutors

Scenario:

A private hair and beauty training organization has recently expanded its provision and has recruited several new tutors to deliver on its programmes, which include NVQ up to Level 3. As some of the recruits are newly qualified, each has been allocated a mentor, with whom they have monthly meetings to address any issues.

Issue:

At a monthly meeting, the mentor is asked by the new tutor for help in formulating learning objectives in the psychomotor domain.

For discussion:

- What advice would you give to the new tutor?
- Design an exercise for the tutor that would assist them in their formulation of appropriate learning objectives.

3.7.2 Case study 2 Placing objectives

Scenario:

A teacher educator in a further education college is to teach a session on professionalism in education and training. The trainees in the class are drawn from a wide range of education and training organizations, such as adult and community learning (ACL), offender learning and work-based learning (WBL).

Issue:

As with much initial teacher education, the practitioner wishes to explore pedagogical theory at the same time as delivering course content; in this case, a demonstration of how the specific learning objectives of the session map against the hierarchy of the cognitive process dimension. See Table 3.7 on p. 66.

(Continued)

(Continued)

Specific learning objectives:

Objective 1 = Identify the definitional criteria which are said to underpin professionalism.

Objective 2 = Summarize the particular features of the profession that have presented obstacles to its advancement.

Objective 3 = Use at least one of the learner-centred methods deployed in the session in own classroom.

Objective 4 = Examine notions of professionalism from other points of view and relate the new material to contradictory research, experience or knowledge.

Objective 5 = Distinguish between a wide range of viewpoints on professionalism and recognize the legitimate differences between them.

Objective 6 = Appraise areas of practice to be developed in the light of recent sector developments and forecast priorities for development.

Objective 7 = Deliver a presentation on the place of ethics as a feature of teacher professionalism.

For discussion:

- Where would you place each of the objectives in the cognitive process dimension taxonomy?

Table 3.7 The cognitive process dimension

The cognitive process dimension					
Remember	Understand	Apply	Analyse	Evaluate	Create

3.7.3 Case study 3 Differentiated learning objectives

Scenario:

Your organization is planning a staff development day following an internal quality inspection. You have been asked to provide a training session on formulating appropriate learning objectives.

Issue:

A major issue arising from the inspection is that, in some sessions, learning objectives were undifferentiated and did not address learner needs.

For discussion:

- How would you devise a training session that will help your colleagues to formulate appropriate and differentiated learning objectives?

Finally some general guidelines to remember when developing learning objectives:

- Avoid vague terms like 'know', 'appreciate'.
- Begin each objective with an action verb.
- Use only one verb per objective.
- Avoid complicated sentences.
- Each objective must be able to be observed, measured and assessed.
- Remember the time factor – over-ambitious objectives are unrealistic in a given timeframe.
- Always ask how the objectives will be assessed.
- Remember the level of learners' learning – if they have progressed beyond the basics, do not formulate lower level objectives for the session, but challenge learners with higher level objectives.

References

Anderson, L. W. and Krathwohl, D. R. (eds) (2001) *A Taxonomy for Learning, Teaching, and Assessing: A Revision of Bloom's Taxonomy of Educational Objectives*. New York: Longman.

Biggs, J. (2003) *Teaching for Quality Learning at University*. Maidenhead: Open University Press/McGraw-Hill Education.

Bloom, B. S. (1956) *Taxonomy of Educational Objectives: The Classification of Educational Goals. Handbook 1: Cognitive Domain*. New York: David McKay Co.

Caffarella, R. M. (2001) *Planning Programs for Adult Learners: A Practical Guide for Educators, Trainers, and Staff Developers* (2nd edn). San Francisco, CA: Jossey-Bass.

Carr, D. (2003) 'Philosophy and the meaning of "education"', *Theory and Research in Education*, 1 (2): 195–212.

Colder, J. R. (1983) 'In the cells of the "Bloom Taxonomy"', *Journal of Curriculum Studies*, 15 (3): 291–302.

Dave, R. H. (1970) *Developing and Writing Behavioural Objectives*, ed. R. J. Armstrong. Tuscon, AZ: Educational Innovators Press.

Dawson, W. R. (1998) *Extensions to Bloom's Taxonomy of Educational Objectives*. Sydney, Australia: Putney Publishing.

Donnelly, R. and Fitzmaurice, M. (2005) 'Designing models for learning', in G. O'Neill (ed.), *Emerging Issues in the Practice of University Learning and Teaching*. Dublin: AISHE, pp. 99–110.

Douglass, J. A. Thomson, G. and Zhao, C.-M. (2012) 'The learning outcomes race: the value of self-reported gains in large research universities', *Higher Education*, 64: 317–335.

Ferris, T. and Aziz, S. (2005) 'A psychomotor skills extension to bloom's taxonomy of educational objectives for engineering learners', *Exploring Innovation in Education and Research*, March 2005.

Giroux, H. (1988) *Teachers as Intellectuals: Toward a Critical Pedagogy of Learning*. Westport, Connecticut, London: Bergin and Garvey.

Guilbert, J. J. (1987) *Educational Handbook for Health Personnel* (6th edn). Geneva. WHO.

Harđarson, A. (2012) 'Why the aims of education cannot be settled', *Journal of Philosophy of Education*, 46 (2): 223–235.

Harrison, R. H. (2009) *Learning and Development*. London: Chartered Institute of Personnel and Development.

Krathwohl, D. R., Bloom, B. S. and Masia, B. B. (1964) *Taxonomy of Educational Objectives. Handbook 2: Affective Domain*. New York: David McKay.

Laurillard, D. (1993) *Rethinking University Teaching: A Framework for the Effective Use of Educational Technology*. London: Routledge.

Mager, R. F. (1984) *Preparing Instructional Objectives* (2nd edn). California: David S. Lake.

Marzano, R. J. (2009) *Designing and Teaching Learning Goals and Objectives*. Bloomington, IN: Marzano Research Laboratory.

Marzano, R. J. and Kendall, J. S. (2007) *The New Taxonomy of Educational Objectives* (2nd edn). Thousand Oaks, CA: Corwin Press.

Mayer, R. E. (2002) 'Rote versus meaningful learning', *Theory into Practice*, 41 (4): 226–232.

O'Houle, C. (2009) *The Design of Education* (2nd edn). San Francisco, CA: Jossey-Bass.

Palliam, R. (2012) *E-Learning and Desired Learning Outcomes, eLearning – Theories, Design, Software and Applications*, ed. Dr Patrizia Ghislandi. www.intechopen.com/books/elearning-theories-design-software- and-applications/ e-learning-and-desired-learning-outcomes (accessed 11 November 2013).

Perkins, D. and Salomon, G. (1992) *Transfer of Learning*. http://learnweb.harvard.edu/alps/thinking/docs/traencyn.htm (accessed 2 November 2013).

Plato (2007) *The Republic*, trans. H. D. P. Lee and D. Lee. London: Penguin Classics.

Ramsden, P. (2003) *Learning to Teach in Higher Education*. London: Routledge.

Ross, V. (2012) 'From transformative outcome based education to blended learning', *Futures*, 44: 148–157.

Simpson, E. J. (1972) *The Classification of Educational Objectives in the Psychomotor Domain*. Washington, DC: Gryphon House.

Wringe, C. (1988) *Understanding Educational Aims*. London: Unwin Hyman.

CHAPTER 4

SELECTING APPROPRIATE AND RELEVANT CONTENT

Ian Rushton and
Anne Temple Clothier

Learning outcomes

After reading this chapter, the reader should be able to:

- Identify the problems and advantages of using learning outcomes.
- Define the connections and relationship between learning outcomes and assessment.
- Identify appropriate learning strategies, taking into account contextual factors.
- Explore some of the possibilities and limitations of managing learning and knowledge.
- Understand the role of the practitioner in relation to the implementation of designing learning and knowledge management strategies.

Chapter outline

This chapter provides an introduction to the concept of learning outcomes, and their application as content. It takes the practitioner through the underpinning theory, the practical application and concludes by presenting a variety of case studies that can be used to further develop practice.

4.1 Underpinning theory

This chapter builds on Chapter 3, where learning objectives have been discussed extensively and reflect the specific knowledge (technical), skill (conceptual or pragmatic) and behaviour (problem solving, time management, group working) that the learner is expected to display on completion of the programme of study. They provide tools for the measurement of cognitive development (knowledge acquisition) and affective development (skills or behaviour) and attempt to provide a framework through which development can be evidenced.

It is useful at this point to distinguish between aims and objectives; according to most authors aims are more about teaching and the management of learning, whereas learning outcomes are more about learning and individuals changing as a result of that learning (see Watson, 2002; Moon, 2004; Burke and Jackson, 2007).

Most educational institutions and private training providers aim to use learning outcomes as scaffolding for development programmes which not only develop cognitive and practical skills but also develop desirable characteristics and attributes in the learner or employee. One line of argument is that this will raise the opportunities for employability and promote good citizenship. As a consequence, it is not only the individual who benefits from a good education, but also the nation and corporate employer, in terms of economic growth and social conformity.

Writers such as Jarvis (2008) suggest that some institutions and employers are interested in socializing the employees into their own corporate culture and values. Furthermore, it is suggested that there are significant differences between the use of learning outcomes within educational establishments, and their use within vocational or business settings (Moon, 2004). The ability of the learner to demonstrate learning at the end of a block of learning is of little use; what is of greater relevance is how the learner carries that learning forward into workplace practice at a later stage and that this is more difficult to control by those who design or facilitate the training programme (Moon, 2004). With the successful application to practice, in terms of work-based competencies, the learners become true members of the organization and conform to the culture and values as well as the directly observable behaviours (Jarvis, 2008).

Can teachers and trainers control learning outcomes in an absolute sense? According to Moon (2004) there are difficulties for the teacher or trainer in that learning outcomes are less susceptible to teacher control as it is not possible to force a learner to learn. With this in mind we now pause to consider the development of independent autonomous learners, and by this we mean learners who are capable of determining what they want to learn, how they want to learn, with the capacity to transfer that learning into new settings; this is an aspirational outcome for many training providers.

4.1.1 Problems with the learning outcomes approach

Although the learning outcomes will measure the end result, a flexible progression route, allowing for individual learning styles and capabilities of learners, is required from the practitioner designing and delivering the programme. The process of allowing learners to construct knowledge through a series of carefully designed learning activities is an outcomes approach that seeks to link learning and assessment, through what Biggs (2003) called 'constructive alignment'. If learners are given a real stake in their own development, by determining their own inputs and outcomes in the process, they may learn better and will be more motivated and enthusiastic about their learning (Knight and Trowler, 2001). Therefore assessment should be specifically designed to allow learners to demonstrate their own specific approach (Brown et al., 1995). However, as Ramsden (2003) suggests it is the assessment not the learning opportunities that form the main focus of learners' attention. This view appears to be supported by Newstead (2002) who suggests that a potential weakness of this approach is that learners themselves tend to over-focus on assessment success to the detriment of learning and that learners become more interested in the mark than anything else. This may encourage a mechanical approach to learning.

Further weaknesses are also identified with focusing on an outcomes approach to development. The European Quality Framework (EQF) itself has suggested that a potential weakness with this approach is that it limits the range of approaches to learning (EQF, 2011). Writers such as Coffield (2008, 2009) suggest there are indeed groups of learners who are 'failed' by the current education system, and criticize an over-reliance on targets and league tables.

A further criticism of the current assessment framework is that learning outcomes have become the sole focus for assessment purposes and that a rigid approach to learning outcomes presents barriers to independent and reflective learning (Burke and Jackson, 2007). There is a danger that the outcome of learning becomes a product, not a process. These authors and others, including Evans (2004), argue for assessment practices that provide opportunities for different kinds of learning, both inside and outside of formal institutional spaces. This emphasis on the recognition of diversity of learning in relation to assessment methods is vital if assessment is to support learning (Brown and Knight, 1994).

4.1.2 Advantages of using learning outcomes

Despite the problems identified above, there are clear advantages in using learning outcomes. The EQF argue that the movement towards adopting learning outcomes provides:

> An opportunity to tailor education and training to individual needs (to promote active learning).
>
> A way of reducing barriers to lifelong learning.
>
> A way to increase the accountability of education and training institutions and systems.
>
> A common language enabling a better dialogue between education and labour market stakeholders. (EQF, 2011: 9)

Learners will quite often expect to be given the learning outcomes from the outset of a course or session and know that these will form the basis of their learning and assessment. This can aid a sense of achievement in fulfilling the learning outcomes.

The following sections of this chapter provide details on how learning outcomes can be used by a practitioner, in different situations, to provide focus.

4.2 Meeting your learning objectives with relevant content

When selecting appropriate and relevant content it is useful to consider a number of key influences including, although not exclusively:

- Learners' entry or start points, including prior experience, qualifications and learning.
- Learners' needs, preferences and aspirations.
- The requirements of the various stakeholders or other interested parties.
- The curriculum 'offer', that is, the nature of the course, programme or curriculum.

4.2.1 Learners' entry points: the known to the unknown

This has been discussed in Chapter 2 although it is worthwhile reiterating the point that not all learners can be assumed to have the same attainments and achievements, let alone the same life experiences, motivation or prior experiences in a learning environment. The underlying thread here is that any course or individual learning session is aimed at leading the learners from the known (that which they already know or can do) to the unknown (that which is, at the start, unknown or which they are not yet able to do and are articulated in the learning outcomes or objectives). Making the journey, or filling the gap, requires not only appropriate teaching and learning strategies but also relevant, meaningful, engaging and context-specific content which should progress learners beyond the immediate needs of the qualification or, indeed, employer needs (Coffield, 2007a: xiv).

Another central concern here is that the content of the course may need to include, for less experienced learners, material that brings them up to the level of *known* that is required for them to benefit from the core material in the course, perhaps even bridging work which gives them a better foothold into the programme.

4.2.2 Learners' needs, preferences and aspirations

Again, as discussed in Chapter 2, we can still sometimes witness boredom or distraction from learners during our sessions. If we have carefully identified their intrinsic motivation for the course and subject at interview stage then the root of disinterest can either be poor teaching and learning (see Chapters 5, 6 and 7 for avoiding this) or learning content that fails to engage.

One of the hallmarks of the further education and skills sector is the presence of the more mature or adult learner who, generally, tends to be more self-directed in their motivation and learning approaches than when they were younger. According to writers such as Knowles (1978) and Mezirow (1981) adult learners expect to be made to work and study hard, through the guidance of the teacher as a facilitator, and that the content needs to be sufficiently challenging in order to satisfy the adult learners' intrinsic motivation. This is where the subject specialist teacher needs to make carefully considered judgements about content and resources that cater, initially, for three levels of ability in the same session:

- the less able or experienced
- the central majority
- the more able who need to be challenged and stretched (see Chapter 3).

Some practitioners select such content with apparent ease, for example, those on BTEC programmes where outcomes and activities are closely located alongside the slightly different grade criteria of Pass, Merit and Distinction, respectively, or AS and A2 programmes graded A–E. Where programmes and awards are not graded so readily, for example NVQs, the practitioner needs to make those same judgements according to what they know of the learners, the subject and the level of the programme.

4.2.3 The requirements of the various stakeholders or other interested parties

Curriculum development in much of the further education and skills sector over the last 30 years has focused on the competence model whereby (and we accept that this is an over-simplification) the learner only receives a certificate once they can do and demonstrate their competence in certain things. Education policymakers in the sector began to develop the competence-based approach to learning outcomes, which rose to prominence in the 1990s, ostensibly in line with the alleged needs of industry and global economic competitiveness. Despite being widely and robustly challenged by commentators at the time, this has become the norm for many courses, especially in vocational areas. This approach has become much more embedded in a wide range of occupations and can be regarded as a relentless 'growth of competence' (Kelly, 2009: 101) and seems to give a privileged position to competence (being able to demonstrate while explaining cursory related underpinning knowledge) as a desirable learning outcome. Yet there are criticisms of this; for example, Dreyfus and Dreyfus (1980) have identified a five-stage skills acquisition model which places *competence* third between *advanced beginner* and *proficient*. Successive UK governments seem to have conflated educational purposes with economic imperatives and shifted the onus for developing the UK workforce onto colleges and training providers in the sector (Orr, 2008) in a relentless momentum that Keep (2006: 59) describes as 'policy hysteria'. Indeed, colleges and providers are expected to respond to government policies (DIUS, 2008) when determining the curriculum and its delivery.

The underlying implication in government policy, therefore, is that choice-seekers from industry (employers) have a central role in directing not only the curriculum offer (see 4.2.4) but also the content. Consequently, the best strategy for vocational tutors when planning content could be to liaise with employers and find out what, exactly, they require and develop their programmes around it.

4.2.4 The curriculum 'offer'

While it is advisable to remain alive to the next governmental policy shift when developing learning content, there are the two touchstones to bear in mind when constructing the curriculum. First, the 'skills agenda' which is unlikely to abate and is what the government believe employers want their employees to be or become, although this privileged position is contested (Pring, 2004; Keep, 2006; Coffield, 2007b; James and Biesta, 2007). Second, 'system outcomes' or learner certification (not to be confused with learner qualification), are the means by which the effectiveness of teaching and learning in the sector can be performatively measured. The reader will be aware of what these look like and how they can create tensions in the practitioner's objectives in providing opportunities for learning that will support the learner to achieve the learning outcome. This may create genuine problems; for example, where vocational tutors regard the industrial visit as essential but the programme does not allow time for this activity. This is where practitioners may turn to alternative approaches in order to retain content that is under threat; they know what learners need.

If learner progress is the primary measure of both the practitioner's capability and the quality of the organization providing the training, then 'what' and 'how much' learners learn is a vital consideration. Enabling all learners to achieve, and creating routes by which they can evidence their ability to exceed, are requirements of 'transformative learning'. By 'transformative' we mean that at the end of the process the learner, or their knowledge, has to some extent 'changed' into something new. This concept goes beyond the notion that learning merely adds to the existing knowledge of the learner, and recognises its capacity to change both views and behaviours. It is widely recognized that the historic processes of transferring knowledge from the 'expert' to the 'learner' have given way to relationships with the practitioner as a facilitator of learning with the responsibility to create a learning forum, which provides multiple routes of engagement and caters for self-directed approaches to knowledge development. As such, the learning outcome has moved from a position of measurement of *transferred* knowledge, to a measure of *developed* knowledge, with the learner at the centre of the process. It requires that the learner takes a proactive stance in that knowledge development, reviewing the information presented and reflecting how they can apply it in new settings. It is the change in the learner's perceptions or meanings that provides personal or professional growth, through appropriate and relevant content and engagement.

Though the outcomes themselves must be measurable, in that their achievement must be demonstrable, they do not necessarily need to be 'gradable' in that the degree to which they have been met is not mandated; they either are met, or they are not. However, given that all assessment needs to be transparent and auditable, it is essential that evidence that the standards are met is collected with a view to making a sample available to an internal or external moderator or verifier.

Once learning outcomes are identified, the practitioner has a number of considerations to make when determining exactly what learning items are going to be made available to the learner. Specifically:

- What is the general outcome desired by this programme?
- How is this broken down into a number of learning outcomes in the assessment process?
- Are the learning outcomes accessible to the learner, both in terms of visibility and language?

Getting a clear picture of what the 'end product' will look like brings clarity to practitioner and learner alike. Once it can be 'pictured' then it is possible to determine how it will be 'measured'.

Although the measurement links directly with the type of assessment used, it has a more flexible relationship with the development of the learning programme itself. 'Teaching to assessment' is not desirable, however developing a learning environment (virtual or otherwise) should create a micro-world of relevant resources, complete with a map and compass, and signposts to paths less travelled for the more adventurous to explore. For example, a good practitioner does not cite the answer to a potential problem to be solved, instead they provide a range of sources that contain the answer, and signpost the way. This may be provided in terms of supportive handouts, reading lists, online sources or case studies. We discuss the appropriateness of each of these strategies later in the chapter while they are also considered in more detail in Chapter 7.

A layered approach to material is recommended:

- a layer of material that fosters inclusivity and is intellectually accessible to all;
- a range of primary and secondary sources that build on this layer, and yet allow the learning preferences of the individual learners to actively determine the types of material and presentation methods selected; and
- signposts to additional resources that require a proactive 'search and locate' behaviour on the part of the learner.

It is through this layering that both inclusion and differentiation needs are met.

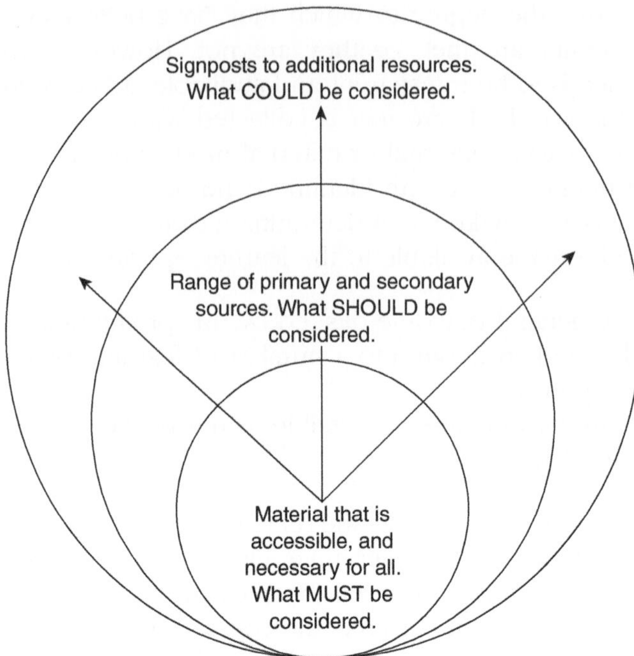

Figure 4.1 The 'onion' layering of material

The *must, should* and *could* elements of Figure 4.1 are referred to later in the chapter, and discussed in more detail.

Despite the vagaries of the dominant business model driving the sector where education is seen as a commodity, learners as consumers and industry as assessment-seeking customers, teaching and training practitioners are still well placed to do what is right for their learners within the 'must, should and could' framework. Here, interested stakeholders (mostly government policymakers, occupational bodies, professional institutions and awarding bodies) dictate what 'must' be learned. However, writers such as Bathmaker et al. (2011) suggest these groups have only a fragile hold on the 'should' and the least grasp on the 'could'. Therefore, it is in the process of designing the learning experience that practitioners have an opportunity to 'make a difference' and have a voice.

4.3 Researching material and content

Any learner with access to the internet will already have more than sufficient information from which to select, to meet the learning outcomes.

What they will need is support in the best way to present evidence, framed as an assessment, to meet the learning outcomes. Therefore the primary role of the practitioner is not to create primary and secondary data, it is to *filter* it. For example, if you were teaching history, it is not necessary to present an 'original' version of the time in question, instead locating first-hand accounts or statistics (primary data) or second-hand accounts or interpretations of statistics (secondary data) will be sufficient.

By carefully selecting material, the practitioner safeguards the learner from 'information overload' and avoids the situation of 'paralysis by analysis' whereby progression is inhibited by the intimidation of self-selection. It is hoped that the practitioner's expert knowledge of both the subject knowledge and the assessment criteria allow them to make informed decisions about a range of suitable subject matter and various types of information representation. The desired outcome is something that neither resembles the shelves in a library, nor highlights the sensational, but instead creates a thematic collection of materials selected to 'define' the area under investigation. The quantity of material made available to the learner should be sufficient to allow various types of people to self-select and produce work and understanding in a way that allows for a diversity of route and style. Too much information and the learner is overwhelmed, too little and there is a danger of 'spoon feeding' or 'teaching to assessment'.

4.3.1 Selecting appropriate amounts of content

A useful consideration, in relation to the volume of content presented, is the length of time it would take a learner to access them all. If the 'notional time' allocated to a task is five hours, how long would it take to access all the resources presented, and respond to them? If the answer is 50 hours, then obviously there is too much material, conversely if everything can be read in three hours, perhaps the practitioner is being overly prescriptive in their selection.

In the same way that individual learners' learning styles vary, practitioners' teaching and training styles vary too; consequently the way learning objectives are developed will reflect the unique collection of attributes and styles of the practitioner and the learners. In addition, the context within which the learning will occur, such as subject discipline, group size, level and context will require consideration. Hence while the practitioner must teach in alignment with the expectations set within a particular course or session or organizational requirement, the aspiration must be to foster teaching that best facilitates learning.

4.3.2 'Need to know' information

The 'need to know' information is critical when deciding content and it tends to fall into three key areas.

Supplying learners with the 'need to know' information regarding outcomes and assessment is the first key element of creating a learning environment where learners feel secure and focused. So to that extent the learning objectives, assessment methods and any relevant grading criteria need to be presented in an unambiguous and transparent manner.

The second element of 'need to know' is the degree and range of support available for the learner as they complete the process – how are they going to be able to access support which will provide feedback relating to their performance in such a way that it will improve and monitor performance before the learning objective is achieved? In this instance it is the practitioner's responsibility to ensure that learners have access to frequent, timely and constructive feedback, as discussed further in Chapter 8, and this should be linked to the transparent and consistent grading criteria referred to above.

The third 'need to know' is the range of materials the learner will need to access in order to develop their knowledge of a given field in order to develop their underpinning 'subject-based' knowledge. This element is covered in more detail later in this chapter. It will require the practitioner to stimulate the learner's interest in, and engagement with, all course material. This is achieved by making it relevant both in terms of their lived experiences and their professional development. The most successful tools will be those that evoke the learner's interest, facilitate participation in selected activities and provide an appropriate level of challenge.

4.3.3 The trap of making things too complex: how the brain works to link new information to existing knowledge

While it is necessary to ensure that a variety of teaching methods are employed in order to appeal to various learning styles of the contemporary learner population, this must also be tempered with an approach that avoids making things too complex. Traditionally practitioners have used didactic approaches (where the expert 'tells' what should be learned, also known as the 'chalk and talk' method) to convey key information and concepts clearly and succinctly; these are usually enhanced by various forms of group-working and collaborative learning. Facilitating effective discussion is a key element to ensuring information has been internalized and processed with a collection of learners. However, two widely recognized 'macro strategies' for teaching are to maximize learning opportunities and to develop learner autonomy. How a practitioner attempts to do this will be shaped by the context within which they practise and the resources available.

A key strategy for building a learning objective, where both these strategies are included, requires the practitioner to consider the skills and knowledge that the learner has as a starting point, and ensure that all subsequent information can add to this in a way that has sense and relevance to the learner. By presenting new information as 'building bricks' of knowledge, time and space should be allowed for reflection as the learner decides where on the existing foundations of understanding this new information should be placed. This space for consideration and assimilation is essential, if the learner is to process and build new understandings. The number of 'bricks' produced by the practitioner, and the speed and frequency with which they are offered, will either enhance an engagement with learning leading to the building of a new house of knowledge, or overwhelm a learner resulting, in effect, in a ruin of a foundation with a disorganized pile of bricks on top. Therefore the scaffolding within a learning objective is paramount.

It is worth noting at this point that the term 'scaffolding' in relation to learning was introduced by Wood et al. (1976) and is strongly embedded and associated with the work of Vygotsky (1978). Essentially, scaffolding describes how learners are supported while attempting to develop a competence, or acquire new knowledge; but that the ultimate aim is that they achieve the capacity to undertake the task independently at the end of the process. This is what Vygotsky calls the 'Zone of Proximal Development'. Vygotsky describes this process as 'the distance between the actual development level as determined by independent problem solving and the level of potential as determined through problem solving under adult guidance, or in collaboration with more capable peers' (Vygotsky, 1978: 86).

Analogies and metaphors, as discussed in Chapter 5, are useful ways of helping a learner grasp a new concept by drawing parallels with similar (more familiar) images or cases; the 'onion' reference in Figure 4.1 is an example of how a familiar image is used to convey a parallel meaning in a new context. Creativity with the way that material is presented supports learners to reflect and to present information in a way that evidences their own capabilities.

4.3.4 Selecting content: identifying what must, should and could be included

Earlier in this chapter, and indeed in the previous chapter, we have emphasized the importance of creating 'inclusive' learning objectives; by this we mean creating an environment where all learners have the capacity to learn and develop to their potential. However, it is also necessary to ensure 'differentiation' is possible, and by this we mean that the differences in learning styles and abilities are both addressed and measured. This is explored in more depth in Chapter 6.

One of the simplest and most popular models for differentiation is presented in the 'must, should and could' formula. Using this template the practitioner selects content, and provides advice, as to what the learner must, could and should be able to achieve and evidence. It provides an effective template to use when designing schemes of work, session plans and in-class activities. Used effectively it will ensure that:

- every learner has covered the 'must' learn content
- opportunities are available for all to rise to the challenges of the 'should'
- for those learners who can be stretched, the 'could' elements are presented as opportunities.

In order for this to occur the 'must' resources need to be supplemented with a range of useful, though not essential, opportunities for further development. See the 'onion' layering of material in Figure 4.1.

4.4 Returning to the skills gap

- What must be covered in order to meet the required skills by the end of the session?
- What material might be relevant and interesting but is not essential (should)?

Layering information in the design of an effective learning objective begins with the 'must'. Essentially this involves considering the skills gap or the difference between existing competence and desired, or required, competence by the end of the session. Using this base point, practitioners assess what 'must' be covered or presented in order for the learning objectives and programme objectives to be met. Consideration will need to be given to any contextual constraints (resources and time) and the opportunities for learner collaboration and engagement. The 'must' is the core scaffolding or central trunk (if we are to change metaphor) to the development of provision. The learner is encouraged to 'climb' from the trunk 'must' onto the lower branches of 'should', and if possible ascend to the higher branches of 'could'. For a variety of reasons not all learners will climb as high as each other. Where they are positioned when the learning objective is complete will form the basis for the template of differentiation

Table 4.1 Learning strategies

Learning outcome	Learning strategy	Suitable for:
The acquisition of knowledge	Conference	A series of one-way presentations, and or workshops, by 'experts' in the field under investigation
	Lecture	A single one-way presentation
	Seminar	A practitioner-led discussion, possibly including a problem-solving activity
	Group work	Learner-led discussion, or problem-solving activity
The acquisition of skill	Demonstration	A practical demonstration of the correct application of a specific process
	Role play	Learners are invited to 'act out' situations or scenarios requiring empathy with 'real life' experiences
	Out of classroom experience	By taking the learner outside of the classroom it is possible to widen their understanding of context, or present them with stimuli that the constraints of the classroom do not allow
	Practical experience	This provides the learner with a full sensory appreciation for the subject under consideration, it also allows for the mastery of technical proficiency of process
	Case study	The simulation provided by case study allows the application of abstract conceptualization of ideas onto a real-life scenario. It therefore facilitates the opportunity to simulate problem-solving conditions and group work
A change in attitude	Critical incident	Learners engage with a specific case study and explore potential outcomes together
	Focused group discussion	Practitioner-led exploration of a particular issue that facilitates critical analysis and refection
	Group discussion	Peer-driven learner discussion which explores, evaluates and reflects on particular issues
	Individual refection	The development of a learning log, CPD file or diary which evidences the learner's ability to reflect on experience and identify changes to personal attitude and behaviour

of achievement, or attainment. The role of the practitioner is to ensure that the opportunity to climb is equal, and that it is the learners themselves who determine the height on completion.

4.4.1 Selecting the appropriate learning method: identifying learning solutions

Earlier in this chapter we suggested that learning outcomes cover three main areas of development. You can refer to Chapter 7 for appropriate learning strategies to meet the needs in terms of delivery.

In Table 4.1 we suggest how certain learning strategies can be used to meet learning outcomes.

These methods of delivery are by no means exhaustive. They do tend to provide an overview of traditional methods of delivery; what they do not illustrate is how changes in technology have increased the tool kit available to practitioners depending on their own level of digital proficiency.

As a practitioner you can access a vast array of information comparing various teaching strategies merely by typing 'appropriate teaching strategies' into a search engine. This will allow you to view material ranging from the online curriculum content of the many organizations in the sector, including subject-specific and professional network virtual learning environments (VLEs). It is possible to refine the search into various disciplines, or indeed in relation to the use of digital technology. For example, Nielsen's (2008) paper can be accessed online, as can Oliver's (2011) work (see Chapter 9 for a more detailed discussion of this). As we said earlier in the chapter, good learners will track down and interpret primary and secondary data themselves. We present signposts to what you 'could' read as well as what you 'should' read. At this point it is now appropriate to consider in a little more detail some potential learning solutions.

4.4.2 Comparison of different learning solutions

Each of these modes of engagement offer different learning solutions. A combination of a range may prove to be the most successful, depending on the developmental level of the learner. The length of engagement related to the learning objective or programme, the proximity to the learner, the practitioner-to-learner ratio may all play a key influence in determining the success of each method. It is worth noting that this method may well provide access to information that is disseminated much faster than the traditional publishing routes. However the credibility of the information will also be varied, so pay good attention as to who is saying what, and try to select recognized and credible sources with which to affiliate.

Table 4.2 New codes of communication with learners (see also Chapter 9)

Learning strategy	Suitable for:	Learning outcome
Blended learning	A combination of online dissemination and engagement and face-to-face classroom based activities	The acquisition of knowledge The acquisition of skill A change in attitude
E-learning	Online provision which provides schemes of work, assessment criteria and resources enabling progression, often supported with access to a specific member of staff as key support for study	The acquisition of knowledge The acquisition of skill A change in attitude
Self-directed training	Research involving the learner to source primary and secondary sources using online resources	The acquisition of knowledge The acquisition of skill A change in attitude
Online closed groups	The creation of online closed groups whereby learners can communicate and support each other as a 'learning set' without the direct involvement of the practitioner	The acquisition of knowledge The acquisition of skill A change in attitude
Linking with affiliated online forums	Directing the learner to engage with specific institutes, professional bodies, journals or websites that provide credible information that will enhance and add to the subject knowledge and skills acquisition	The acquisition of knowledge The acquisition of skill A change in attitude
Blogging	Here the learner keeps a public reflective journal to evidence the learning and development that has taken place	The acquisition of knowledge The acquisition of skill A change in attitude
E-portfolio	The private production of an electronic portfolio that is subsequently shared with an assessor to evidence the learning and development that has taken place	The acquisition of knowledge The acquisition of skill A change in attitude

Blended learning may provide greater autonomy for the learner to aspire to 'could' objectives, using time management and organizational skills to match their levels of commitment. If the 'must' objectives and provision are clearly presented, and the 'should' clearly signposted with adequate practitioner support, the 'could' will be determined by the range of additional activities engaged with.

4.5 Selecting the best learning methods

It is vital that learning methods reflect the content of the learning. Thinking about the sorts of behaviours you wish your learners to emulate by the end of the learning should help identify the most appropriate learning method. For instance, when learning about teamwork, there must be some elements of working together with other individuals in a team situation during the course, to help them put their new skills into practice.

It is essential that each and every learning method or strategy selected is chosen to reflect its suitability regarding the content of the learning required. The practitioner is required to consider the development level of the learner, and the sorts of behaviour, skill sets and attitudes they are hoping to embed in the process and learning outcomes. In order to successfully achieve this, practitioners must have an understanding as to how this particular collection of learners will achieve skill and cognitive development, and pay due regard to the experience they are fostering. To effectively manage this process an awareness of 'learner culture' is important. By this we mean the personality of the group, and how the members behave with each other. By proactively encouraging a culture that is inclusive, proactive, facilitates good communication and is supportive, it is possible to model the behaviours that you wish your learners to emulate by the end of the learning process.

4.5.1 Using your own experience

Using examples from your own professional development will provide illumination as to how learners may also engage with continually reflecting on their own practice. Similarly any research you may have done in terms of your own subject knowledge development may well provide signposts to additional resources and methods of engagement. A desire to work with, and be receptive to, ideas presented by others can be demonstrated through projects you have undertaken, showing an impact on professional development and evidencing relevance and application. However, citing examples is no substitute for experience, therefore if the development of interpersonal skills or group working is an integral aim or objective there is no substitute for creating learning experiences which present the opportunity for participation and refection. A simple 'schedule' of group activities is insufficient; instead the learners need to be taken through a developmental process that allows them to transform from a collection of individuals to a cohesive group operating in a climate of trust, openness and shared understanding. Many induction procedures or 'ice-breaking' activities are specifically designed with this in mind. A simple exercise of 'interviewing the person next to you, to then introduce them to the group' is often used to help build cohesion. It is a simple yet effective way of trying to foster the cohesive and supportive environment that enhances good learning opportunities. It is evident that the practitioner has a pivotal role to play in creating this climate for learning.

4.5.2 Using group work

Group work is especially effective at reinforcing learning and ensuring that learning outcomes relating to knowledge and skill acquisition are reinforced, and in addition opportunities for changes in attitude are developed and evidenced. The practitioner can hear this evidence as learners explain and articulate their knowledge and beliefs to other members of the group. As they present their ideas to others, not only does it develop their cognitive ability and assist them in memorizing what has been learned, it also provides the practitioner with an opportunity to identify any skills and knowledge gaps that may hinder the learner achieving the learning outcomes. See Chapter 2 which includes discussions on group work from a learner or participant-centred perspective.

It can be argued that group work is also a way to foster the development of the 'professional' and 'vocational' learner by modelling behaviours that will become part of everyday practice at the end of the programme of study. It provides a forum to develop an awareness of the views of others, their research and experiences, and to use this to develop new understandings. This skill is vital in order to move the learner from a position of responding to the practitioner, to one where they synthesize their knowledge with peers and make effective contributions to teams. Not only does this expand their knowledge base, it also develops a confidence in undertaking tasks and taking responsibility for themselves. It is likely that positive engagement with these activities will bring intrinsic rewards and increased motivation. In addition, working with a broad range of abilities and approaches will provide a working experience of 'inclusive' education, again modelling what is to come.

4.6 Summary, case studies, discussion questions and learning activities

In summary, this chapter has outlined key features of selecting appropriate and relevant content. We suggest that the acquired skill, knowledge and behaviour that you, the subject specialist, have can both inform what is relevant and appropriate content and give you a voice, however muted, as Biesta (2007: 20) argued: 'Educational professionals need to make decisions about what is educationally desirable'.

Below are four pairs of case studies followed with activities and questions: each case study is an example of a particular approach to selecting appropriate and relevant 'must, should and could' content; and each activity is a corresponding exercise for you to complete individually or as part of a team.

4.6.1 Case study 1 Skill development

Tom teaches practical benchwork to BTEC National Diploma Engineering apprentices for a private training provider on a day-release basis. Among the plethora of skills that the apprentices *must* develop in the workshop, Tom and his colleagues believe that the ability to file true (for example, filing an accurate square end on a 25mm wide piece of mild steel) is fundamental to accuracy, precision, tool dexterity and other skills that follow. Despite carefully and repeatedly demonstrating the correct technique, Tom's learners seem to be taking longer to develop the required skill and technique than previous groups; a concern shared by his colleagues who bemoan a lack of patience and attention in 'today's learners'. While watching an internet video of computer-aided machining, an idea dawned on Tom: why not get the learners to video themselves filing then compare what they see with the demonstration (self-assessment)? They could use their mobile phones (motivation and new technology) and swap with each other (peer assessment and competition) and tutor–learner dialogue could provoke a much clearer assessment of learner understanding at each workstation (dialogic formative assessment). Tom thought that the *should* skills (for example, correct stance in order to avoid tiredness) and the *could* skills (for example, using the full stroke of the file to promote the life of the tool) could emerge during the dialogue. He also thought that an extension to the proposed approach could be to have learners play the role of assessor or critical friend while watching internet videos of diverse filing operations.

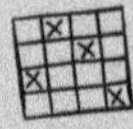

Activity 1 Skill development

Think of one skill that either you or your learners need to develop as part of their programme of study then complete the following table according to the *must*, *should* and *could* framework.

Table 4.3 Skill development

Skill title			
Question	**Must**	**Should**	**Could**
What are the features associated with that skill?			
How can I promote more learning/less teaching of the skill?			
How can I give learners more ownership of assessment?			
How can I challenge the more able learners?			
How can I support the less able learners?			
What are the extension activities that could come out of this?			
Which resources can be utilized? Which resources do learners already have access to?			

4.6.2 Case study 2 Knowledge development

Liz teaches a research methods module to mature undergraduates on a Higher Education Institution (HEI) Social Sciences programme in a general FE college. Liz is comfortable in both her own knowledge and teaching skills, is considered by the college to be an 'outstanding' teacher, spends each summer sourcing current resources and has been commended by the HEI for the depth and quality of her formative and summative feedback to learners. Yet she is troubled that some learners appear to struggle with, and seemingly misunderstand, basic terminology relating to the module. For example, why are some learners not 'critical' and why do some not *synthesize research evidence* as the module ability outcomes stipulate? Liz decided to prepare a pre-module activity, using terminology from the module specification, which she sent by email to the next group requiring them to complete a range of short preparatory tasks as follows:

1. Carefully read the attached module specification.
2. Define (write a short sentence for each) the following eight terms (be prepared to share these with peers at the first session):

- Argument
- Analysis
- Synthesis
- Formulation
- Hypothesis
- Question
- Criticality
- Evaluation

3. Write a 100-word summary of the process you went through in Task 2 (above).
4. Identify an area of interest that can be your research focus for the module assignment. Write this as a concise research question.
5. Email your outputs from tasks 2, 3 and 4 to me by (date).

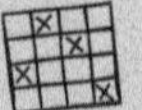

Activity 2 Knowledge development

Identify one of the core documents (for example, module or unit specification, programme handbook or core specification) that you issue to your learners and then answer the following questions:

- Is the level of language accessible to a learner commencing your course? (For example, if you are in any way unclear about what a particular outcome/active verb or term really means, a learner might find such terminology inaccessible). You *must* put a highlighter pen through any that you are slightly concerned about in order to make the outcomes achievable for your learners.
- For every term or use of language that you feel is somehow 'fragile', write a definition (which you *should* provide to your learners) and carefully craft one example (which *could* further clarify its meaning for your learners).
- One of the greatest barriers that teaching practitioners face is the knowledge that language fails us in many ways. For example, we often cannot articulate what we understand when explaining a concept in the same way that our learners often cannot explain or write what they mean, know or intend. With this in mind consider other documents, induction materials and written resources which you have previously considered to be self-explanatory.

4.6.3 Case study 3 Behaviour development

Jen has been teaching employability skills to Entry Level 3 groups in a Pupil Referral Unit (PRU) for the last five years. Although she teaches to the awarding body's list of learning outcomes and received huge praise from the recent external verifier's monitoring visit, thus reinforcing her belief that she adequately covers the *must* know element, she harbours a nagging unease that she *could*, indeed *should*, do something more around developing learners' affective skills in preparation for the world of work. She finds that teaching to the unit outcomes (basically, a portfolio of evidence) is easy but the learners tend to exit the programme with the same thinking and feeling that they had when they reluctantly enrolled.

The unit comes to a conclusion with a mock job interview role play with Jen as the interviewer although, regardless of how authentic she tries to make it (for example, sending them a formal appointment letter to home and spending time on what constitutes appropriate dress, presentation and hygiene for the interview), the learners never seem to take it seriously. There is no one else available at the PRU and Jen feels that this is both a missed opportunity and a focus for development. It was while Jen was running through her mental

(Continued)

(Continued)

Table 4.4 Feedback sheet

Interviewee name: Date:

Aspect	Strengths	Areas for development
Appearance		
Body language		
Verbal language		
Responses to questions		
Interest and motivation		
Additional comments		
Key to highlighted points	You *must* develop this before your next interview You *should* develop this to enhance your interview style You *could* develop this to give you an edge over others	

checklist of who she knows in Human Resources departments in various organizations who might be free to conduct the interviews for her, that she spotted the gift on the doorstep – one of the 'Big Four' supermarkets was building a huge store round the corner and was recruiting new staff, although they would be fully staffed before her learners completed the programme. The rhetoric surrounding the store development included a community-based social justice message that Jen thought worthy of exploiting so she approached the regional manager and negotiated the following remit.

- Conduct a 10-minute job interview, at 20-minute intervals, with each learner in the group (10 minutes to complete the feedback sheet and the whole thing will only take half a day per year).
- Provide both positive and developmental feedback comments to each interviewee.
- Colour-code the development points using three different highlighter colours.

Jen thought that it would be especially useful if the regional manager could conduct two interviews (see for example Table 4.4) of the same learners – one with feedback and a later one to measure the extent to which each had acted on the feedback, although she conceded that this might be pushing such benevolence despite the benefits to the supermarket of the PRU being a possible feeder organization in the future. Nonetheless, she was optimistic that the promise of a 'proper' job interview at the end of the course (subject to appropriate on-course behaviour and attendance) could have a positive and motivational effect on learner behaviour with the next group.

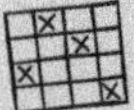

Activity 3 Behaviour development

The authors of this chapter spent many years as teaching practitioners challenging inappropriate behaviour without success until we began to understand that for learners:

THINKING + FEELING = BEHAVIOUR

Now, we focus on identifying why learners think and feel the way that they do and working with those two components to bring about

(Continued)

(Continued)

the desired behaviours. For example, we have found that: positive reinforcement (praising good behaviour and drawing less attention to bad behaviour) tends to encourage good behaviour in 'attention seekers' because that is all they get recognition for; making the learning enjoyable (even occasionally using humour) makes learners look forward to the next lesson; and getting to know a little of the learners and their culture helps to develop rapport (however we have found that we always have to show something of ourselves before they do).

With this and your 'difficult' learners in mind, complete Table 4.5

Table 4.5 Typical behaviours

Typical behaviours	Thinking or feeling?	Possible strategies for working with that thinking or feeling

4.6.4 Case study 4 Organizational development

Alan has worked for an organization helping unemployed people back into work for the last four years and staff responsibilities have recently been 'rationalized'. One of his new responsibilities is to design and implement the organization's in-house mandatory Continuing Professional Development (CPD) programme consisting of quarterly training days which, previously, he and colleagues had little enthusiasm for. With the help of some 'dog and tennis ball' escapism (see 2.9.3 Activity: Diverse needs in Chapter 2), Alan has tried to breathe new life into the next training day by moving away from an over-reliance on PowerPoint presentations and 'telling' staff. In his preparation for his first training day, which he had moved to the car park, Alan produced a set of verbatim teaching notes (fearful of freezing at the outset) which began as follows:

> Good morning and well done for being on time. Good to see some new faces among us – we dinosaurs look forward to learning much from what you bring to the company and today is one of those times and spaces where you have a voice. Use it well.
>
> Speaking with colleagues has taught me that, overwhelmingly, the two best features of any CPD event or conference are the coffee and the networking. Hence, coffee is on tap on the table near the door (help yourself at any point during the day) and we're going to be working with each other, and frequently changing those groups, throughout the day so that we network as widely as possible.
>
> We are in the car park for a number of reasons: there is no PowerPoint out here; we won't be distracted by phones or incoming email; the forecast is for sun until this afternoon – so we should make the most of it; we have plenty of writing surfaces (the chalk is for the floor and the dry-wipe pens for car windows, hence this window spray and cloths); the smokers can work in smokers' corner: because it gives us an opportunity to look at things differently, and we need to. Exit questionnaires from our clients suggest that some of the features of our work are not as we perceive them, but more of this later. What is important is that we become more aware of what we bring to the table and how we use those skills. We are this company's greatest resource and today is about developing us so that the clients benefit.
>
> I have my own thoughts about what we need to do differently but CPD isn't about me – it's about all of us. So, get yourself a coffee, form a group of three with some people you don't usually work with and make sure one of you has a mobile phone. You have five minutes then I'll tell you what we're doing next.
>
> Thank you for doing that quickly. In your groups, and given the resources available to us in this space, you have three minutes to negotiate the CPD that you want from today (an extended lunch and early finish are not CPD). There are two conditions here: first, everyone in your group has a voice; second, one of you must video the discussion on a mobile phone.

(Continued)

(Continued)

Thank you for your work there. There is a Frenchman by the name of Jacques Rancière who doesn't teach anyone anything but is a bit like Socrates who just seemed to ask questions all the time, which led people to discover their own answers. It sounds clever but I don't think it's too difficult to do so we are going to give it a try. Rancière just asks three questions: what do you see? What do you think of it? And what do you make of it? What we're going to do now is that you swap the mobile phone with another group, watch their video and, individually, try to answer Rancière's three questions. Having got as far as you can, share your thoughts with the others in your group and record the group's thoughts in some way. You have 20 minutes from now.

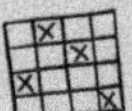

Activity 4 Organizational development

- Read Alan's case study again, very carefully, at least twice.
- Answer Rancière's three questions concerning this case study.
- Borrow a dog and a tennis ball, take yourself off somewhere and apply Rancière's three questions to your own professional role.
- List three things that you can develop, change, stop doing or begin to do as part of your next CPD:

  1. One thing that must change is ...
  2. One thing that should change is ...
  3. One thing that could change is ...

- Against each of the above three changes, suggest ways in which they can be realized within your organization's CPD framework.
- Against each, state a date for when they can be achieved.
- Now go and do them.

See Chapter 10 regarding how to develop this further.

References

Bathmaker, A.-M., Ecclestone, K. and Cooke, S. (2011) 'But is it "proper" knowledge? The vexed question of "knowledge" in broad vocational education', paper presented at the *Journal of Vocational Education and Training* 9th International Conference, 8–10 July 2011, Worcester College, Oxford.

Biesta, G. (2007) 'Why "what works" won't work: evidence-based practice and the democratic deficit in educational research', *Educational Theory*, 57 (1): 1–22.

Biggs, J. (2003) *Teaching for Quality Learning at University*. Maidenhead: Open University Press/McGraw-Hill Education.

Brown, S. and Knight, P. (1994) *Assessing Learners in Higher Education*. London: Kogan Page.

Brown, S., Race, P. and Smith, B. (1995) *500 Tips on Assessment*. London: Kogan Page.

Burke, P. J. and Jackson, S. (2007) *Reconceptualising Lifelong Learning: Feminist Interventions*. London and New York: Routledge

Coffield, F. (2007a) 'Foreword', in D. James and G. Biesta (eds), *Improving Learning Cultures in Further Education*. Abingdon: Routledge.

Coffield, F. (2007b) 'Running ever faster down the wrong road: an alternative future for education and skills', keynote lecture at the 6th Annual Conference, The Consortium for Post-Compulsory Education and Training, 22 July, Leeds.

Coffield, F. (2008) *Just Suppose Teaching and Learning Became the First Priority*. London: Learning and Skills Network.

Coffield, F. (2009) *All You Ever Wanted to Know about Learning and Teaching But Were Too Cool to Ask*. London: Learning and Skills Network.

DIUS (2008) *Further Education Colleges: Models for Success*. London: Department for Innovation, Universities and Skills.

Dreyfus, S. E. and Dreyfus, H. L. (1980) *A Five-stage Model of the Mental Activities Involved in Directed Skill Acquisition*. Washington. DC: Storming Media.

EQF (European Qualifications Framework) (2011) *Using Learning Outcomes. European Qualifications Framework Series: Note 4*. http://ec.europa.eu/education/lifelong-learning-policy/doc/eqf/note4_en.pdf (accessed 2 October 2013).

Evans, M. (2004) *Killing Thinking: The Death of the Universities*. London: Continuum.

James, D. and Biesta, G. (eds) (2007) *Improving Learning Cultures in Further Education*. Abingdon: Routledge.

Jarvis, P. J. (2008) *Democracy, Lifelong Learning and the Learning Society: Active Citizenship in a Late Modern Age*. London and New York: Routledge.

Keep, E. (2006) 'State control of the English education and training system: playing with the biggest train set in the world', *Journal of Vocational Education and Training*, 58 (1): 47–64.

Kelly, A. V. (2009) *The Curriculum: Theory and Practice* (6th edn). London: Sage.

Knight, P. and Trowler, P. R. (2001) *Departmental Leadership in Higher Education*. Buckingham: Open University Press/SHRE.

Knowles, M. (1978) *The Adult Learner: A Neglected Species*. Houston, TX: Gulf.

Mezirow, J. (1981) 'A critical theory of adult education and learning', *Adult Education*, 32 (1): 3–24.

Moon, J. (2004) *Linking Levels, Learning Outcomes and Assessment Criteria*. www.aic.lv/bolona/Bologna/Bol_semin/Edinburgh/J_Moon_backgrP.pdf (accessed 2 October 2013).

Newstead, S. (2002) 'Examining the examiners: why are we so bad at assessing learners?', *Psychology Learning and Teaching*, 2 (2): 70–75.

Nielsen, S. M. (2008) 'Half bricks and half clicks: is blended onsite and online teaching and learning the best of both worlds?', in M. S. Plakhotnik and S. M. Nielsen (eds), *Proceedings of the Seventh Annual College of Education Research Conference*. Miami, FL: Florida International University, pp. 105–110.

Oliver, M. (2011) 'Technological determinism in educational technology research: some alternative ways of thinking about the relationship between learning and technology, *Journal of Computer Assisted Learning*, 27: 373–384. doi:10.1111/j.1365–2729.2011.00406.x.

Orr, K. (2008) 'Room for improvement? The impact of compulsory professional development for teachers in England's further education sector', *Journal of In-Service Education*, 34 (1): 97–108.

Pring, R. (2004) *Philosophy of Educational Research* (2nd edn). London: Continuum.

Ramsden, P. (2003) *Learning to Teach in Higher Education*. London: Routledge

Rancière, J. (1991) *The Ignorant Schoolmaster: Five Lessons in Intellectual Emancipation*, trans. K. Ross. Stanford, CA: Stanford University Press.

Vygotsky, L. S. (1978) *Mind in Society: The Development of Higher Psychological Processes*. Cambridge, MA: Harvard University Press.

Watson, P. (2002) 'The role and integration of learning outcomes into the educational process', *Active Learning in Higher Education*, 3 (3): 205–219.

Wood, D., Bruner, J. and Ross, G. (1976) 'The role of tutoring in problem solving', *Journal of Child Psychology and Child Psychiatry*, 17: 89–100.

CHAPTER 5

USING METAPHORS IN TEACHING, TRAINING AND LEARNING

Mohammed Karolia

Learning outcomes

After reading this chapter, the reader should be able to:

- Appreciate some of the theories that underpin the use of metaphors in teaching and training.
- Understand how to use metaphors in practice.
- Identify models of metaphors and how to use them.

Chapter outline

The need to ensure content is clearly explained and articulated within sessions should be at the forefront of the minds of practitioners. Preparing sessions often results in an inordinate amount of time being spent on developing visual, auditory and kinaesthetic resources in an attempt to capture learners' imaginations and cover learning objectives. However, as 'meaning-making machines', learners learn best when they are able to relate with, connect to and explore content in a way that makes sense to them and which, at times, visual, auditory and kinaesthetic learning resources may not always be able to achieve. This is where the use of similes, metaphors and stories can be used as a means of capturing, utilizing and maximizing learning. This chapter suggests that metaphors, similes and stories share a number of important similarities and connections. They are all used to explain and solve a wide variety of events, situations, concepts and problems. Hence it aims to explore how similes, metaphors and stories can be more widely used in learning and development practice.

5.1 Underpinning theory

Wormeli (2009) states that metaphors are so unconsciously common that they become fundamental to what and how we think, and given their significance, metaphors and similes should be one of the primary considerations when designing learning. The word 'metaphor' originates from the Greek phrase *metapherein* which means 'to transfer or carry over' something (Wormeli, 2009). In the context of language and everyday conversations the use of metaphors refers to the way in which people carry over or translate the meaning of one idea, concept or thought to another idea, concept or thought. Metaphor, it is suggested, is a fundamental mechanism of mind, 'it allows practitioners to use what they know about practical, physical and social experience to provide understanding, understanding of many other topics' (Lakoff and Johnson, 2008).

So what is a metaphor? Lakoff and Johnson (1980: 5) in their seminal text *Metaphors We Live By* define metaphors as 'describing one thing in terms of another, whereby we refer to understanding an unfamiliar concept, event or state of affairs in terms of something more familiar'. Kovecses (2002: 39) expands on this to describes metaphors as 'the result of associating certain concrete and abstract concepts to each other, not by a pure flight of fancy, but because they entail or implicate each other'. Geary (2011) observes that individuals on average can utter up to six metaphors in a minute. This, when combined with the notion of how metaphors are endemic, helps to highlight the importance and value of using metaphors as a means of explaining new and unfamiliar learning via means of something that is more familiar and easily understood by learners.

It is argued that the endemic nature of metaphors only becomes apparent when observing how individuals, in their everyday conversation, discuss and talk about their experiences and attempt to convey their thoughts and ideas (Geary, 2011). More often than not, they will refer to aspects that are familiar to them as a means of simplifying the same understanding to the other person. For instance, everyday metaphors such as 'a storm in a teacup' would often be used to communicate to someone how an event is perceived as being more significant than it actually is, or 'in the blink of an eye' is used to stress something happening very fast. In addition to everyday conversations, metaphors can also form archetypes and narratives of how people may live their lives (Lakoff and Johnson, 1980, 2008). Their notion of 'conceptual metaphors' suggests that our thoughts and subsequently our actions are guided by subconscious 'conceptual structures' that impact on the way we think, act, interact and live our lives. For example, consider the metaphor of someone who describes their life as 'living in a palace' to someone who is 'drowning in a sea of sorrows'. This then suggests that metaphors are used to give meaning to what is happening in people's lives.

Similes, metaphors and stories can all be used as powerful ways to promote learning as they resonate with the way in which individuals think and comprehend their experiences. At a basic level, the mind seeks to understand phenomena and experiences via a process of building connections and associations with what is already known and understood. This is a process that aids in recalling and remembering information. This then draws on the notion of how metaphors are used to 'describe one thing in terms of another' and feeds into the process of understanding something via a connection or association with something else that is already known. This in turn helps learners to better understand a subject. Our mind also has an inherent tendency to want to close the loop or avoid the 'cliff-hanger' scenario whereby there is a sense of uncertainty about what is understood. This sense of uncertainty can be filled by framing an experience and learning about our 'own map of the world' which, in turn, can be impacted by and influenced by, the metaphors and narratives that are referred to in interpreting experiences.

Within a teaching or training context, the importance and relevance of metaphors is further emphasized by Saban (2006). He identified 12 functions of metaphors in teaching, which included the role of metaphors as a pedagogical device to reframe content, focusing on or filtering content that is of importance to encourage discussion or as a tool to summarize and clarify learning.

As a medium of reflection, metaphors can be used to promote critical thinking and explore different perspectives, the content being covered and the different interpretations of the key issues, as well as encouraging learners to form their own conclusions of what has been learnt.

As an 'instrument of discovery' metaphors can be used to engage learners' imaginations and promote creativity due to the many ways in which metaphors and in particular stories (as extended metaphors) can be interpreted to aid learning. In summary, as a 'springboard for change' metaphors can be used to identify, challenge and shift learners' frame of reference due to the powerful way in which metaphors can shape learners' concepts and perceptions of their experiences and the world.

5.2 Differences between similes, metaphors and stories

Many have suggested that there is little in learning that has as much influence on learners' success as the metaphors and similes practitioners use to make unfamiliar concepts clear (Wormeli, 2009). They can be used to transform learners' thinking and actions, but they can also open their minds to new ideas. While the generic term 'metaphors' has been used to refer to describing one thing as another in this chapter, it is important to understand how similes and stories can also be considered as metaphors. It is also important to acknowledge how they differ and to ensure they are used appropriately within a teaching and training context.

Similes

Similes can best be described as 'comparing one thing to another as a means of helping the other person to understand the relevance or significance of the things being compared' (Saban, 2006: 10). On the other hand, Wormeli (2009: 5) describes a simile as: 'A comparison between two unlike objects or ideas'. The things being compared do not have to follow any logic or specifically relate to each other, aside from stressing how the comparison being made is of significance. For example, 'as clear as mud', 'you're as cold as ice', 'your voice is like music to my ears' or 'your explanation was like spaghetti'. These are all examples of similes where one thing is compared to another. Note, the words 'as' and 'like', which signify the presence of simile, often feature in the use of similes and aid in comparing one thing to another.

Metaphors

Metaphors convey similarities by substituting one thing for another, thus the substitution of one concept for another by means of metaphors creates understandings (Marks, 2011). In other words metaphors offer comparisons, and are figures of speech that can help convey one thing in the form of another by additional use of correlations, parallels, likeness, significance and similarities of the message being conveyed. For example, 'you're biting off more than you can chew', 'too many cooks in the kitchen' and 'walking on egg shells' are also examples of metaphors which a person can use as a means of better expressing or conveying what they wish to say.

Stories

Stories can be considered as extended metaphors; a story can have embedded within it several similes and metaphors, all of which are used to communicate a key message. Stories are memorable and can be rich in substance and be significant; they offer a powerful way to communicate, as they not only contain factual happenings but also can be absorbed and used to engage the whole group. Therefore it doesn't matter if the story is true or a myth as long as the story is used in context, and it is relevant and aids in reinforcing learners' understanding.

5.2.1 The use of similes, metaphors and stories

Moving onto how similes, metaphors and stories can be used in teaching and training, Figure 5.1 offers a process that can be followed as a means of incorporating the use of metaphors within your classes or sessions. The diagram is aimed at giving you suggestions of how to integrate the use of metaphors in your teaching practice. It would be useful to experiment with the process in the diagram to determine how best metaphors can enhance your practice.

Guidance on how to maximize each of the above four steps are discussed in more detail below.

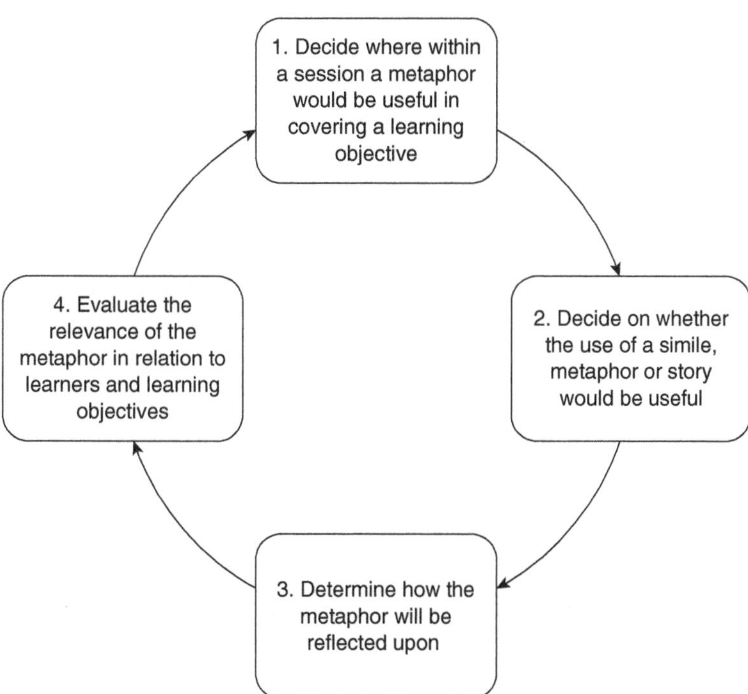

Figure 5.1 Incorporating similes, metaphors and stories

5.2.2 Using metaphors to cover a learning objective

It is often said that all practitioners want learners to fully understand a topic, but in order for this to happen they need to become more proficient at showing them how to imagine what has been discussed and then describe it in visual terms. So when thinking about the use of a metaphor as a teaching and training method within a session, it is useful to think about using them as a learning technique in the same way as inviting group discussion in order to generate creative ideas or question and answer techniques. All these techniques are regarded as teaching methods to help reinforce a specific aspect of knowledge, skills, attitudes or learning objective and as such are used to add variety to a session while keeping in mind the need to meet learning objectives.

Similes, metaphors and stories all work on the premise that the brain works by making links and associations. Hence it is useful to review a session to determine and identify how learners have or can associate what they need to learn with something they already know. However, these associations do not necessarily link to existing concepts or new or existing learning; they can be as diverse as the range of experiences a learner may have in a day, though the key consideration is that learners are able to associate aspects of a metaphor with the content that will be covered in the session. Once potential associations have been identified, it is useful to consider how the association can be used to cover or reinforce a learning objective, or to explore views and emotions of what is being taught. Hence, any aspect of a session where learners already have formed or have potential associations with what needs to be taught, presents an opportunity to use a metaphor activity within a session.

5.2.3 Is simile, metaphor or story useful in teaching and training?

As discussed earlier, while the word metaphor has been used as a catch-all phase to discuss how one thing can be described, similes and stories can also be considered as metaphors and, as such, can be utilized differently within a session. For example, as similes aim to compare one thing to another via the words 'as' or 'like', within a session this phenomenon can be used whenever the practitioner feels it would be helpful for learners to explore how one concept or aspect being taught compares with another. Similes can also be used to determine learners' thoughts about a particular issue by comparing one thing to another to gauge the depth of emotion or understanding of the issue. Simple sentence completion exercises that require learners to complete phases such as 'life is like …', 'management to me is like …', 'my thoughts about "x" are like …' can be quick and effective in gaining valuable data about the current understanding and comprehension of the issues being taught. On the other hand, metaphors and stories (which in essence are a form of extended metaphors) can be used where a greater degree of exploration or understanding is needed from the learners about the subject being taught. For example and as mentioned earlier, due to the metaphor's ability to better convey correlations, parallels, likeness, significances and similarities of the message, a metaphor or story can be used to highlight potentially difficult or abstract ideas which may otherwise be difficult to comprehend. Therefore, once a potential area of a session is identified where greater clarification or exploration of a subject may be helpful, the practitioner needs to think about potential association, either actual or fictional, that may exist, which can be developed into a metaphor to help explain the topic.

A useful starting point that can aid this process would be what Rees (2013) identifies as the four universal metaphors that correlate with how individuals describe and comprehend their experiences:

- Issues/factors of importance are considered 'big' in size. For example, 'a massive job', 'it's a big deal'.
- Emotions are conveyed as being 'up' or 'down'. For example, 'that sinking feeling', 'as high as the sky', 'down in the dumps'.
- Emotional attachments are related to proximity. For example, a 'close family', 'distant relations'.
- Time is linked to space. For example 'looking ahead' now, that's 'behind me now'.

Other useful potential avenues where associations of relevance can exist are:

- local and cultural contexts and events
- current news events and items
- movies, TV programmes, songs
- real or fictional stories and fables.

Once an association has been established, consideration needs to be given to the '*thread*', '*channel*' and '*attributes*' of the metaphor to ensure that the metaphor to be used will be appropriate and relevant to covering the intended learning objectives.

The 'thread' of the metaphor refers to the key concept that needs to be explored in more depth as part of a session and can be a segment of knowledge, skill or attitudes that needs to be covered during the session. For example, within a session on communication skills, the practitioner may want to emphasize the negotiation skills as the 'thread' that needs to be covered in more depth or, within a session on communications and information technology (ICT), the importance of 'internet security' as the 'thread' may need further explanation.

The 'channel' crucially refers to the metaphor that will be used to explore the 'thread' in more depth. It is important when using a 'channel' that its 'associations' are relevant and promote understanding. Hence, to emphasize the importance of questioning skills within a communication skills session, a scenario of a 'road journey' can be used as a 'channel'. This will help you to steer round obstacles and adapt to the terrain and environment in which the key elements of good negotiation skills are explored. Similarly, the way in which a bank keeps its money safe and secure can be used as a potential 'channel' through which to explore 'internet security'.

The 'attributes' of the metaphor refers to how there needs to be an understandable and recognizable connection between the 'thread' and 'channel' of a metaphor. A poor metaphor is one where the connection between the 'thread' and the 'channel' is difficult to understand and the association vague and unclear. It is essential to ensure that the 'thread', 'channel' and 'attributes' of the metaphor or stories to be used within a session are congruent. It is also helpful to ensure that the use of the metaphors is of value, relevant and significant in reinforcing the learning.

5.3 Key considerations in selecting metaphors

As mentioned above, the success or otherwise of the use of metaphors in learning is dependent on the relevance and context in which the metaphors are used. Delivering your sessions through metaphors, similes and narratives should be a conscious choice to scaffold learning by making meaningful connections among topics. This can be done using artefacts relevant to the topic, so as to enable learners to think critically about the topic. Wormeli (2009) suggests that doing this will enable learners to make the 'invisible visible' through explicit comparisons and applying knowledge from one topic to another, to help learners to move beyond memorization to deeper learning that lasts. Thus, it is important to ensure that any metaphors used within sessions are clearly understood by the learners. Hence, consideration needs to be given to the factors outlined in Table 5.1.

While consideration of the above variables will ensure that the metaphors have a positive impact in teaching and training, they can also

Table 5.1 Considerations in the use of metaphors

Age of learners	What factors would the learners within the particular age group relate to and be able to associate with? For example, middle-aged middle managers are likely to have very different associations to everyday events and phenomena than a group of 16–18 year-old A-level college students
Locality/cultural differences	Some metaphors, as well as being context specific, may only be understood or relate to a particular locality or community and hence care needs to be taken to ensure metaphors are as inclusive and generic as possible
Occupational context	Just as specific vocations use jargon and acronyms to convey and communicate key messages, they may also refer to metaphors which are only understood by those familiar with the vocation or organization in which they are used. Therefore, it is better to refer to generic metaphors when working with diverse groups of learners and only resort to organizational or industry specific metaphors when there is a degree of certainty that those present will be able to relate to and associate with the metaphor
Use of humour	Special care also needs to be taken in the use humorous metaphors and the underlying messages they may convey. While humour can greatly aid in building rapport and relaxing learners, the use of unintentionally humorous stories and metaphors can have the opposite effect due to humour being a very personal construct that differs from person to person and hence consideration again needs to be given to the points listed above to ensure they do not impact on learners negatively

guard against the use of an ill-judged metaphor that can cause some confusion rather than clarification. Due to the potential for time saving that metaphors have to offer practitioners, there can be a tendency to rely on them too heavily within a session. This can be counter-productive as familiarity in itself can present a barrier to learning. As with any other teaching strategy, metaphors need to be used in moderation and in conjunction with other teaching methods. Therefore, metaphors should be used to aid learning and reinforce a learning objective where learners have already formed ideas about, or have potential associations with, what needs to be taught. This is not to say that metaphors cannot be used to convey new content or knowledge.

Another key consideration to note when using metaphors in teaching is the time commitment needed to effectively maximize the value of using them. While the use of similes and sentence completion exercises may not be too time-consuming to complete within a session, the time needed to review, reflect on and debrief the metaphor may impact on the session as a whole, particularly with regards to the use of metaphors or stories as extended forms of metaphors.

5.3.1 Determining how the metaphor will be reflected upon

Many agree that metaphors make the world intelligible to people by providing a mental referent by which information is categorized and understood by the brain (Marks, 2011). Therefore once a simile, metaphor or story has been used or referred to within a session, it is essential to reflect on the learning gained from working with metaphors to both identify what has been learnt and to help evaluate whether the metaphor has helped to cover or reinforce a learning objective. The process of reflecting on metaphors can follow popular models of reflection stipulated by Kolb (1984), Gibbs (1988) and Brookfield (1995); however, whichever model of reflection is used, as a practitioner it is essential to consider how the metaphor will be both 'reviewed' and 'debriefed', with review specifically focusing on how learners themselves reflect on their learning and the debrief stressing the role of the practitioner in the process.

With regards to encouraging learners to actively reflect on and review learning from metaphors, it may be useful to make learners aware of the components of the metaphors by briefly informing them of the differences between the 'thread', 'channel' and 'attributes' of a metaphor and how each of the components aided or informed the learning through the use of metaphors. The practitioner can guide this process by acting as a conduit to ensure there is a balance between the level and depth a metaphor is reflected upon and analysed and the learning objectives that need to be stressed or covered within the session. It may also be useful to inform learners of how to specifically review the learning from a metaphor prior to the review process and the need to explore the learning in terms of the:

- finer details of subject
- 'big picture' or 'blue sky thinking' of a subject
- logistics behind the metaphor and what needs to be learnt
- creative aspects of what the metaphor reveals.

It is necessary to take time to stress and inform learners how the review process is conducted, in addition to ensuring the review process keeps within the boundaries of the instructions given. This can pay dividends in ensuring learners maximize the opportunities available to them via the use of metaphors. With regards to the practitioner's role in debriefing the use of a simile, metaphor or stories exercise, it would be better for the practitioner to direct the debrief via the use of questions in preference to directing learners towards what they needed to have gained and learnt from the exercise. Taking time to consider the use of Jensen's (1998) 'recall', 'process' and 'application' questions as part of the preparation process can greatly aid the debrief process and again maximize the learning to be gained from using metaphors.

Recall questions such as, 'what did you do … / when you … / what happened? / describe what …' can all help learners recollect and bring to the fore the key learning gained from the use of and review of the metaphors and assist the practitioner in gauging the level of understanding of the group in relation to the learning objectives.

There are crucial 'process' questions that can be used to dissect, analyse and explore the learning via questions such as: how does 'x' link to 'y'? What do 'x' and 'y' have in common? How are they different? These help to add another level of analysis and review of the metaphor that is steered by the practitioner in addition to the review and reflections of the metaphors completed by the learners. Application questions are aimed at moving the learners towards linking the analysis of the metaphors to practise and exploring the implications the metaphors have in furthering learners' thinking and understanding of the learning objective. Taking time to consider how learners are likely to respond to a metaphor activity, the likely metaphors that will be explored and discussed and how these can be debriefed prior to the session by preparing a list of recall, process and application question can greatly aid in ensuring the metaphors activity helps in working towards covering the learning objectives of the session.

Another skilled method of completing the debrief comprises of the use of the 'clean language' model by asking questions that specifically aim to explore and analyse metaphors used by individuals in describing and comprehending their experiences. The 'clean language' model, originally devised by David Grove, stems from Grove's observation of how clients, whom he counselled within a therapeutic setting, would often revert to using metaphors that had personal significance and relevance to them as a way of better conceptualizing their experiences. This observation led Grove to devise a set of questions, which was further developed by Lawley and Tompkins (2000) and Sullivan and Rees (2008) and which practitioners can use to identify and explore the metaphors used by learners in a way that prevents them from knowingly or subconsciously interpreting the metaphors (as signified by the term 'clean language'). While the specific use and application of the clean language model is beyond the remit of this chapter, further details can be found in the reference list at the end on this chapter.

5.4 Evaluate the relevance of metaphors in relation to learners and learning objectives

As with all learning activities and exercises, it is important to evaluate the effectiveness of the level to which the learning activity and exercises helped in covering the set learning objective (see also Chapter 8 on evaluation). The use of any simile, metaphor or story within a session should be aimed at introducing new concepts, exploring existing concepts or reinforcing the concepts and content that have been previously covered within a session or part of the curriculum. Having a clear understanding of the precise and specific knowledge, skills or behaviour that a metaphor needs to introduce, explore or reinforce prior to the session can aid this process, especially if some consideration is given to the degree of understanding that can be measured and is required from the metaphor activity. For example, the popular and well-known Bloom's taxonomy of understanding levels (Anderson and Krathwohl, 2001) can be used prior to a session to gauge the depth of understanding required of learners with regards to whether learners are required to remember, understand, analyse, apply, evaluate or create new understanding from exploring a simile, metaphor or story within a session (Marks, 2011). Alternatively, industry and awarding bodies specific assessment criteria can also be used to evaluate the level to which a metaphor activity aided the achievement of a learning objective. The key message is to ensure that some thought is given to how a metaphor activity will aid learning within a session with regards to set learning objectives and how the success of the metaphor activity will be evaluated during and after the session.

5.5 Worked example of the use of metaphors in teaching and training

To further understand how similes, metaphors and stories can be used in practice, the learning objectives below show how each can be utilized within a generic 'stress management' session that is delivered over a day. Although, the worked example that follows specifically focuses on a session on managing stress, the principles discussed and the guidelines given can equally be transferred to other hard and soft skills subjects and used accordingly.

The stress management session around which the case study is centred has attached to it the following learning objectives:

1. Identify a definition of stress.
2. Recognize the signs and symptoms of stress.

3. Compare different stress coping strategies.
4. Compile personal action plan for managing stress.

With the above learning objectives in mind, a facilitator would proceed with preparing a session that works towards covering the above learning objectives and this is where the use of similes, metaphors and stories should be considered as a teaching method in the same way as individual, group or brainstorm activities would.

Objective 1: In deciding whether and where similes, metaphors and stories can be used as an appropriate learning and development strategy, the first step in the process is to consider where potential associations exist in relation to what learners need to know (learning objectives) and what they may know and recognize already. Most people would have some experience and understanding in defining to some degree what stress means to them and hence this association can be exploited via the use of a simile and an exercise whereby the learners complete the sentence, 'Stress for me is like ...' as a means of covering and exploring learning objective 1.

Objective 2: Similarly, learners are likely to have some comprehension and association of how to manage stress either in themselves or through observing others and hence a metaphor activity whereby learners are asked to identify metaphors of good and bad examples of managing stress from themes associated with local or cultural contexts, current news items, movies, songs or real and fictional stories can be used to help cover learning objective 2. Finally, as a means of encouraging learners to compile and follow through on their personal action plan for managing stress (objective 4) a metaphorical inspirational story can be used to close the session and help cover the final learning outcome. A more detailed explanation of how examples of the use of similes, metaphors and stories can be used to facilitate the stress management session follows below.

While the use of a simile sentence completion exercise (Stress for me is like ...) would help cover the learning objective 'to be able to identify a definition of stress', consideration needs to be given to how the exercise will be conducted, reviewed and debriefed. As it would be useful to gauge learners' immediate thoughts and feelings about how they experience stress, it would be helpful to time-limit the activity and give learners no more than a couple of minutes to complete the sentence to avoid the scenario whereby they may give a more considered response in relation to what is expected of them by the tutor or peers. As the responses to the sentence completion activity are likely to be personal, the exercise would be better reviewed in pairs or small groups with the learners given the brief to focus on how the responses to the exercise are similar to or different from each and the likely significance of the impact of this on the way they define and experience stress. The practitioner-led debrief can be launched via the use of recall questions such as 'Would anybody like to share their sentences?', followed by process questions which can explore the similarities and differences between sentences. The practitioner can focus in on the four key metaphors identified by Rees (2013) with regards to whether the similes chosen by learners are big or small in size, give a future or past perspective, have any attachments associated with them and in particular, given the simile is aimed as exploring stress, whether any emotions conveyed are perceived to be either high or low, to help focus the debrief discussions led by the practitioner.

Objective 3: The metaphor activity whereby learners are asked to identify metaphors of good and bad examples of managing stress from themes associated with local or cultural contexts, current news items, movies and songs, or real or fictional stories can be used to help cover the learning objectives linked to being 'able to compare different stress coping strategies'. It is important to research and prepare beforehand examples of potential metaphors or similes that learners can relate to and associate with. Once these have been identified it would be helpful again to allow peers to review, reflect on and compare different metaphors and the relevance and significance of them. The practitioner can aid this process by informing learners of the presence of 'threads', 'channels' and 'attributes' within the metaphor and which can also be used by the practitioner to debrief the exercise and further shed light on the 'finer details' of the metaphor with regards to how different learners manage stress in different ways again via the use of process and recall questions, which can be prepared and thought through beforehand.

Objective 4: Finally, to help close the session the use of an inspirational story as an extended metaphor can be used to gain some commitment towards compiling a personal action plan for managing stress. Again it is essential to refer to a story that is relevant, within context and one that learners within the group are able to identify and associate with. As a closing activity, there may not be time to thoroughly review the story, however, as a minimum it would be helpful for a practitioner to prepare a list of process and application questions such as 'How is the story similar to the way in which you intend to manage stress?', 'Is there a better way of managing stress than mentioned in the story?', 'What would happen if you were to manage stress in this way?' to help debrief the activity and get learners to think creatively about how they can manage their stress in relation to the lessons learnt from the story.

All learners can learn to identify and use metaphors, similes and stories to deepen understanding in a learning environment. However, practitioners as well as learners need good models of metaphorical thinking. Therefore, when using them as a teaching method to build on learning, it is useful to work through the following case studies, activities and questions as an example of how to utilize the use of similes, metaphors and stories in your sessions.

5.6 Summary, case study, discussion questions and learning activities

The use of similes, metaphors and stories provides immense opportunities and potential in enabling practitioners to engage with and work with learners in a way that is meaningful and relevant to them. However, as with all teaching and training strategies, prior thought and consideration needs to be given to the way in which metaphors are used appropriately within a session.

As with any new skill, the use of metaphors as a key learning and development strategy takes time and will require practice and the ability to reflect your experiences, to fine tune and perfect your practice. However, the advantage of doing so will be that you are inherently working with the very ways in which your learners perceive, think, comprehend and experience the world, which can only help you work towards meeting learners' needs and learning objectives. Consequently, Plato advocated, we should be the ones who show learners and each other that the flickering shadows on the back wall of the cavern are not all there is to reality. Recognizing and moving beyond our current metaphors may be the best gift we provide to our learners; their enthusiastic response, 'Oh, now I get it!' is music to a practitioner's ears (Wormeli, 2009: 145).

It would be useful for you to follow and reflect on the case study and activities below.

5.6.1 Case study Associations of similes, metaphors and stories

Imagine that you are working with a group of accounting technician learners on the importance of communication and interpersonal skills. This is a subject that is not integral to their course but still of importance to their personal and professional development.

Key issues:

As the learners perceive the session and the subject being taught to be a by-product of the actual course, you envisage some hesitancy in

(Continued)

(Continued)

the way in which the learners are likely to engage in the session. You have taught a similar session before which resulted in a general lack of interest and participation by the learners. This is not helped by the fact that there is a lot to cover within this three-hour session.

Having reflected on your last experience of delivering the session, in addition to making some amendments to the lesson plan, you wish to make further use of the learners' life experiences as a way of delivering the session content and to link theory to practice. However, since the learners are not likely to want to discuss personal life experience within a large group setting or even a small group, you consider that the alternative use of similes, metaphors and stories can help to provide the bridge in overcoming the learners' hesitancy within the session.

Questions:

To help ensure similes, metaphors and stories are used effectively within a session, you need to consider the following questions:

- Are there aspects of the session where associations may exist in relation to the content and learning objectives that need to be covered?
- How can these associations be explored in more depth via the use of a simile, metaphor or story?
- Once a simile, metaphor or story has been identified, how can the 'thread', 'channel' and 'attributes' of the metaphor be fully explored and reviewed as part of the learning exercise?
- How can the effectiveness of a metaphor activity be evaluated against learning objectives?

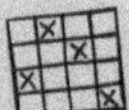

5.6.2 Activity

- Split the group of learners into smaller groups (no more than six in a group).
- Then get your learners to demonstrate a metaphor of what they have learned in the session (this should take no more than 10 minutes).
- Get them back together and share and discuss the metaphors each group identified (check for similarities, relevance and connectivity).

5.6.3 Summary of the key processes

The diagram below summarizes the key processes of using metaphors, which were discussed within this chapter.

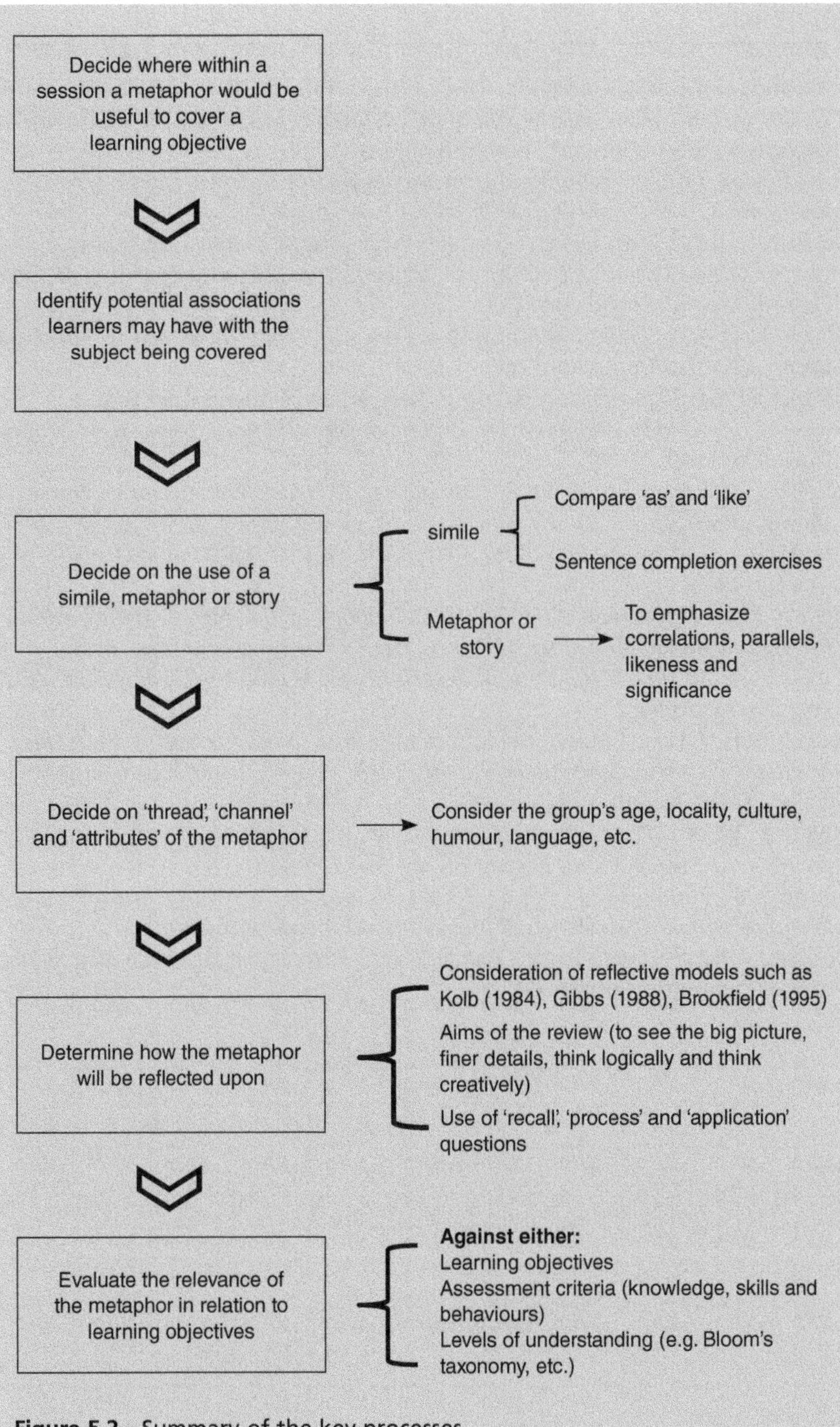

Figure 5.2 Summary of the key processes

References

Anderson, L. W. and Krathwohl, D. R. (eds) (2001) *A Taxonomy for Learning, Teaching, and Assessing: A Revision of Bloom's Taxonomy of Educational Objectives*. New York and London: Longman.

Brookfield, S. (1995) *Becoming a Critically Reflective Teacher*. San Francisco, CA: Jossey-Bass.

Geary, J. (2011) *I Is an Other*. USA: New York: HarperCollins Publishers.

Gibbs, G. (1988) *Learning by Doing: A Guide to Teaching and Learning Methods*. Oxford: Oxford Polytechnic FEU.

Jensen, E. (1998) *Sizzle and Substance: Presenting with the Brain in Mind*. San Diego, CA: The Brain Store Inc.

Kolb, D. (1984) *Experiential Learning*. New Jersey: Prentice-Hall Inc.

Kovecses, Z. (2002) *Metaphor: A Practical Introduction*. New York: Oxford University Press.

Lakoff, G. and Johnson, M. (1980) *Metaphors We Live By*. London: University of Chicago Press.

Lakoff, G. and Johnson, M. (2008) *Metaphors We Live By*. London: University of Chicago Press.

Lawley, J. and Tompkins, P. (2000) *Metaphors of the Mind: Transformation through Symbolic Modelling*. London: The Developing Company Press.

Marks, M. P. (2011) *Metaphors in International Relations Theory*. New York: Palgrave MacMillan.

Rees, J. (2013) 'Four hidden metaphors in action', *X-Ray Listening Newsletter*, 7 August. www.xraylistening.com/blog/2013/08/07/four-hidden-metaphors-in-action/ (accessed 10 August 2013).

Saban, A. (2006) 'Functions of metaphor in teaching and teacher education', review essay in *Teaching Education*, 17 (4): 299–315.

Sullivan, W. and Rees, J. (2008) *Clean Language: Revealing Metaphors and Opening Minds*. Carmarthen, Wales: Crown House Publishing.

Wormeli, R. (2009) *Metaphors Analogies: Power Tools for Teaching any Subject*. Maine: Stenhouse Publishers.

CHAPTER 6

DESIGNING LEARNING DELIVERY

Louise Mycroft and
Jane Weatherby

Learning outcomes

After reading this chapter, the reader should be able to:

- Explore some key principles and theories of learning.
- Identify barriers and motivation to learning experienced by learners.
- Understand the importance of planning for differentiated learning.
- Identify strategies for developing effectiveness in teaching, learning and assessment.

Chapter outline

This chapter explores a values-based approach to designing the delivery of learning sessions. It explores some principles and theories of learning and the barriers and motivations that adults experience when accessing education. It sets out a process for reflexive, differentiated planning and suggests why this is crucial to the effectiveness of teaching, learning and assessment. Finally, the chapter explores how sessions can be constructed, to engage and enthuse individuals and bring purposeful learning to life.

6.1 Underpinning theory

This chapter explores approaches that are deliberately reflexive; they encourage you to apply learning to your own practice, to help you figure out for yourself why, as a practitioner, you do what you do. Rather than describing the traditional approaches to the theories of learning (behaviourist, cognitivist, humanist) which are incorporated into other chapters in this book (see, for example, Chapter 9), and can be explored in many texts (see for example, Jarvis et al., 2004), we draw on the work of bell hooks, Stephen Brookfield, Paulo Freire, Nancy Kline and others in order to think reflexively and for ourselves and to write in our authentic voices. While hooks, Brookfield and Freire may be identified as taking a critical approach, Kline has focused on coaching models in the pursuit of individual and organizational improvements. Each of these writers and educators has encouraged us to question some of the most commonly held assumptions about teaching, training and learning, and it is this reflexive process that underpins our approach.

6.2 Assumptions about learning delivery

The phrase 'learning delivery' is a convenient way to describe the process of teaching and learning, and one that has become familiar to those working in education. The danger is that, in using a metaphor that makes learning sound like a parcel to be posted to the recipient, practitioners may fall into what Freire (1970) dismisses as the 'banking' concept of education. While the use of the term is understandable, after all, teaching, training and learning involves the transfer of knowledge and understanding, and 'delivering learning' can sound snappy and neat, but it misses something vital.

For over a hundred years there has been an argument that the process of teaching adults should be seen as distinct from that of teaching children and the work of Knowles (1970; 1980) was instrumental in popularizing this idea. In more recent years educational writers, such as Brookfield (2000), have challenged the assumption that methods for effective learning differ according to age or maturity, while acknowledging that many of Knowles' ideas about what constitutes effective learning remain helpful;

for example, the recognition that learners bring a valuable resource to the classroom, in the form of their experience and knowledge. This is the essential stuff of discussions, case studies, metaphors and storytelling (see Chapter 5), which, in turn, highlight the real-life application of learning and have potential to bring the experience of absent identities into the classroom setting, thus increasing the diversity of perspectives. The concept of 'delivering' learning can so easily overlook our capacity to be what Freire (1970) calls 'practitioner-learners' where both learners and practitioners are engaged as joint creators of knowledge.

6.3 Barriers to learning

Knowles' concept of the self-motivated learner, choosing to enrol in a traditional class, has significantly fallen away; this is because increasingly more young people and adults are required to attend vocational training; for instance, work-based programmes such as health and safety, mandated parenting, substance misuse and employability training. After a lifetime's experience, adults sometimes face barriers which can affect their motivation and achievements, but assumptions can be made here, too, including untrue assumptions, identified by Kline (2009) as being limiting to growth.

When practitioners on community education programmes discuss barriers to education, the discourse is frequently around what is most visible: wheelchair access or childcare, for example. While these issues can undeniably create barriers if not addressed, the focus on certain characteristics as 'problems' both diminishes the individual learner and reduces inclusive practice to a focus on difference. Mindful of Ecclestone and Hayes' (2009) counsel against the therapeutic turn in education, there is, nevertheless, an argument to be made for considering the less visible needs of all learners. There is much in academic literature about 'persistence' (see, for example, McGivney, 2004), which, while important for success rates and the future viability of courses, carries a flavour of 'sticking it out' until the bitter end. More hopeful (to use a bell hooks' 2003 term) is to consider 'resilience' in adult learning, defined by Hoult as: 'the mysterious and elusive quality which explains why some people are able to withstand massive disadvantage and still succeed, while others fall by the wayside' (2011: 1). This entails being mindful of all aspects of approach and practice that may have an impact on learners. This might be anything from making sure the language and images in course literature are reflecting a range of identities, through to the simple act of leaving the door open to help welcome learners. These courteous actions are rooted in values such as compassion, diversity, respect and empathy and are the practice principles of the reflexive, or, as Hyland (2009) defines it, the 'mindful' practitioner, who will be aware of why they are doing what they do, in order to welcome learners into the classroom or training room for the very first time.

The reflexive practitioner aims for each learner to be there in an authentic way; that is, as themselves, from their first engagement with the learning group. hooks (1994) suggests that all learners in a class should understand they have a duty to contribute to the learning process, and practitioners, in turn, should show learners that they are valued. Fundamental to this is recalling and using each learner's name correctly, one of our most powerful acts as a practitioner; this is even more powerful if you can enable learners to quickly remember one another's names.

It is given that assumptions formed on meeting others can stick fast and where learners are carrying untrue limiting assumptions about themselves, the impact of this is magnified. Debriefing with co-workers after the initial session, or meeting to evaluate sessions with learners, gives an opportunity to bring assumptions out into the light and identify what might be hidden to the self or from others, limiting and untrue. Kline's 'Thinking Environment' work (2009) is based on the exposure and incisive questioning of untrue limiting assumptions; Activity 3 at the end of this chapter can be helpful when first meeting each learning group. Separating what's truly known about the self from what is assumed about others is a fascinating task for that initial debrief.

6.4 Learner motivation

'So, why do you want to do this course?'

How many times are learners asked this question as part of an opening exercise? The goal is to gain information about learners and their motivation, and perhaps to give learners a confidence-boosting chance to speak. Trainers and practitioners find themselves teaching in contexts where learners are compelled to attend, by their organizations, their managers, the changing requirements of their role or because they will get into trouble in some way if they don't. (Note: it takes a confident learner to admit this during an opening round, or an angry, disaffected and resentful one.) It may be disappointing to find out that learners are only in your session because they have to be, but reassuring learners that they can be honest about their motivation, without incurring the practitioner's wrath, is important; for one thing, such knowledge provides a valuable insight into how best to support resilience when learning becomes especially challenging. Acknowledging the potential frustration of learners who have not chosen to attend may go some way to mitigating its impact and demonstrates your respect for learners' different starting points.

Individual motivation is also, partly, what shapes personal goals, and taking steps towards achieving these, in turn, helps increase resilience. Identifying the personal benefits of learning is important, both for practitioners and learners, but exploring some of the wider benefits can have a deep and powerful impact on learners' approaches. At this juncture Cutts' model of Win/Win/Win (2010) can be used in asking learners to consider how their learning can be used in the wider world, in their group, their organization, their family or community, to create positive change. The opportunity to express wider goals and aspirations can help foster a sense of connection and community within groups of learners, and this sense of belonging and commitment to peers can further contribute to resilience.

The capacity for teaching and learning to effect change in the real world has its roots in Freirean philosophy, as well as in the notion of 'really useful knowledge' (Thompson, 1996): knowledge that enables learners not only to reflect on the circumstances of their lives, but to act to bring about fruitful change. The concept of the learner inherent in this idea is one who is engaged, active, motivated and liberated by their learning, and who has come to recognize the freedoms and constraints placed upon them by their social, economic, political and cultural environment. Such learning may not be necessarily easy, or immediately enjoyable. Both hooks (1994) and Brookfield (2000) point out that the most powerful and challenging learning may leave learners unsettled and unsure.

One further assumption merits some thought; that is speaking early in the course will automatically put people at their ease. Brookfield (2000) points out that 'rounds' where learners take turns to talk, may well have the opposite effect, and instead create dread around what to say. Does this mean rounds shouldn't be used? Well, no, just that, as with all other components of a session, their purpose and impact is something the practitioner makes a mindful judgement about, in order to balance caution with Kline's assertion that 'no-one has truly arrived in a room until they have spoken' (2008).

'Really useful knowledge' connects with the work of Dweck, Zimmerman and others around the expert or 'self-regulated' learner. Dweck's concept of 'growth mindset' (2006) has resonance for adults (and younger learners) who have spent a lifetime believing they lack intelligence. The practitioner's role is to scaffold growth in confidence of each learner, drawing on the metaphor identified to describe Vygotsky's (1962) 'zone of proximal development' by Wood et al. (1976). Again, studies in child psychology offer perspectives on a concept which is amplified by the longer life experience of adult learners.

6.5 Subject specialist knowledge

It had previously been accepted that most practitioners could teach a range of subjects; in recent years this has shifted, under the weight of increasingly stringent expectations in terms of subject specialist qualifications and experience, particularly in formal learning environments, such as further education colleges. In community learning, however, it is still possible to teach a much broader range of subjects than would normally be expected in an FE college as the community development legacy is about engaging and involving learners with topics they choose. Here, the concept of 'really useful knowledge' is a lived reality.

The transmission of knowledge is an important aspect of teaching, but it is not everything. Teaching is reduced to a performance when learning does not effectively take place: put simply, teaching is not teaching when assessment of learning isn't present too. While it is essential that practitioners know their subject well enough to feel confident in teaching it, a practitioner brings much more than the transmission of facts. The practitioner's job is to distil their subject knowledge to the essentials that learners need to know; not to dumb-down, but to free facts from opinions in order that learners can apply essential learning to their personal contexts and make sense of it for themselves.

This chapter will not teach you how to improve knowledge and skills in your chosen subject area, or how to learn enough about another subject in order to teach it. However, what we think you should be able to do is consider the following: *do you know enough to be credible in your subject, at the level you're teaching or training?* If you experience any mental squirming in response to that question, then Activity 5 at the end of this chapter may be helpful for you now.

6.6 Why planning is important

One of the paradoxes of teaching is that freedom needs boundaries. The truth is that 'winging it' will only take practitioners so far. For most of us, not being quite sure of our ground when we are teaching is profoundly undermining to our confidence; this relates to process just as much as it does to content. Planning is important, and it is the process that is important, including the opportunity to mindfully express your teaching values by thinking through your intentions. Through this process of reflection, it becomes possible to identify limiting assumptions and also, of course, those assumptions that hold good and true. As each learning session is unique and almost anything can happen when you are in the learning space, you will be significantly more prepared to rise to the challenge if you have thought through your session in advance. The discipline of planning develops reflexive self-awareness, knowing why you do what you do.

The increasing quality assurance regulation of the sector has led to some planning which has been over-detailed in terms of activities and resources and is virtually meaningless with regard to the important stuff: blanket statements about differentiation and diversity, for example, which become invisible once they are stamped onto a session plan template for ease of use.

What is crucial is to consider reasons for the decisions made in delivering the learning session. Quality assurance people may not always use the language of 'reflection', but they are certainly looking for its presence when they observe teaching and learning. Doing things by accident is not an option, whether they happen to work out or not; it evidences neither intent nor good judgement and can be easily diagnosed where a session lacks momentum and purpose and where learning is, as it inevitably will be, haphazard.

So it does not matter whether your session plan is a mindmap or a diamond or a timetable-plus, or if it is colour-coded or hand-drawn or in hieroglyphics. Use whatever format you choose as a framework for your thinking. There are fashions in session planning, as in everything else, and it is good to revisit your practice on a regular basis. The internet abounds with planning templates; indeed, it abounds with pre-written lesson plans which not only take away the process of working through assumptions and intent, they also take away much of the joy of teaching too; the process of creativity being reduced to the delivery of someone else's ideas. Robinson (2006), drawing inspiration from the life of Richard Feynman (2006), advocates creativity in teaching and training, to ensure the personalization of education for the benefit of all learners. Creativity does not always mean something which is brand new; for us it means thinking around what will most enhance the learning process for each individual.

If you have the opportunity to work with a group of learners over a period of time, and the context is appropriate, it can be useful to do some values-work at the beginning of the course, enabling learners to reflect more deeply on their learning experience, gaining insight into their response to the content, and how they operate as individuals. We agree with Price (2013) that the opportunity for values-led learning is often missed in formal education. Table 6.1 provides a list of values that you might want to consider in terms of their role in the learning process.

Table 6.1 List of values

balance	contentment	efficiency	growth	mastery	serenity
belonging	co-operation	empathy	happiness	openness	simplicity
boldness	creativity	equality	helping society	originality	strength
calmness	curiosity	faith	honesty	perfection	success
challenge	democracy	fairness	honour	prudence	support
cheerfulness	diligence	fidelity	humility	reliability	teamwork
commitment	discipline	fluency	irreverence	rigour	thoroughness
community	diversity	freedom	justice	self-actualization	tolerance
compassion	effectiveness	grace	making a difference	self-reliance	usefulness

It is one of the privileges of teaching to work with a group of learners over a period of time. Facilitating one-off sessions presents a different challenge. If you are delivering a one-off session it can feel initially refreshing to be liberated from the responsibilities of formative assessment and relationship building. Many freelance practitioners work happily and successfully delivering one-off sessions for much of their time; others feel frustrated by the limitations of relationship building in this context. There is no reason to give up on the possibilities of learner reflection, however. Depending on your situation, a social networking group might be one way of extending the learning experience for learners who are left wanting more.

6.7 Planning for differentiated learning

Differentiation from the learner's perspective is, essentially, the right to learn and to be provided with challenges for learning at the most appropriate level where growth proceeds most effectively. As practitioners, we work through this physically with our trainees using the practical activity at the end of this chapter (Activity 9). We believe that the only ethical approach to differentiation is one that is, as far as possible, ipsative: the learner is in charge of setting their own personalized learning goals in addition to those goals you have set in the learning outcomes for the session (more on this below). The 'as far as possible' caveat recognizes that there may be learners who, for reasons of mental ill-health, learning disability or abject lack of confidence are not currently in a position to negotiate their own learning. However, we believe it should be an aspiration of practitioners to take an ipsative approach with *every* learner eventually. Ipsative literally means 'of the self' and it hands back to the learner the power taken away from them in traditional forms of education (again, what Freire (1970) describes as 'banking' – the idea that learning means depositing information in empty minds). For the practitioner, this can be scary, but rewarding. As Price (2013: 202) says, 'Commit to giving learners the freedom and responsibilities of adults, and they'll behave like them.'

Ipsative learning takes away much of the need to make assumptions about learners' abilities; although there is plenty of room for disagreement between learner and practitioner, this is generally the essence of scaffolding (believing in the learner's ability for them until they can believe in it themselves). There are always learners who overestimate their ability; challenging and supporting such people, through the humbly unsettling time of unlearning and relearning, is a skill of great judgement.

When learning is genuinely differentiated to the individual, for example in the process described below, diversity is respected if not, at this stage, promoted. Informal discourse often limits the application of the term 'diversity' to ethnicity, or maybe disability, with gender, sexuality and age occasionally brought into view. Yet diversity in its broadest sense of 'variety' or 'difference' has innumerable aspects. Taking the standpoint that each learner is a unique human being, with myriad aspects to their identity, what becomes important is that individuals are able to join the learning experience *as* themselves. This means planning for diversity of opinion, as well as demographic diversity. It also means that it is impossible to truly personalize differentiation, without the involvement of the learner. You can't *do* differentiation to someone.

The process of planning for differentiated learning begins with shaping the outline of the course or session. Once the decision is made to pursue either a one-off session or a series of sessions (this may not be your decision), it is worth approaching your planning differently in each case to reflect this. More than one session suggests the use of a 'scheme of work', where all the key assessment information can be seen at one glance (examples can be easily found on the internet). Session plans are then developed for each session. For a one-off session, a single plan can combine both functions.

The first action is to write the learning outcomes you intend all learners to meet (see Chapter 3). Think of it as a roadmap; this is not a mystery tour. If you're going to Edinburgh, that's where you are going, no matter what route. The learning outcomes are the destination ('Edinburgh'); anything else is the route. Just as you would not normally get on the train without knowing where you're going, writing the learning outcomes first will anchor you to your destination, and will ultimately shape the activities you plan. Clear learning outcomes are one additional factor in motivating learners. They want to know what they will be able to do as a result of coming on your course or session, and getting this right is the first step in the planning process.

Estimating the time needed is an art, not a science. In our experience, it is more common to pack too much into a session than to underpopulate it. When planning a new session, do not expect more than a best guess, timings should *always* be a guideline, rather than a rule. It is useful to have an activity prepared in case you are short on timing, or the context to be able to finish the session early. Check your activities are ones that contribute to achieving the learning outcomes in your plan, and that all your learning outcomes can be met. Do not infantilize learners by giving them something to do just to fill the time, or bore them by letting activities drag on. If you are likely to run out of time, promise yourself in advance which activity can be done later, or outside the session (if an activity can be missed out altogether ask yourself why you were doing it in the first place. Did you make what Brookfield (2000) calls a 'common sense assumption'?) Making a pact with yourself beforehand about what to drop if you run out of time prevents you from wavering on the day. To do justice to your practice and intent, be sure to indicate this in some way on your session plan.

Ideally, and if your selection process is effective, the learning outcomes you write (or inherit) before the course begins will keep most learners in their comfort zone, allowing them to have confidence in their potential for achievement. If all learners have the potential to meet all learning outcomes, planning for differentiation happens when learners are given the opportunity for further stretch through ipsative goal setting. The process described in Table 6.2, for planning differentiated learning, is one way to approach this.

A differentiation rubric can be used by the practitioner to anticipate extension activities (all learners *must*/most learners *should*/some learners *could*). Each learner will have a copy of the rubric included in an

Table 6.2 A process for planning differentiated learning

Stage	What	Why
1	Write a scheme of work, with basic learning outcomes for each session (or a single session plan, for a one-off session)	Establishing the destination ('Edinburgh') and connecting to qualification criteria
2	Confirm selection for the course and design initial assessment activities into the first session	Ensuring that everyone who attends can comfortably achieve the pre-written outcomes, with appropriate teaching and support
3	Design an individual learning plan (ILP) which enables learners to either a) produce individual additional learning goals or b) highlight what they want to additionally achieve on a differentiation rubric	Developmental process aspires to self-identified additional goals; until then, the rubric provides the learners' further stretch goals in your words
4	Build in opportunities to monitor and adjust goals	ILP remains 'live' and meaningful; learners see that they are making progress, which builds confidence
5	At the end of the session or course, learners summatively evaluate the achievement of goals and produce an action plan for future learning	Contextualizing achievement into a lifetime of learning opportunities

Table 6.3 Differentiation rubric example: seeking volunteering opportunities

Learning outcome all learners *must* ...	Stretch 1 most learners *should* ...	Stretch 2 some learners *could* ...
Identify one area of charitable interest	Based on your research, narrow down the definition	Find out about the history of charitable work in this area
List local organizations connected with one area of charitable interest	Write a paragraph about each of these organizations	Choose one organization and research their current work
List personal volunteering skills	Produce a CV for volunteering	Write a letter of application to the charity of choice

individual learning plan (ILP). As part of an initial assessment, they will then highlight the level of 'stretch' they hope to achieve.

Clearly, an ILP is key to the management of differentiated learning and is to be recommended over the 'one size fits all' approach. We believe that as much thought should go into producing a course-specific ILP, which encourages ipsative goal setting, as goes into the planning of teaching activities. Appropriately broad initial assessment activities, resisting the tendency to focus solely on functional skills, provide a platform for getting to know learners as individuals. Remember that one of the most powerful things a practitioner can do to provide differentiated learning is to remember and use each person's name.

What differentiation is not, is the categorizing of individuals into groups, labelled 'kinaesthetic' or 'pragmatist'. It is not the mindless stereotyping of 'young people' or 'dyslexic learners'. It is useful, of course, to keep in mind that any learning group has a range of learning styles present (see section 6.8) and that it is both ethically and legally critical to provide any additional learning support which is necessary to level the playing field for learners with disabilities or learning difficulties. Ultimately, differentiation is grounded in the professional relationships you as a practitioner have, with each individual who comes to you to learn.

It is worth reiterating that differentiation only becomes truly personalized when the practitioner begins to get to know their learners as individuals. By extension, it is not good practice to write every session of a course before getting to know your learners. Write the scheme of work (which is detailed as far as the learning outcomes and overall assessment strategy) and write the first couple of sessions, by all means, but leave the rest until you know who your learners are and have started to get to know what they need from you as learners.

6.8 Learning styles

The notion that learners innately favour a particular style of learning started to gain currency as practitioners became more interested in the idea of an individualized approach to learning. It seems common sense that, just as people have individual preferences and talents for many activities, they also have preferences for types of learning. This shift of focus from practitioner to learner enabled the prevalence of some traditional methods, including rote learning and copying from the board, to be roundly challenged. For practitioners, recognizing that there may be a range of learning styles in a class fosters the desire to provide a variety of learning activities, in an attempt to better meet learners' needs.

A number of different models and tools to uncover learning styles have been developed, and we are going to focus on three examples here.

6.8.1 Honey and Mumford

One of the most popular is a questionnaire developed by Honey and Mumford (*The Learning Styles Questionnaire*, no date). It is based on Kolb's cycle of reflection (1984) and categorizes learners as: 'activists' (who prefer to learn by doing something, such as problem solving), 'reflectors' (who like to listen, watch and reflect on what's happened), 'theorists' (who prefer a logical and structured approach) or 'pragmatists' (who need to see the immediate and practical benefits of their learning). Honey and Mumford (1992) suggest that learners may have characteristics of more than one learning style, and that the context of their learning can also influence which learning style is dominant at any one time.

6.8.2 VARK

Neil Fleming's VARK model is also widely used, which defines learners as visual, auditory, read/write or kinaesthetic (Fleming and Mills, 1992). Visual learners learn best by looking at graphics, or diagrams, rather than by reading information; auditory learners do best by hearing, so they tend to like lectures or pod-casts; reading and writing learners prefer text-based approaches; and kinaesthetic learners learn best through hands-on activities. The VARK approach suggests that learners need to choose learning methods that match their personal learning style and avoid those that do not.

6.8.3 Gardner's multiple intelligences

Howard Gardner's theory of multiple intelligences has had an influential impact on ideas about teaching and learning (1983, 2004, 2011). The theory suggests that intelligence is complex, and, rather than being a single attribute, is made up of seven distinct strands: linguistic (language and words), logical-mathematical (number, logic and calculation), musical (music and rhythm), bodily kinaesthetic (physical movement and ability), spatial (visual, awareness of space), interpersonal (relationships with others) and intrapersonal (self-awareness). Gardner later extended this list, but these seven are the ones most frequently cited. One of the most important of Gardner's arguments is that people have different levels of intelligence across the range, so, for example, someone may be gifted in language skills, but less so when it comes to spatial awareness.

Each of the theories and models above, as well as others, has something intriguing to offer, and against an expanding cultural landscape around individualism, self-awareness and self-help, it is easy to see how learning styles theory has dominated the literature around teaching and learning. This may not be the only reason; unreflective practitioners may be drawn to the learning preference that most suits them, which brings with it the potential for that preference (whichever paradigm you use) to dominate the learning experience. Being forced to consider a breadth of styles when planning learning has been a healthy move for practitioners and one from which learners have benefited. Effective teaching and learning involves variety and interest, and rather than blaming learners for their lack of learning, practitioners have been asked instead to reflect on the efficacy of their teaching. The notion of learning styles is appealing because it seems to provide a quick and easy solution to the complex question of how learning takes place, especially when the answers elsewhere appear messy or contested. Increasingly, learning styles questionnaires have been seen as essential, diagnostic assessment tools when learners enrol on courses.

The danger here is that the results are accepted uncritically by learners and practitioners. Labels of any kind can act to self-limit opportunities for learning ('I'm a kinaesthetic learner, so this is not meeting my needs'), rather than providing learners with deeper insight into their personal learning processes, or encouraging self-reflection or dialogue about why some learning activities are appealing and others not. Other than encouraging variety, the question of how information about learners' preferred styles really makes an impact on teaching styles also remains unclear. A research report commissioned by the Learning and Skills Research Centre (Coffield et al., 2004a) has persuasively challenged the assumption that learning styles can be diagnosed through a questionnaire, or that the findings of such questionnaires provide some sort of scientific basis on which learners should base their approach to learning or their career, or that pedagogy is genuinely informed by the diagnosis of learning. After analysing 13 commonly used models, the report concludes that their reliability varies widely and that the claims made for their value are often overly generous and based on very weak research. While arguing against the uncritical use of learning styles questionnaires as tools to enable learning, the authors' caution against wholesale rejection of the notion that learners have different needs when it comes to learning. What they call for instead is a greater focus on developing 'an overarching and agreed theory of pedagogy' (Coffield et al., 2004b: 61)

We have the opportunity now to find a balance. One question is this: how can variety enhance effective learning, while at the same time challenging learners to broaden their learning style? Broadening learning style preference is, of course, yet another example of 'stretch'. Although

Coffield and colleagues' research indicated that the science behind many familiar learning styles diagnostics was neither valid nor rigorous, it certainly seems as though individuals have sensory modality preferences, possibly formed through experience. Running through the many paradigms which have been extensively developed has been done effectively elsewhere (see, for example, de Bello, 1990); the learning here is to interrogate your own practice, to ensure that you are not restricting your learners to your own learning preference.

6.9 Teaching and training delivery

Creating engaging and interactive learning experiences, which benefit learners' ability to achieve their pre- and self-determined learning outcomes, is the ultimate aim of any practitioner. Teaching is not teaching without assessment and everything we do as practitioners, including the rapport, trust and openness we build with learners, should be to this end. As novice practitioners, our focus is inevitably on our own performance; it takes confidence to focus on the experience of our learners as being central to effective delivery of learning and assessment. Early educational thinkers were concerned with the practitioner's perspective; later Sotto (2001) and others moved pedagogical thinking towards the learner experience, a healthy paradigm shift. Now, a more balanced canon of thinkers helps us return to our own performance as practitioners and gives us the opportunity to analyse a range of delivery styles.

Across a range of ages, the Socratic approach has a great deal to offer. Socrates promoted a dialogic approach to learning, more recently redefined by Sennett (2012). Dialogic discussion explores the middle ground, in a meeting of open minds with no expectation of consensus. Socratic education uses focused questioning to explore this space and finds an echo in Kline's 'incisive questioning' (2009). The Community Philosophy movement (Sapere, 2013) also uses Socratic questioning as the basis for exploring a philosophical question and sets out to explicitly develop skills around dialogic disagreement and challenge, useful for enabling diversity of opinion to be both heard and respected. Socrates used the metaphor of midwifery to describe the process of facilitating the birth of ideas and the terms 'facilitator' and 'enabler' are often used in community education to describe the teaching role; indeed, many adult tutors feel more comfortable describing themselves thus, rather than as practitioners.

The very best practitioners use stories and metaphors to bring life and colour to the process of learning, and help us express complex ideas (see Chapter 5). Patchen and Crawford's (2011) work highlights how the analysis of teaching metaphors may illuminate practice and the constraints under which practitioners may find themselves working with learners.

Increasingly, the field of lifelong learning is seeing a growth in dual professionalism and also portfolio-based freelance working (Price, 2013). Practitioners may teach in community venues and workplaces, each with its own organizational culture. Where this culture clashes with the values of the practitioner, tension will arise. Working in a place or in a way that is at odds with your ethics and values is deeply unsettling. We all have expectations placed on us as practitioners, for example funding and performance targets driven by national policy and interpreted locally.

6.10 Learning activities

To return to an earlier metaphor, activities are stops along the route and must come second to the destination. If you find yourself thinking of activities before you've written a single learning outcome, *stop right now*; remember that teaching is not teaching without assessment. Each activity should contribute to each learner reaching the destination and if you have not decided what that is yet, you need to reconsider your planning process. Write the learning outcomes first, and then you can decide on the route.

Outstanding learning sessions have momentum and variety, where individuals are moving towards their destination with purpose and satisfaction, even in the unlearning moments and where challenge occurs. It is beneficial to mix the group up too; this develops resilience, as learners get used to sharing a common purpose with different individuals and grow to appreciate diverse viewpoints, once the group culture is established via ground rules and custom and practice as a respectful and supportive one.

In providing a diverse session, you are aiming for a situation where the individual learner is 'stretched' (where they feel challenged and excited by their learning but not overwhelmed by it) and this is what makes the balancing act of teaching such a nuanced one. Dixon et al. (2009: 124–126) provide an overview of research behind popular teaching interventions, which may help you make decisions about potential effectiveness. They adapt Hattie's (2009) table of the effect sizes of selected teaching interventions. Hattie's meta-analysis took an evidence-based approach to establishing what works in teaching. A few points bear closer inspection. First, it's heartening that Hattie identified formative feedback as being significantly effective. Good quality, differentiated feedback continues the dialogue between the practitioner and the individual learner and provides opportunities for developing confidence and self-knowledge. Second, team teaching has a low effect score. This may be true of traditional educational contexts. Dual professionals, working in empowerment settings such as parenting programmes, may refute this finding, citing the importance of having a safety net when exploring emotive or sensitive topics with vulnerable people. Third, it is certainly possible that technological advances might have improved the effectiveness of e-learning since Hattie's meta-analysis in 2009 (see also Chapter 9). Price (2013) argues that recent advances such as MOOCs (massive online open courses) will enable individuals to take control of their own learning, something which Dixon et al. (2009) would clearly welcome, given their identification of learner-led activity making a significant contribution to effectiveness.

Common sense assumptions hold great power over the choice of learning activities. It is easy to get drawn into 'what practitioners do', without considering either evidence of effectiveness or what assumptions you are making. The reflective practitioner will keep the destination in mind and question their own choices with transparency and openness. Any session is only ever planned in theory. In practice, the best laid plans come second to the learning needs of the individuals in front of you. And be brave; as Price (2013: 203) says:

> No learner ever had his entire education ruined because of a learning innovation that didn't come off. But I can show you plenty of learners whose curiosity and imagination were strangled by being trapped in a repetitive, uninspiring, unimaginative learning enclosure.

Sessions can be memorable for all sorts of reasons; you want the session to be remarkable for the only right reason: that deep and memorable *learning* happened, which has been retained and which has provided learners with some insight about the subject or themselves. There is some evidence that the brain more easily retains what it absorbs at the beginning and end of a learning session (Sousa, 2011), so start strong and end strong and make sure that what goes in the middle is the most memorable of all.

Finally, a word about assessment (see also Chapter 8). An important question to ask yourself as a practitioner is how do you know what your learners are learning? Of course, the answer to this may not be straightforward. Asking learners what they have learned in a lesson may not elicit an impressive response; sometimes learning deepens and gels after the session has finished. Tests and quizzes may measure the sharpness of learners' memories, but not necessarily measure their learning; or learners may not recall a lot of facts, but they may learn they do not like tests. Despite these misgivings, a focus on assessment necessitates a shift in perspective from teaching to learning, and it is this which is the most important aspect of the session dynamic. Teaching is not teaching without assessment, no matter how creative or reflexive it is, so it is imperative that when planning your session, you plan assessment.

6.11 Summary, case study, discussion questions and learning activities

In this chapter, we have presented and explored learning using a range of theories which are recognized as taking a critical approach or coaching model; essentially we have taken a values-based approach to delivering learning, which explored assumptions inherent in the language we use and in common sense practice. We define ourselves as teaching for a social purpose; teaching, that is, to change the world via a reflective, mindful approach to planning and assessment and to our relationship with learners. You may not define your practice in this way. Whether you do or not, we hope that you have taken inspiration from a way of working which enables you to teach to your values and to take satisfaction in the benefit this will bring to your learners, and to the communities in which they live and operate.

6.11.1 Case study Practitioners and personal skills presentation

It's the start of the day, and the room is full of practitioners from a range of subjects and contexts: private organizations, universities, work-based training providers, libraries, community halls, shops, cafes, hospitals, gardens and woodlands. There are people here who teach courses on catering, ICT, art, ESOL, trade union skills, sport, philosophy, broadcasting, first aid, personal and organizational development, mathematics and music.

Each will give a presentation on the development of their personal skills as part of a continuing professional development (CPD) programme. This may seem a dull and daunting prospect, but the passion and excitement today is palpable.

The issue is to establish a sense of collective values and to challenge assumptions participants have made about one another, and about what is or isn't 'teaching'. Learners present how they teach to their values and for a social purpose.

The outcome is that the social purpose element brings the group together. This connection is at the heart of our philosophy, an awareness of the pervasiveness of social inequality (Newman, 2006a and 2006b). So, for example, the art tutor is teaching elderly people in sheltered accommodation, the chef is teaching people with mental ill health. Underlying these topics is a whole other raft of benefits, a growth in confidence, a thirst for further knowledge, and the simple joy of participating in the collective process of learning.

Questions:

- What might be some of the issues that arise as participants present and explore their values in the group?
- How do you incorporate values in your own teaching and working practice? How do you justify this? Does this present any particular problems?

Activity 1

What do you picture, when you imagine yourself teaching or training? Are you standing at the front of a group of people? Are you researching, planning, designing activities? Are you talking with learners, or at them? What does your autobiography as a learner teach you about what teaching is?

Activity 2

Reflect on the strategies you use for memorizing learners' names. How effective are they? How can you improve the speed at which you remember and use each learner's name, sincerely and with confidence? How can you better enable learners to remember and use each other's names?

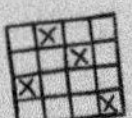

Activity 3

Think about a learning group with whom you have recently begun working. What assumptions are you making about the group that may be limiting and untrue?

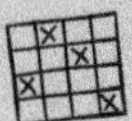

Activity 4

What assumptions do you make about what motivates your learners? How can you better enable learners to develop resilience, whatever their motivations?

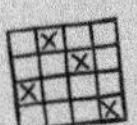

Activity 5

What are you assuming about the knowledge you have of your own subject(s)? What does subject credibility look like for you? What are the steps you can and do take to ensure that your subject knowledge is up to date and relevant?

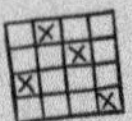

Activity 6

Is planning something you look forward to, or does it always feel like a chore? Does the template you use allow you to think mindfully through your intentions? Does it help you express those intentions with clarity? Think through how planning might become more useful to you and beneficial to your learners.

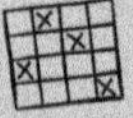

Activity 7

Do an internet search for 'session plan' or 'lesson plan' and choose one which looks very different from your usual template. Work through it with a familiar session in mind. After the activity, take some time to reflect, perhaps in dialogue with a colleague, perhaps alone. What is your freshest thinking about your familiar session?

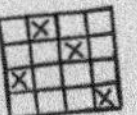

Activity 8

Designate the front of the training room as the 'comfort zone', the back of the room as the 'panic zone' and the space in between as a continuum of 'stretch'. Present verbal scenarios to learners (for example, public speaking, bungee jumping) and ask them to place themselves in the room, according to how that makes them feel, less mobile learners could nominate someone to be their 'runner'. Once the activity is flowing, you can present scenarios relating to the challenges of the course or session; for example, 'Your first observation'. You will learn much about individuals from this exercise and also about how people feel differently in different situations. Your learners will also learn something about themselves, about each other and, if you join in, about you.

Activity 9

With a colleague or critical friend, identify an uninterrupted period of time and ask them to listen to you while you think through your differentiation strategy. Be careful in your thinking to hunt down and expose any untrue limiting assumptions you are making about yourself, your learners or the learning environment. It is helpful if your thinking partner commits to not interrupting you during this time (even if you fall silent for a while).

References

Brookfield, S. D (1995) *Becoming a Critically Reflective Teacher.* San Francisco, CA: Jossey-Bass.

Brookfield, S. D (2000) *The Skilful Practitioner.* San Francisco, CA: Jossey-Bass

Coffield, F., Moseley, D., Hall, E. and Ecclestone, K. (2004a) *Learning Styles and Pedagogy in Post-16 Learning: A Systematic and Critical Review.* London: Learning and Skills Research Centre.

Coffield, F., Moseley, D., Hall, E. and Ecclestone, K. (2004b) *Should We Be Using Learning Styles? What Research Has to Say to Practice.* London: Learning and Skills Research Centre.

Cutts, N. (2010) *Love at Work.* Burley-in-Wharfedale: Fisher King.

de Bello, T. (1990) 'Comparison of eleven major learning styles models: variables, appropriate populations, validity of instrumentation and the research behind them', *Journal of Reading, Writing and Learning Disabilities International*, 6 (3): 203–222.

Dixon, L. Harvey, J. Thompson, R. and Williamson, S. (2009) 'Practical teaching', in J. Avis, R. Fisher and R. Thompson (eds), *Teaching in Lifelong Learning*. Maidenhead: McGraw-Hill, pp. 119–141.

Dweck, C. S. (2006) *Mindset. How You Can Fulfil Your Potential.* New York: Ballantyne Books.

Ecclestone, K. and Hayes, D. (2009) *The Dangerous Rise of Therapeutic Education.* Abingdon: Routledge.

Feynman, R. P. (2006) *Don't You Have Time to Think?* London: Penguin.

Fleming, N. D. and Mills, C. (1992) 'Helping learners understand how they learn', *The Teaching Professor*, 7 (4). Madison, WI: Magma Publications.

Freire, P. (1970) *Pedagogy of the Oppressed.* Harmondsworth: Penguin.

Freire, P. (2009) 'An incredible conversation'. www.youtube.com/watch?v=aFWjnkFypFA (accessed 10 November 2013).

Gardner, H. ([1983] 2011) *Frames of Mind: The Theory of Multiple Intelligences.* New York: Basic Books.

Gardner, H. (2004) *Changing Minds: The Art and Science of Changing Our Own and Other People's Minds.* Harvard: Business School Press.

Hattie, J. (2009) *Visible Learning: A Synthesis of Over 800 Meta-analyses Relating to Achievement.* Abingdon: Routledge.

Honey, P. and Mumford, A. (1992) *The Manual of Learning Styles.* Maidenhead: Peter Honey Publications.

hooks, b. (1994) *Teaching to Transgress: Education as the Practice of Freedom.* Abingdon: Routledge.

hooks, b. (2003) *Teaching Community: A Pedagogy of Hope.* Abingdon: Routledge.

Hoult, E. (2011) *Adult Learning and la Recherche Féminine: Reading Resilience and Hélène Cixous.* Basingstoke: Palgrave Macmillan

Hyland, T. (2009) 'Mindfulness and the therapeutic function of education', *Journal of Philosophy of Education*, 43 (1): 119–131.

Jarvis, P., Holford, J. and Griffin, C. (2004) *The Theory and Practice of Learning* (2nd edn). London: Kogan Page.

Kline, N. (2008) Keynote speech at *Creating a Thinking Environment*, The Northern College for Adult Residential and Community Learning, Barnsley, 21 May.

Kline, N. (2009) *More Time to Think.* Burley-in-Wharfedale: Fisher King.

Knowles, M. S. (1970) *The Modern Practice of Adult Education: Andragogy Versus Pedagogy.* Englewood Cliffs: Prentice Hall/Cambridge.

Knowles, M. S. (1980) *The Modern Practice of Adult Education: From Pedagogy to Andragogy.* Englewood Cliffs: Prentice Hall/Cambridge.

Kolb, D. (1984) *Experiential Learning.* New Jersey: Prentice-Hall Inc.

McGivney, V. (2004) 'Understanding persistence in adult learning', *Open Learning*, 19 (1): 33–46.

Newman, M. (2006a) *Teaching Defiance Stories and Strategies for Activist Educator.* San Francisco, CA: Jossey-Bass.

Newman, M. (2006b) *Throwing Out the Balance with the Bathwater*. http://infed.org/talkingpoint/newman_throwing_out_the_balance.htm (accessed 10 November 2013).

Patchen, T. and Crawford, T. (2011) 'From gardeners to tour guides: the epistemological struggle revealed in teacher-generated metaphors of teaching', *Journal of Teacher Education*, 62 (3): 286–298.

Price, D. (2013) *Open: How We'll Work, Live and Learn in the Future*. UK: Crux Publishing.

Robinson, K. (2006) 'Do schools kill creativity?' www.youtube.com/watch?v=iG9CE55wbtY (accessed 2 November 2013).

Sapere (2013) *Community Philosophy*. www.sapere.org.uk (accessed 2 November 2013).

Sennett, R. (2012) *Together: The Rituals, Pleasures and Politics of Cooperation*. London: Allen Lane.

Sotto, E. (2001) *When Teaching Becomes Learning*. London: Continuum.

Sousa, D. A. (2011) *How the Brain Learns*. Thousand Oaks, CA: Corwin.

The Learning Styles Questionnaire. www.peterhoney.com/content/learningstyles-questionnaire.html (accessed 8 November 2013).

Thompson, J. (1996) 'Really useful knowledge: linking theory and practice', in B. Connolly, T. Fleming, D. McCormack and A. Ryan (eds), *Radical Learning for Liberation*. Maynooth: MACE, pp. 15–26.

Vygotsky, L. (1962, revised 1986) *Thought and Language*. Cambridge: US MIT Press.

Vygotsky, L. S. (1978). *Mind in Society: The Development of Higher Psychological Processes*. Cambridge, MA: Harvard University Press.

Wood, D., Bruner, J. and Ross, G. (1976) 'The role of tutoring in problem solving', *Journal of Child Psychology and Child Psychiatry*, 17: 89–100.

CHAPTER 7

PREPARATION AND DELIVERY OF LEARNING

Wayne Bailey and Mohammed Karolia

Learning outcomes

After reading this chapter, the reader should be able to:

- Appreciate the role of planning when delivering learning.
- State ways in which to manage presence when delivering learning.
- Identify ways to engage learners within a teaching or training environment.

Chapter outline

When we think about delivering learning, we might initially think about: a practitioner's quality of communication; their use of voice; the appropriateness and inclusiveness of their language; their body language, their use of gesture; eye contact; their listening and observation skills; the confidence they exude and their presence. While these are key ingredients when delivering learning and will be considered within this chapter, we also need to give some thought to the key part planning has to play in any session interaction or delivery that takes place. In the first part of this chapter, we concentrate on how delivery can be enhanced by the planning that is undertaken, both before and after a session is delivered. In particular, we give consideration to teaching and training strategies, and the resources that will be utilized, both while delivering and after the session and evaluation. Within this section reference is made to Reece and Walker (2007), Simpson and Gravells (2010) and Hattie (2012). In the second part we consider the work of Jensen (1998, 2008); Silberman (1998), Meier (2000) and Atkinson (2004) and pay particular attention to delivery issues and discuss how a practitioner might prepare to teach, manage their presence and ensure that learners find sessions engaging. In the third part of this chapter we offer a worked example that briefly considers planning issues before moving onto specific delivery issues. This should be read in conjunction with Chapter 6. The context for the worked example is a session that introduces the concept of mentoring to a group of learners who may want to implement mentoring schemes within their organizations. To help justify the strategies that are utilized, the work of Sadler (1989), Cowley (2005), Wallace and Gravells (2007), Scales (2008) and Ollin et al. (2010) are incorporated. Finally, a case study is presented that offers a scenario, a problem and some associated questions that will require the reader to apply some of the strategies outlined in this chapter.

7.1 Using planning to aid delivery

Think for a moment about a session you have observed as a practitioner, or took part in as a learner, that inspired you, that was delivered effortlessly but with energy, that engaged, challenged and motivated learners and which met their needs. What was it that allowed that particular practitioner to deliver meaningful learning? For even those who find that teaching or training is highly enjoyable and satisfying, we can only deliver in a meaningful way because of the planning we undertake.

In order to deliver meaningful learning, practitioners need to give a great deal of thought to the planning process. Detailed planning is a key ingredient when preparing to deliver learning that is engaging, active and inclusive. While there are several planning documents that can help to ensure that learning is delivered in a meaningful manner, such as a scheme of work or session plan, within this chapter we intend to briefly consider three planning elements that can have a particular influence on delivery aspects. In this section of the chapter, we will outline how and why the various issues influence and impact upon the delivery of learning, focusing on:

- teaching and training strategies
- the resources that will be utilized
- incorporating formative feedback and evaluation into the session.

7.2 Choosing appropriate teaching and training strategies

As a practitioner, there are many teaching and training strategies that can be utilized within a teaching and training environment to aid the delivery of learning, and the choices that you make will influence the impact that the session has on your learners. A strategy includes a variety of methods and it is important that you consider the needs of your learners and the environment in which they learn. There are many teaching and training methods to choose from when developing a teaching and training strategy, too many to fully discuss within this chapter. However, when deciding upon an appropriate strategy, you might want to give some thought to the following:

- the learning outcomes set
- the teaching/training environment
- resource availability
- the size of the group.

It is important to note that to engage your learners, you need to make sure that they are actively involved so careful consideration should be given to the choice of teaching and training methods. When choosing a method give some thought to the effect it will have on the way learners' learn, but even more importantly, evaluate the impact that the chosen method has on your learners (Hattie, 2012). Remember some methods will be more successful than others, in particular situations and with particular learners. Make sure that you consult the learning outcomes that have been set for the session, as they need to be considered when choosing teaching methods, and remember that different methods will test different delivery skill sets. An effective practitioner should be able to choose from a repertoire of pedagogic techniques that might include:

- buzz groups
- case studies
- games
- group work
- group discussion and debate
- group and individual presentations

- lectures
- question and answer
- quizzes.

Clearly, different methods will require the practitioner to call upon different skill sets. For example, group work will require the practitioner to facilitate an interactive approach within a training room. Delivering the information in a manner that allows this method to be a success will take planning. Alternatively, a 15-minute 'practitioner talk' input or the facilitation of an active question and answer session will call upon different delivery skills. The actual application of some of the methods outlined above is discussed in the worked example that can be found later in this chapter.

7.3 Using resources

There are many different types of resources that can be used within a learning environment to aid the delivery of learning. The learning resources used by a practitioner might include people, objects, information and learning technologies and resource material (Simpson and Gravells, 2010). It is important when a practitioner chooses the resources that they complement their overall strategy and help to meet the learning outcomes that have been set. Colleagues or staff from other organizations who have a particular expertise in a specific area might be included. Objects might include toys, which could be used in an early years or childhood studies session, or sports equipment to enhance a coaching session. Learning technologies might include the use of a virtual learning environment (VLE) that can be used to facilitate discussions or be used as a repository for other resource material. Social networks, tablets, mobile devices or interactive whiteboards can also be utilized (see Chapter 9). Resource materials might include handouts, quizzes, books and journals.

Any resource that a practitioner intends to use during a session should help to:

- enhance learner perception
- promote understanding
- reinforce learning and help with the retention of key facts
- motivate learners
- provide variety in learning
- make effective use of time.

The resources that are used need to be simple, interesting and to the point (Reece and Walker, 2007: 157–158).

Without doubt, the ways in which the use of these resources are communicated and explained to learners is paramount. Even the most well-designed or thought-out resource can be rendered useless, if consideration is not given to the explanation of the resources to those learners using them which, in turn, can mean that the session learning outcomes may not be met.

7.4 Evaluation

Ongoing evaluation is a good way for a practitioner to find out what learners think about the way learning is delivered in a session. Evaluation is a useful way in which to ascertain whether a particular session has been a success or a failure. Evaluation can take place at the beginning of a session, during the session and after the session. A practitioner can evaluate through the use of questionnaires, discussions, individual reflection and peer observation. Evaluation is considered in detail in Chapter 8, and within the worked example later in this chapter.

Below is a diagram summarizing the different stages of delivering learning.

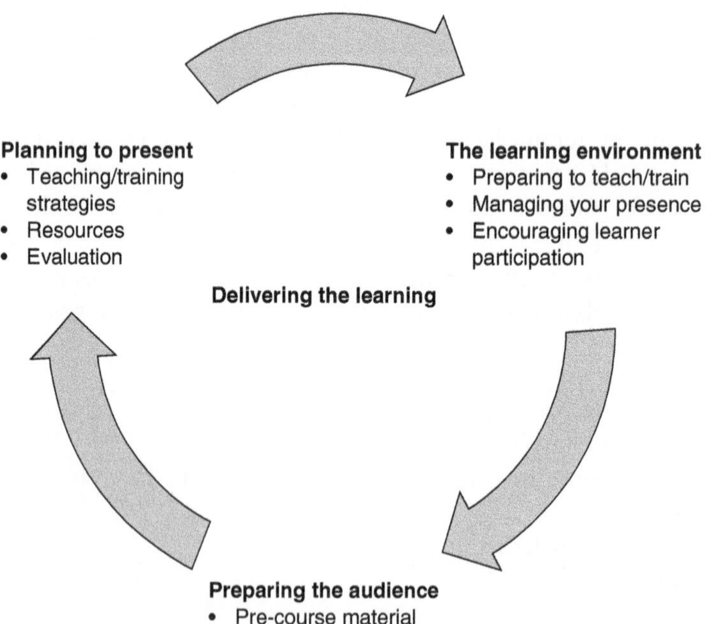

Figure 7.1 Delivering the learning

7.5 Delivering learning considerations

As part of the preparation process, in addition to preparing schemes of work, lesson plans and learning resources, it is also important to consider and prepare yourself to help create as conducive a learning environment as possible. While there are many variables that need to be taken into account to achieve this, for the purposes of this chapter the following three themes are explored in more depth:

- preparing to teach or train
- managing your presence
- encouraging learner participation.

7.5.1 Cohort considerations and the learning environment

In preparing to teach or train, two key issues needs to be considered: those relating to the learners in the group (referred to as the 'cohort'), and where the teaching or training is to be delivered (referred to as the 'learning environment').

Diversity issues

During the preparation stage of the session, Silberman (1998) stresses how it is important to know your group and consider who the learners are. This process can be aided by giving some thought to the size of the group, as this would have an impact on the strategies chosen to help cover or reinforce learning outcomes and the diversity of the group with regards to aspects and issues linked to gender, culture, ethnicity and disabilities.

Where possible research the composition of cohort prior to the session and as part of the preparation efforts, for example, by reviewing applications forms completed by learners or via initial introductions that help to introduce the session, the practitioner and the learning to be covered. Such a process would also allow learners to get in touch and express any concerns they may have or aspects they would like you to take on board while delivering the session.

With regards to gender, culture and ethnicity, while this may not be an issue in need of consideration for some learning contexts, if the learning to be covered as part of a session is gender sensitive or where there exists particular religious sensitivities, then it is important for the practitioner to consider how these will be managed to ensure that these do not become a barrier to learning. While much depends on the level of feelings associated with different aspects of diversity among the cohort, the practitioner would need to be attuned and be sensitive, and more importantly, research the likely impact issues of diversity may have on their session. The research would be undertaken once a practitioner has knowledge of the likely composition of the cohort, which as mentioned earlier would be important to determine prior to the session.

There are many definitions of disabilities, but disabilities can be considered with regard to those that are seen (visible) or unseen (not apparent at first sight). For example, the use of a white stick, wheel chair or hearing aid may indicate the presence of seen disability which would be apparent at first sight, whereas dyslexia, allergies, asthma and epilepsy would be hidden unless disclosed either during or prior to the session via an application form. Again, it is important for the practitioner to research the likelihood of learners with disabilities being present in the session and ensure that the use of different teaching and training methods and resources does not impact or hinder their learning.

The Equality Act 2010 requires practitioners to 'pay attention to the needs of learners from diverse groups within your course design' and suggests completing equality impact analyses as a means of ensuring that due consideration is given to inclusivity and accessibility. It requires institutions to change their practice by anticipating the changes they need to make and be proactive in making adaptations. More importantly, the Equality Act 2010 asks practitioners and institutions to make 'reasonable adjustments' to their practice to ensure learners are not disadvantaged in any way and have equal rights and equality in opportunities to learn. These 'reasonable adjustments' must be put in place prior to the session and not during or after the session, which again stresses the need to ensure that the practitioner researches and take steps to get to know the group and the diversity that exists within the group.

If it is not possible to research the group prior to a session, needless to say it is important to keep in mind the need to be 'user-friendly' at all times with regards to the way lesson plans are devised, learning resources are compiled and the manner in which learners are encouraged to participate within a session. This is a good guideline to follow.

The learning environment

With regards to the learning environment, consideration can be given to ways in which the furniture is arranged within the room, and the decorations that can aid the learning process as visual, auditory and kinaesthetic stimuli can assist in making learners feel comfortable, which in turn helps to enhance the retention of learning from the session (Jensen, 2008).

Where it is possible to rearrange the furniture, consider how the learning methods planned for the session can best use the space and furniture available. For example, if the practitioner intends to get the cohort to discuss issues in small groups, a less formal 'bistro' arrangement would be helpful. Whereas if the practitioner intends to complete a series of practical kinaesthetic activities, then moving tables and chairs against the wall may be more helpful. Alternatively, if the focus of the session requires learners to complete the presentation or delivery of specific context then a more formal setting may be appropriate. Regardless of the room layout chosen, it is important to be flexible and to modify the learning environment in a way that aids the learning process and coverage of the learning outcomes (see examples in Figure 7.2).

Consideration should also be given to how pictures and posters can be used as learning resources. Thinking through how the use of pre-prepared pictures (either on flipchart, infographic or poster) may convey a message can considerably help reinforce a learning outcome and help learners comprehend and remember what needs to be learnt, as can decorating the wall with pictures and flipcharts that learners have designed and produced themselves. The use of a specific theme for a session and its associated pictures can further aid this process. For example, a beach theme can be used to promote a sense of air and openness about a session via pictures, posters and sounds associated with beaches being placed around the room.

The use of music too can help create an ambience or induce a state conducive to learning. For example, calming music for moments of reflective learning and high tempo, high beat music for exercises requiring energetic participation (see examples below) can be used. Music (or more precisely the beats of the music) can affect the heart rate and breathing patterns, which in turn influence the mood and emotional state of learners (Meier, 2000). While the use of music can greatly aid learning, two important caveats need to be borne in mind when considering the use of music during sessions. First, it is important to remember how learners may have associations (sometimes powerful emotional associations) with music or particular songs. These associations can potentially hinder or create a barrier to learning and therefore it may be better to avoid the use of songs in teaching/training and play classical music or tracks that promote a sense of relaxed alertness wherever possible. Second, do be aware of how copyright issues also need to be considered when deciding to play music in sessions. The Performing Rights Society (www.prsformusic.com) gives guidelines of the use of music within educational establishments and should be consulted prior to using audio recordings within sessions.

<table>
<tr><th>U Shape</th></tr>
<tr><td>Advantages<ul><li>Useful for whole group discussions</li><li>Good learner visibility</li><li>Facilitator has full view of learners</li></ul>Disadvantages<ul><li>Formal and business-like</li><li>Does not encourage small group work discussions</li><li>May present some difficulties in facilitating small group tasks</li></ul></td></tr>
<tr><th>'Bistro' Pattern</th></tr>
<tr><td>Advantages<ul><li>Informal and encourages participation</li><li>Useful for sessions which require teamwork or small group discussions</li><li>Facilitator can circulate and be part of group discussions</li></ul>Disadvantages<ul><li>Obstructed or poor visibility of AV equipment and other group members</li><li>May encourage side conversations</li><li>Can help to create sub-groups</li></ul></td></tr>
<tr><th>Circle</th></tr>
<tr><td>Advantages<ul><li>Encourages learner involvement</li><li>Can help create a sense of informality</li><li>Facilitator may appear to be part of the group training–learner contact</li><li>Minimum side conversations or sub-group formations</li></ul>Disadvantages<ul><li>Some participants may feel uncomfortable and hence not participate</li><li>Difficult to bring and use any AV resources</li><li>Difficult for learners to make notes</li></ul></td></tr>
<tr><th>Theatre</th></tr>
<tr><td>Advantages<ul><li>Useful where sessions are predominantly delivered as a lecture or formal presentations</li><li>Good visibility of AV resources</li></ul>Disadvantages<ul><li>Can be seen as very formal and school-like</li><li>Does not encourage small group work</li><li>Some learners can hide their lack of participation in the session</li><li>Unless the back rows are elevated, can lead to poor visibility</li></ul></td></tr>
</table>

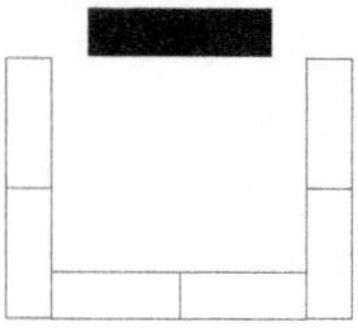

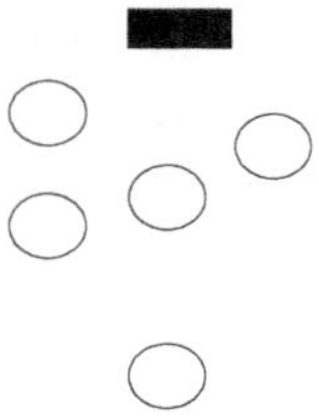

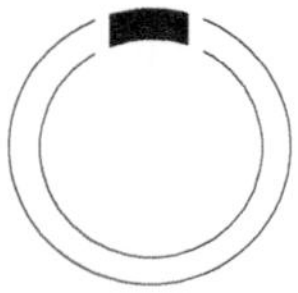

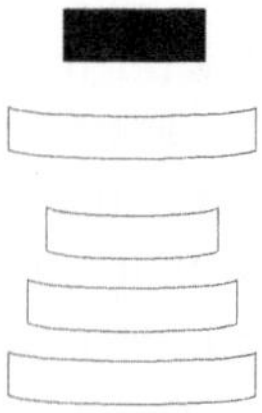

Figure 7.2 Popular room layouts

Music resources

Relaxing

- *The Four Seasons* (Vivaldi)
- *Water Music* (Handel)
- Claire de Lune (Debussy)
- *Trois Gymnopédies* (Eric Satie)
- Piano Concerto 21 (Mozart)
- Pachelbel's Canon
- Oboe Concertos (Vivaldi)
- Air on G String (Bach)
- *Chariots of Fire* (Vangelis)

Energetic

- 'Rocky' theme
- 'Miami Vice' theme
- 'Superman' theme
- Prelude in D Major (Bach)
- Concerto for Two Pianos (Mozart)
- Suites for Orchestra (Bach)
- 1812 Overture (Tchaikovsky)
- 9th Choral Symphony (Beethoven)
- Chronologie, Part 4 (Jean Michel Jarre)
- Quatrième Rendez-Vous (Jean Michel Jarre)

Books and collections

Jensen, E. (2005) *Top Tunes for Teaching*. Thousand Oaks, CA: Corwin.

Jensen, E. (2000) *Music with the Brain in Mind*. San Diego, CA: The Brain Store Inc.

Jackson, N. (2009) *The Little Book of Music for the Classroom: Using Music to Improve Memory, Motivation, Learning and Creativity* (Independent Thinking Series). Carmarthen, Wales and Bethel, CT: Crown House Publishing.

Roberts, R. (2000) *Mozart for Accelerated Learning: Unleash Your Potential through the Genius of Mozart* [CD] Carmarthen, Wales: Crown House Publishing, 1899836616.

Roberts, R. (2006) *Mood Music: Three Classical Collections Designed to Accompany and Enhance Different Training Activities* [CD] Carmarthen, Wales: Crown House Publishing, 1845900189.

7.5.2 Managing your presence

Managing your presence is about the way in which practitioners present themselves in class in terms of their physical and mental state, moods and appearance, each of which can have an impact on the way learners perceive the practitioner and how the practitioner interacts with the learners.

A key factor that can impact on a practitioner's ability to have 'presence' with a group is fear. Fear and anxiety of working with a group and fear that each and every move of the practitioner is being judged negatively by learners, can undermine a practitioner's confidence. Such an expectation (even if false) can present itself with such intensity that it can detract from a practitioner's ability to teach, or train, effectively and confidently.

While no guaranteed method of managing your presence exists, there are factors that can help. For example ensuring time is taken to be mindful of your body language and breathing patterns can help (Atkinson, 2004). When individuals are anxious, they tend to breathe quickly and shallowly from the chest which in turn results in a distressed state where the person may breathe more quickly and in an inconsistent manner. Taking the time to breathe in a more controlled way from the abdomen can help to bring about a sense of calmness and in turn a more relaxed state of being.

The use of visualization exercises can also help manage anxieties by replicating the sights, sounds and feelings prior to an event in the mind's eye so as to gain a sense of familiarity of the event beforehand. Hence, taking the time to prepare thoroughly for the session is helpful in terms of:

- visiting the room where the session is scheduled
- running through the session in the mind's eye in terms of what needs to be said and done
- predicting how learners might respond to questions
- considering how the practitioner in turn responds.

These can go a long way in helping a practitioner manage the fears and anxieties they have about delivering the session. A practitioner can also give some thought to the pace, clarity and tone of their speech.

Body language can also help to instil an air of confidence and build on your personal presence. Presenting with an upright open posture, looking up and promoting a sense of positivity will help to generate an affirming frame of reference that can transmit and encourage the same optimistic outlook in learners. A key point of note is to remember to be 'natural' in the way in which you behave, conduct and present yourself. Forcing a smile and a confident posture, in a way that would be unnatural and incongruent, would severely impact on the effective delivery of a session.

The appearance of a practitioner can also aid or hinder the way in which they promote and convey their presence as well as instil or diffuse confidence in how learners perceive the practitioner. The key factor to remember here is how learners' expectations help to shape their perception of the practitioners with whom they work. Therefore, it is important to give some thought to how learners might perceive your role as a practitioner and dress accordingly.

7.5.3 Encourage learner participation

When delivering, in addition to thinking about the use of different learning methods and resources, some thought also needs to go into how best to engage learners so that not only are they covering and learning new content, but they are also active in the learning process.

An aspect of session preparation that can hinder this process is the need to focus on covering the stated learning outcomes and working towards devising activities, exercises and resources that predominantly focus on covering the learning outcomes of the syllabus or curriculum without acknowledging how they engage the learners in the learning process.

Taking time to think through the learners' 'what's in this for me?' need and then taking steps to communicate this to a group at the beginning of a session may help them engage with the session by illustrating the value of their learning. This process can be further aided by being responsive to what learners need to know, both in relation to the set learning outcomes, and also with regard to the hidden curriculum (additional work that is covered which aids learning, but may not be part of the stated curriculum) which at times may better resonate with and engage learners.

It is also important to address any fears learners may have about what is to be taught. Fear can be limiting in many ways and is the primal emotion that can cause learners to either fight or fly when faced with anything they perceive as dangerous, regardless of whether it is real or imagined (Jenson, 2008). A simple 'hopes and fears' exercise to help to elevate these fears, and working towards actually addressing them by reassuring learners of the learning journey, may help.

In addition to addressing fears, it is equally important to promote the benefits of the learning to be undertaken and ensuring learners are informed of what they will gain from the session, or alternatively, completing an exercise where they convey their expectations and what they hope to gain from the session to generate a sense of 'buy-in' which might otherwise be missed.

The practitioner's ability to engage emotions is another crucial factor that can help to encourage learner participation. In addition to the use of music, which was discussed earlier, the use of positive feedback and giving learners opportunities to succeed in their learning (without making it too easy) can help to engage emotions due to a sense of moving forward and in acknowledging their success at doing so (Reece and Walker, 2007).

In addition to working towards meeting the learners' 'what's in this for me?' need, another factor that can hinder learners from engaging in the learning process is a sense of uncertainty and unease about the session and what is about to transpire; a sense of unease that, if left unattended, can fester into a major barrier to learning. Therefore, it is important to commence a session via an agenda that clearly communicates the learning outcomes of a session, an overview of the activities to follow and the practitioner's expectations of how the group will engage with the session. Further ensuring that each learner has the resources they need to equally participate in the session will go some way towards gaining buy-in from the group at the start of a session.

7.6 Preparing the audience

Ensuring that your learners are prepared for a session is important if meaningful learning is to take place. One way in which to raise the curiosity of your learners is by using pre-session material; this can include some form of pre-reading, viewing online videos, session handouts and pre-session tasks, exercises and activities. Using such materials is one way to prepare your learners, whether room-based, virtual or blended. Pre-session materials help to give learners a taste of what is to come in the actual session.

7.7 Delivering the learning: a working example

The following worked example helps to demonstrate how some of the above principles of delivering learning work in practice. The session that is the focus of this worked example is an introduction to mentoring session, which is aimed at a group of learners on a degree-level course. Within the example, consideration is given to specific delivery issues, taking account of the make-up of the group, the course application process, inclusivity and room layout issues. The choice of learning outcomes are also discussed, along with the teaching and training methods that were adopted, the resources that were used, formative assessment and the opportunities provided to evaluate, both while delivering and after the session. Table 7.1 outlines the session plan used.

Table 7.1 Session plan: Introduction to mentoring

Course title Mentoring in Organizational Contexts	**Subject** Introduction to mentoring	
Name of learning group	**Time and duration of session** 9.30am–4.30pm	**Date of session** 1*/**/20**

Prior action needed
Learners should have read the pre-session material on mentoring models that was available on the VLE

Aim(s)
The aim of the session is to enable learners to have an appreciation of mentoring principles and practices

Learning outcomes (By the end of the day learners will be able to ...)
1. Evaluate definitions of mentoring 2. Have an awareness of the ethical issues that impact on mentoring 3. Discuss principles of effective mentoring practice 4. Create a poster that considers key mentoring principles

Assessment
• Main session objective made clear on flipchart paper throughout the day • Plenary quiz to check and recap on the learning that has taken place • Practitioner assertive questioning to help draw out and assess learners understanding • Students' oral contributions • Reciprocal teaching • Poster presentation *Note* At the beginning of the day learners are placed in 'buzz groups' and are asked to pick a type of mentoring out of a hat. Throughout the day each buzz group will create a poster, at key milestones in the day. The focus of the poster will be the type of mentoring chosen from the hat. For example, one buzz group will choose learning mentors and the focus of their poster will be learning mentors. The decisions that the group make at each milestone about definitions, models, phases, ethics and evaluation must be made with that particular context in mind. Each group will present their poster and then be questioned by their peers and the practitioner.

(Continued)

Table 7.1 (Continued)

<table>
<tr><th colspan="3">Session content</th></tr>
<tr><th>Practitioner activity</th><th>Learner activity</th><th>Time</th></tr>
<tr><td>Practitioner input
Practitioner introduces themes that will be considered throughout the day and the concept of 'key milestones' linked to:
• What is mentoring?
• Mentoring models
• Phases of mentoring programmes
• Mentoring and ethics
• Evaluation of mentoring programmes</td><td></td><td>10 mins</td></tr>
<tr><td>Whole class activity
Practitioner gives consideration to definitions and modules of mentoring. The models considered include:
• The Apprenticeship Model
• The Competency Model
• The Reflective Model
• The Counselling Model
• The Model of Helping
Practitioner to use assertive questioning strategy and ask students questions about specific definitions and models to draw out understanding. For definitions and models refer learners to the pre-reading.</td><td>Learners placed in buzz groups (four learners in each group) to discuss models of mentoring. Ask the groups to think about whether the models could/should be used within their particular context and which models were most appropriate and why? The intention is for the learners to justify their arguments and opinions.
Groups need to be prepared to feed back to the wider group.
MILESTONE 1 Definitions and Models</td><td>90 mins</td></tr>
<tr><td>Pair-work
Practitioner to discuss the possible phases of a mentoring programme. The practitioner gives each pair a case study in an envelope. Each case study relates to a specific example of mentoring, in a specific context (such as a learning mentor in a secondary school or a business mentor who mentor new business start-ups). Each pair reads the case study, answers the questions and justifies the most appropriate phases for their particular mentoring programme.</td><td>Learners work in pairs and use the information provided in their envelope and attempt to provide a response to their task. Selected pairs share their findings with the group.
MILESTONE 2 Phases of mentoring programmes</td><td>60 mins</td></tr>
</table>

Reciprocal teaching The practitioner introduces ethical considerations that must be taken into consideration within a mentoring relationship. Each member of the buzz group are asked to read through and be prepared to teach other members of their group, each learner is given one of the following areas: • control • competence • conflict of interest • confidentiality The purpose of this is to allow learners to develop their abilities to question, summarize and clarify key elements linked to ethical considerations.	Learners review their given areas and decide how best to teach its key elements to the other three members of their buzz group. MILESTONE 3 Ethical considerations	60 mins
Practitioner input Practitioner gives consideration to the purpose of evaluation and outlines why it is important. Practitioner to use assertive questioning technique to stimulate discussion.	Learners are asked to consider evaluation issues and to add to their poster. MILESTONE 4 Evaluation of the mentoring programme	30 mins
Poster presentation and plenary After all key milestones have been completed the practitioner recaps the purpose of the milestones and asks the learners to get their poster together. The aim of the activity is to allow learners to synthesize what they have learnt throughout the day. Plenary quiz: practitioner recaps on key issues from the day and takes questions from learners. The day finishes with a 20 questions quiz (all questions are discussed after the quiz) and the winning team gets a prize.	Learners prepare their posters and present to the group. Each group must be prepared to field questions. Learners to take part in the quiz.	90 mins

Evaluation

A Post-it® exercise will be carried out at the end of the session. An A3 sheet will be placed on each of the four walls in the classroom, learners will be asked to think

(Continued)

Table 7.1 (Continued)

about the question on each sheet, to write their answered on different Post-its and stick at least one on each sheet as they leave the session. They will be asked to think about: • What have you learnt? • How do you feel about what you have learnt? • What can you now do? • What would you kick out of the session? After reflecting on the session, it will also be evaluated following Scales' (2008) checklist.

7.7.1 Prior to the session

During the preparing-to-deliver stage of the introduction to the mentoring session, the first step in the process was to consider the nature and make-up of the group. Not so much in terms of the group size, as this was considered during the lesson planning and preparation stages, but in terms of the gender, culture, ethnicity and disabilities of learners within the group. As the learners within the group completed application forms prior to commencing the course, the first step in this process was to review the forms to determine any potential diversity or disability issues that needed to be dealt with. Once these were determined, it was important to research how particular elements of these aspects of diversity needed to be considered prior to and during the session. For example, with regards to cultural and religious considerations and diet, some of the learners expressed an allegiance to a particular faith, so it was ensured that particular diets were catered for (for example, Halal, kosher).

With regards to disabilities, it was important to remember that both practitioners and institutions are required to make 'reasonable adjustments' to the way in which they train and deliver sessions where it is evident that the person has a disability (either seen or unseen). If it is not possible to determine participant's disabilities prior to the session, steps will need to be taken to identify these during the session. However, practitioners must be aware that some learners may not feel comfortable disclosing the presence of a disability to their peer group and hence care needs to be taken to invite learners to seek help in a way that does not draw attention to them by mentioning the support available as part of the domestic arrangements at the start of the course. An alternative approach is to ask learners to come and speak to the practitioner privately, outside of the normal session times. As a result of the application process two learners within the group were identified as having dyslexia. In order to accommodate the learners with dyslexia, a multi-sensory approach was planned with learners being asked to look, listen, say and do when carrying out a variety of activities throughout the day. A glossary of terms useful for the course was also issued to the learners (Scales, 2008).

Taking the time to familiarize yourself with the room where the learning is scheduled helps to build a sense of familiarity of what is known and, in turn, can potentially develop an air of confidence in the way in which the session will be delivered. Hence as part of the preparations for delivery, the practitioner visited the room prior to the session, not only to arrange the furniture to the needs and context of the session, but also to visualize where the learners were likely to sit (as discussed above) and how the practitioner was going to work and engage with them. If time allows, actually delivering a mock session in front of an empty classroom or training room can be a useful preparation exercise and in this particular instance a 60-minute mock session was delivered in front of a colleague. The learners were also asked to undertake some pre-session reading pertaining to definitions of mentoring and coaching. This was made available on a VLE.

7.7.2 Delivery of the session

Throughout the session itself the learners considered some key issues relating to mentoring. By the end of the six-hour session (across one day) learners developed a poster that took account of the key issues linked to an introduction to mentoring. At key learning milestones during the session learners were invited to develop a poster that they presented to the group in the final section of the session. The milestones took place after each topic was covered, the topics include:

- What is mentoring?
- Mentoring models
- Phases of mentoring programmes
- Mentoring and ethics
- Evaluation of mentoring programmes

As mentoring is a conversational activity, the practitioner arranged the room to reflect this via the use of a 'bistro' layout to give learners an opportunity to talk to each other as well as potentially complete skills-based activities in pairs or small buzz groups. The walls of the room were decorated with examples of famous mentoring relationships (for example, Margaret Thatcher mentored John Major, Ivan Lendl mentors (and coaches) Andy Murray, Bradley Wiggins is mentored by Shane Sutton and Sir Richard Branson was mentored by Sir Freddie Laker), and quotes which emphasize the way in which mentors work and assist their mentee were also included. Flipcharts were used to list information about key aspects of mentoring as well as record the learners' responses to activities as a means of signposting the work covered. A part of the wall was left bare for the posters that were to be developed at key milestones during the day.

On the day of the session, the practitioner thought through the likely expectations of the learners and this informed their style of dress. As mentoring tends to have an organizational bias in the perspective attached to it, a more formal style of dress was chosen as the learners came from organizational settings where this type of dress was the norm. Alternatively, if the mentoring session was to be delivered to a group of youth workers, it may have been helpful to consider a style of dress that was less formal in attire and to have adopted a more casual-smart look.

Once in the room, in discussing the day ahead, a clear agenda was set, whereby the practitioner informed the group of domestic arrangements for the day, learning outcomes, timing of events (breaks, lunch) and expectations of the group. The practitioner's clear signposting of these further helped the facilitation of an effective opening to the session and the day ahead. At the commencement of the mentoring session, to allay learner fears and to build rapport with the group and further create a sense of certainty about what is to follow, a 'hopes and fears' exercise was used to help this process. It is important that a practitioner takes time to allay the fears in class wherever possible before positively moving on with the session by matching how hopes and expectations match those of the learning outcomes and the day ahead. This activity helped to engage learners' emotions and to create a climate conducive to learning.

After careful consideration, the following learning outcomes were devised for the session and shared with the learners.

By the end of the session learners should to be able to:

- evaluate definitions of mentoring
- develop awareness of the ethical issues that impact on mentoring
- analyse principles of effective mentoring practice
- create a poster that considers key mentoring principles.

In order to ensure that learners were actively engaged throughout the mentoring session, several creative teaching and training methods were used to help make sure that the session was interesting and motivated the learners. The aim was to make sure that learners became curious about mentoring and the mentoring process within their particular context. The intention was for them to retain their curiosity throughout the session (Cowley, 2005). Assertive questioning techniques were utilized during the session, both to the group as a whole (targeted questions) and to specific groups, while they were preparing their poster during the milestone activities. For example, during the session buzz groups were used (four learners in each group) to discuss models of mentoring. The groups were asked to think about whether the models can and should be used within their particular context and which models were most appropriate and why. The intention was for the learners to justify their arguments and opinions.

During the activity the groups were monitored to ascertain how each was doing. An individual was nominated to feed back to the group. Questions that were asked included, 'Why do you think counselling skills might be utilized within your context?' 'What are your reasons for discounting coaching within your context?' After each group had fed back, a full group discussion was facilitated, led by the practitioner, in order to arrive at a general consensus. It was very important that learners' work was acknowledged by the practitioner. While facilitating the groundwork, the practitioner was mindful of the limitations of group work, but they were facilitated in such a way that ensured they were not 'hijacked by determined individuals' (Petty, 2009: 233), nor did the practitioner allow individual learners to hide within their group.

A second training method that was used relating to ethical considerations was reciprocal training (Hattie, 2012). Each member of the buzz group was asked to read through an explanatory handout and be prepared to teach other members of their group. Each learner was given one of the following areas:

Control

Competence

Conflict of interest

Confidentiality. (Wallace and Gravells, 2007: 59)

The purpose of this method was to allow learners to develop their abilities to question, summarize and clarify key elements linked to ethical considerations. It is worth noting that these skill-sets had been developed during the previous sessions.

Another method that was used after all key milestones had been completed was the learner poster presentations. It is worth mentioning that, as mentoring can be viewed as a reflective activity, relaxing background music was played to help create an ambience and help induce a state of mind conducive to reflecting on learning during the key milestones and while learners were preparing their posters. Low-energy music and in particular classical music was used to help in this respect. Care was taken to ensure that the learners did not have associations attached to the music.

The purpose of a poster was to foster a creative environment to help encourage creativity in the group as well as creativity in learning. The practitioner developed ideas to try and devise an activity that would allow the learners to synthesize what they had learnt during the introduction to mentoring session, but that actually allowed them to physically create something. Robinson (2001) suggests that for something to be creative it needs to be original, of value and requires imagination. The practitioner was keen that the activity would allow learners to foster their own creativity. By approaching the session with a creative frame of mind the practitioner hoped that this would filter through into what was happening within the room. As a creative practitioner, the intention was to 'light a fire' and make the learning seem 'worthwhile and exciting' (Cowley, 2005: 58).

While formative assessment (see Chapter 8) was utilized throughout the session, the poster feedback session allowed the practitioner to check learning in a holistic manner. For example, a combination of assertive questioning, reciprocal training and group activities had been used when considering definitions of mentoring, the principles of effective mentoring and ethical issues that impact on mentoring, so the practitioner was able to confirm that learners had understood specific mentoring issues. However, it was the poster that allowed learning to be checked in a holistic manner. Feedback is vitally important and has the potential to either motivate or to demotivate learners. The feedback given made it clear what constituted a good introduction to a mentoring poster (this was also discussed prior to the task) and how their poster compared with what was deemed to be a good poster and how they might bridge that gap (Sadler, 1989, in Ollin et al., 2010). The feedback session showed the practitioner that learning had taken place as each group had been able to synthesize key points from the different elements of mentoring that had been discussed.

While delivering the introductory mentoring session the practitioner paid attention to his breathing and body language; the delivery of a 60-minute mock session helped to ensure that the practitioner not only was prepared with regards to the structure and content of the session, but also was mentally equipped and familiar with how he intended to deliver the session. The mock session also allowed the practitioner to think about the pace, tone and clarity of the delivery. In this particular instance a colleague was able to observe the session and offer constructive feedback, one of several evaluation strategies used by the practitioner.

The session was evaluated (following Scales' (2008) checklist) at several stages both throughout the session and afterwards. The practitioner asked the following evaluation questions noted by Scales (2008: 294) after the session:

- How did you feel at the end of the session?
- How do you think your learners felt?
- Was there a buzz about the session?
- What was the learners' non-verbal communication like?
- Did they look as if they were enjoying themselves?

A self-assessment evaluation checklist as devised by Scales (2008: 296) was also filled in by the practitioner that evaluated:

- the planning that was undertaken
- the start of the session
- the communication skills of the practitioner
- the teaching and training methods and strategies utilized
- the learning that took place during the session
- the resources used
- the use of assessment
- the end of the session.

The Post-it® exercise carried out at the end of the session (see Table 7.1) revealed that, while on the whole feedback was positive, with the learners enjoying the fact that they were actively involved throughout and working in buzz groups, there were things to consider. For example, some learners had not liked the idea of such assertive questioning. The practitioner made a point of explaining the purpose of, and reason for, that particular method of assessment at the next session and this enabled the practitioner to get some 'buy-in' from the learners. See Chapter 8 for further discussion about assessment and evaluation.

In addition to the above worked example, the case study and questions below are given as a further example of how to prepare and deliver learning with the key questions that can be considered to aid this process.

7.8 Summary, case study, discussion questions and learning activities

The old adage 'by failing to prepare, you are preparing to fail' could not be more true when delivering teaching and training sessions. While often a high degree of time and effort is spent on planning the mechanics of the session, at times the same might not be said of the way practitioners prepare to actually deliver the session. This chapter aimed to stress the importance of planning when delivering learning, particularly when choosing appropriate strategies and learning resources; giving due consideration to the learning environment; taking into account diversity of the learners; working towards managing your presence; encouraging learner participation; and evaluating learning. Failing to take these into account can be the difference between a session being rated good or outstanding.

7.8.1 Case study The micro-teaching session

The scenario:

As a new learner on a Postgraduate Certificate in Education (PGCE) course, you have been asked to deliver a 15-minute micro-teaching session on the subject of your choice within the first few weeks of commencing the course and view this as the perfect opportunity to demonstrate to your tutors your confidence, commitment and ability to complete the course.

The problem:

You feel nervous and anxious, questioning your ability to demonstrate to your tutors your commitment to the course. You decide to see your mentor to discuss your preparation.

Discussion questions:

To help you to achieve your aim, to be able to confidently demonstrate your commitment and ability to complete the course, your learning mentor has asked you to think through the following questions prior to the micro-teaching session:

- Have you considered the learning outcomes and what you want learners to learn?

- Has time been taken to research the composition of the group and the needs of individual learners?
- Are the teaching and training strategies chosen fit for purpose and do they cover the learning outcomes?
- Will the learning resources used during a session enhance learner perception, promote understanding, aid reinforcement and motivate the learners?
- Is it possible and necessary to revise the room layout to match the learning needs of the group and teaching and training strategies chosen for the session?
- Have you considered how you are going to evaluate the session and give learners immediate feedback on their understanding/progress?
- Have you prepared 'yourself' to deliver the session in terms of your presence, state and dress?

Consider this scenario, or any similar situation where you have been asked to lead a teaching or training session, and reflect on how you would answer these questions.

References

Atkinson, M. (2004) *Lend Me Your Ears*. London: Vermilion.

Cowley, S. (2005) *Letting the Buggers Be Creative*. San Diego, CA: The Brain Store Inc.

Hattie, J. (2012) *Visible Learning for Teachers: Maximizing Impact on Learning*. London and New York: Routledge.

Jensen, E. (1998) *Sizzle and Substance: Presenting with the Brain in Mind*. Thousand Oaks, CA: Corwin Press.

Jenson, E. (2008) *Brain Based Learning: The New Paradigm of Teaching*. London: Sage.

Meier, D. (2000) *The Accelerated Learning Handbook*. New York: McGraw-Hill.

Ollin, R., Thompson, R. and Tummons, J. (2010) *Assessment in Teaching in Lifelong Learning*. Milton Keynes: Open University Press, pp. 163–180.

Petty, G. (2009) *Teaching Today: A Practical Guide*. Cheltenham: Nelson Thornes.

Reece, I. and Walker, S. (2007) *Teaching, Training and Learning: A Practical Guide* (6th edn). Sunderland: Business Education Publishers Ltd.

Robinson, K. (2001) *Out of Our Minds: Learning to Be Creative*. Oxford: Capstone Publishing Limited.

Sadler, D. (1989) 'Formative assessment and the design of instructional systems', *Instructional Science*, 18 (2): 119–144.

Scales, P. (2008) *Teaching in the Lifelong Learning Sector*. Milton Keynes: Open University Press.

Silberman, M. (1998) *Active Training* (2nd edn). San Francisco, CA: Jossey-Bass Pfeiffer.

Simpson, S. and Gravells, A. (2010) *Planning and Enabling Learning in the Lifelong Learning Sector* (2nd edn). Exeter: Learning Matters.

Wallace, S. and Gravells, J. (2007) *Mentoring in the Lifelong Learning Sector.* Exeter: Learning Matters.

CHAPTER 8

EVALUATING AND ASSESSING LEARNING

Glenys Richardson and Alison Iredale

Learning outcomes

After reading this chapter, the reader should be able to:

- Identify a range of assessment methods appropriate to a specific course or session.
- Relate assessment strategies and methods to specific learning situations and purposes.
- Distinguish between assessment and evaluation.
- Examine and apply models of evaluation.
- Self-assess to identify strengths and areas for development.
- Identify professional development opportunities as an assessor.

Chapter outline

This chapter examines assessment and evaluation and how they are essential tools for the learning and development practitioner. This chapter intends to support practitioners to understand the differences, similarities and relationship between these two strategies. It is often difficult to separate the two, but one way is to think of assessment being focused on the learner, whereas evaluation includes the practitioner, the organization where the learning is taking place and wider organizations and interested parties, such as external awarding and regulating bodies.

8.1 Underpinning theory

This chapter builds on previous chapters and discusses theories on assessment and evaluation in learning and development. When we talk about assessment we are thinking about methods and activities that are designed to judge how close a learner is to achieving the learning outcomes. Evaluation is a broader set of activities designed to judge how effective the session is in supporting learning and achievement and the wider context in which learning takes place. This chapter focuses on theories, models and ideas drawn from Kirkpatrick and Kirkpatrick (2006), Sadler (1989), Black et al. (2003), and others.

8.2 Principles of assessment

In this section we define assessment according to both recent and established principles and ideas, followed by an overview of different types of assessment. Finally we show how a range of assessment methods can be used in a well-planned session. This leads on to thinking about evaluation and its place in learning and development.

The relationship between assessment and learning is a contentious one, particularly when some courses separate them for practical reasons, as if one can be done independently of the other. Formative assessment describes a series of assessments over time, leading to a final, summative assessment; however, learning is not linear, it is more likely to be a messy process involving remembering theory, practising routines, building theoretical connections, perfecting techniques and even forgetting what we have learned so far! Recent research (please see references for further reading) has provided two more holistic ways of thinking about assessment, one is that of assessment being for learning, and the other is assessment of learning. There is another way of considering assessment *as* learning, or authentic assessment, where the focus is on regular practice of a task, possibly in the workplace. Let us now define these terms in more detail.

8.2.1 Formative assessment

Sadler (1989) developed a theory of formative assessment, which argued for the development of practices that enable learners to monitor the quality of their own work so that they can improve on their performance. Only through authentic experiences can learners gain the evaluative expertise necessary, and the design of assessment tools needs to include authentic evaluative experiences. More recently formative assessment has been thought of as Assessment for Learning (often abbreviated to AfL). This set of principles is derived from the work of the Assessment Reform Group (1999) whose aim was to use research and evidence about assessment to inform assessment practice, mainly in primary and secondary schools. However, the outcomes and resources developed by the groups began to inform learning and development practitioners more widely. See also Black and Wiliam (1998) and Black et al. (2003).

8.2.2 Feedback on learning

John Hattie's research, using meta studies about the influences on learner learning, has helped practitioners to think more about the power of feedback in assessment practices (Hattie, 1999). Although most of the research was conducted in schools, the findings and recommendations are transferrable to most learning environments. Simply put, Hattie, in answering the question 'What has the greatest influence on learner learning?' used effect sizes, a statistical measure of improvement on grade performance. From his research he identified 'feedback' as providing the greatest effect size. Using feedback to improve performance allows both tutor and learner to evaluate the success of a particular activity.

8.2.3 Summative assessment

Given that learning and assessment go together, the idea that it is possible to assess learning is disputed, particularly if we consider learning as an active process rather than the product of an action taken by the tutor. The best way to define assessment of learning is that it serves to inform the tutor about the success or otherwise of a planned activity. At the end of a session, a course, or in preparation for the next stage of a course, tutors and organizations can use the results of an assessment to make decisions about achievement and progression. It must be noted here that where formative assessment is a process directly related with learning and development, summative assessment has more indirect effects on the learning, but often has a powerful effect on the learner.

8.2.4 Authentic assessment

Learning and development often take place in real settings, such as the workplace or while carrying out 'authentic' tasks. In these settings learners find meaningful activities and assessment are more likely to be valid, that is relevant to both the activity being assessed and the interests and ambitions of the learner.

8.3 Assessing the learning

A series of learning theories (see the work of John Watson (1878–1958), Ivan Petrovich Pavlov (1849–1936), Edward Thorndike (1874–1949), and B. F. Skinner (1904–1990)) assume causal, behavioural links between learning and achievement of knowledge or skill, where the practitioner 'conditions' the learner to respond appropriately (correctly) to a given stimulus, such as a question or a test. More recently researchers and many practitioners draw upon social learning theory and view learning as a socially constructed activity where the learner 'tests' his or her ideas against what is already known about a topic, and how competent he or she is before the new activity. John Dewey (1859–1952), Lev Semyonovich Vygotsky (1896–1934) and Jean Piaget (1896–1980) bring experiential theories to bear on how we relate assessment to learning. Transforming ideas into practice requires personal skills as well as technical expertise gained over time. Hence how we transform ideas into practice is not just about planning sessions but more about the development of skills.

8.3.1 Methods of assessment

However we view assessment, the methods that we choose will depend on their purpose. We should agree a starting point with the learner, giving them credit for learning, experience and achievement that is related to the forthcoming session; this can be referred to as initial assessment (see Chapter 2). We should review their progress during the session, engaging the learner in this process so that they can set goals for the rest of the session. We should establish what has been learned as a result of the session, and agree a way forward. Three questions, each with an example response, may help you to do this:

1. What do I want my learners to learn?

   Sample response: I want my learners to learn about assessment so that they can choose the most appropriate assessment methods for their session.

2. How can I support their learning?

   Sample response: I will support them by providing activities that allow them to experience and reflect on three common methods of assessment.

3. How will I know that they have learned?

   Sample response: I will know that they have learned about assessment when they choose, discuss and justify an appropriate assessment method for a given scenario – either a real session that they are planning, or one provided.

Once these questions have been answered it is time to build into the session methods of assessment that will support the learner to achieve their desired outcomes and goals.

Table 8.1 offers a list of the main methods of assessment used on most courses/sessions, showing how well these can work for the various purposes in any learning context.

8.4 Evaluating the learning session

Evaluation is about making judgements as to worth and value and is not synonymous with assessment. Assessment can inform evaluation but is only one component in making a broader judgement. To give an extreme example, imagine a session in uncomfortable surroundings, with an uninspiring practitioner, poor quality learning resources and the focus is on a topic which the learners had already covered very thoroughly. The learners all scored high marks in the test which was set, but they had certainly not enjoyed the session and no new learning had taken place. A fair evaluation of the session would recognize that it was in many ways unsatisfactory, despite the test scores. In evaluating a learning session, we need to think about the purpose of the evaluation and what criteria we will judge against. We must also consider the different viewpoints of the people with a stake in the session, the learners, the practitioner and the organization.

8.4.1 Models of evaluation

The individual practitioner can usefully evaluate their own learning sessions, with a view to improving their delivery skills. Later in this chapter we make some suggestions for ways in which you can approach this, by using a self-assessment checklist, by gathering feedback and by videoing your session. Practitioners may also benefit from evaluation of and feedback on their performance by others. The models and methods

Table 8.1 Main methods of assessment

Assessment methods	Initial assessment	Assessment *for* learning	Assessment *of* learning	Assessment *as* learning	Authentic assessment
Recognition of prior learning portfolio of evidence A collection of statements and/or artefacts organized in relation to the course criteria, often by cross-referencing	Sets the starting point for learning from the learners' perspective, rather than the course	Tutor agrees and aligns prior learning with course outcomes Learners can construct their own learner journey and achieve at their own pace	No significant learning takes place in the session The emphasis is on providing accreditation of prior learning	Learner reinforces learning through the assessment activities Gaps in knowledge are identified, leading to an individual learning plan	Helps to connect the learner to meaningful learning
Interview A structured conversation based upon the entry criteria of the course/session	Helps to identify whether the learner can benefit from the course/ session	The learner is able to self-assess against the entry criteria for the course	Tutor can make a judgement about whether the learner is ready to benefit from the session or course	Both learner and tutor are able to agree the starting point for the session	
Knowledge/skills audit A matrix, or simple checklist that represents the outcomes of the course	A useful tool for short training courses and portfolio-based courses It can be used as part of a self-selection strategy, enabling tutors and learners to decide whether this course is right for them	Depending on the regularity of the audit it can support courses where personal and/or professional development are part and parcel of the course	As a self-assessment tool this is useful to establish whether the learner already has the knowledge and skills required, enabling accreditation/ recognition of prior learning and experience	The results of the audit, when carefully analysed can become a powerful reflection tool	As long as the criteria on which the audit is based are valid (i.e. related to the learners situation and context) learners can connect their future learning to the 'real world'

Assessment methods	Initial assessment	Assessment *for* learning	Assessment *of* learning	Assessment *as* learning	Authentic assessment
Observation Usually related to 'performance' based tasks in the workplace or real environment	Where this is done sensitively, with trained observers who understand the context this allows both tutor and learner to decide whether the course will be of benefit in the short term	Feedback from observations allows for reflective conversations where meaningful learning can take place based upon experience	Where the criteria are clear and authentic this can be part of an overall assessment strategy	Learners can be encouraged to integrate theory and practice through the feedback tutorial following an observation	As part of a reflective process observation of progress and/or performance can capture learning points that are more difficult to achieve with other methods
Self/peer assessment The course or topic criteria are used as a developmental tool, to support the learner's understanding of the summative method	Learners need to thoroughly understand the assessment criteria to be able to make best use of this method as a starting point for further study	This is a powerful method as it allows for the use of feedback to reflect on experience	The summative value of this method will depend on the type of course/ session	Learners need to be able to use the criteria to discuss how the assessment impacts on the learning for the course/session	Where the criteria are authentic to the situation and context learners can use this method to set realistic goals
Assignment A selection of activities, typically written, such as essays and reports based on a set topic related to a course	The tutor needs to design highly inclusive criteria for this method to provide a fair assessment of a learner's starting point	The learner has an opportunity to explore areas of particular interest, and to apply ideas in an intellectually stimulating way, as long as the assignment allows for a range of opportunities across the course	The tutor can assess the depth of engagement and understanding of one topic if the method includes opportunities to research the topic in depth	Application, analysis, synthesis and evaluation, can all be learned through this method	This depends on the way that the assignment is written. If there are options and choices within the tasks it can be a realistic measure of competence

(Continued)

Table 8.1 (Continued)

Assessment methods	Initial assessment	Assessment *for* learning	Assessment *of* learning	Assessment *as* learning	Authentic assessment
Simulation activities Based on a real or realistic situation or performance of a task Usually there are opportunities to introduce variables to support decision-making skills	This method is often used as an initial assessment during interview It allows the tutor to assess the entry knowledge and skills of the learner in a 'realistic' situation	The learner gains a great deal from this method about their current level of knowledge and skill, depending on how closely the task reflects 'real life' situations	Clear criteria need to be established, not just relating to performance but also the process, to allow a fair judgement to be made	Real time or computer-based problem solving, where changing circumstances are included within the simulation are useful for both learner and tutor	The closer to 'reality' the better for this method, depending on how practicable this is
Case study Learners work through a series of 'realistic' set problem(s) from which a number of solutions are available in the case study narrative; constrained assessment	A good way of assessing how well a learner can apply theories and principles to real-world situations They require careful criteria to be useful at entry to a course or programme	Both tutor and learner can identify gaps in knowledge and skills as long as the criteria are shared and understood beforehand	The criteria need to be based upon what is the correct response, rather than a range of opinions; otherwise it is difficult to make a fair judgement of performance from this method	The process, if used as a formative tool, can be useful for assessing understanding, allowing learners to make links between theory and practice	The timing of this method is important; if introduced too early learners can struggle to see the 'relevance' of the situation to their practice
Project work A series of planned activities around a specific problem/ issue designed to assess collaboration skills over time, usually ending in a summative assessment	Rarely used because of the significant amount of work needed, and as such it lacks feasibility	This method provides opportunities for the learner to develop ideas and skills learned in a controlled way, supported by a clear plan for progression of learning throughout the project	Tutors can make judgements about the performance of a cohort, allowing for fair summative assessments based on both the process of the project and the final product	Tutors can use the criteria to identify differentiated opportunities in future sessions to support the learner in planning for attainment of summative goals	A good method depending on the levels of engagement of each learner for group projects

Assessment methods	Initial assessment	Assessment *for* learning	Assessment *of* learning	Assessment *as* learning	Authentic assessment
Reflective journal/ personal and professional development plan A record of learning and personal/ professional development over a period of time; it can combine text, artefact and images and usually features a narrative journey; it can include action planning and target setting	Not usually used unless it is part of a portfolio of evidence	A valuable method as it allows learners to focus on their own learning and development, loosely based upon the criteria, but also capturing a greater range of evidence	As a formative method it is difficult to extract the summative assessment criteria for this method	Both tutor and learner can use the narrative journey to discuss the links between theories, principles and practice	As it derives from personal experience and critical incidents during a course it is highly authentic, but may be difficult to assess
Quizzes/games Short, often fun activities based on the topic of the course/session	As part of an icebreaker session these can provide information for the tutor in planning during the course/ session (for example, in pairing and grouping learners)	Both tutor and learner benefit from these non-threatening yet often challenging activities	Not used for summative purposes	The learner is able to reflect on their progress without the 'high stakes' of other more formal methods	Authenticity is not as important for this method to be successful The lack of 'reality' can often reduce stress and anxiety

of such evaluations can be questioned; Scriven (1995: 128) lists numerous approaches and comments: 'all models in use are invalid, and seriously so'. Scriven himself went on to develop a model emphasizing the developmental aspects of evaluation (Scriven, 2001). Eisner (1985) advocated a connoisseurship model: education as an art form, which can be appreciated and can benefit from an expert critique.

Curriculum evaluation takes account of the wider issues, going beyond the evaluation of practice. There is an extensive literature on curriculum evaluation and in this section we will consider a few of the more influential models.

Writers who take a product perspective on the curriculum advocate specifying behavioural objectives and designing learning programmes to achieve the stated goals. Evaluation is then concerned with measuring how effectively these have been achieved. Tyler's (1949) model is the most influential of this approach. Stufflebeam (1983) devised the CIPP (Context, Input, Process and Product) model of evaluation, which is orientated towards evaluation as a tool for decision making.

Kirkpatrick developed a four-level model of evaluation, which has been very influential on subsequent writers and practice (Kirkpatrick and Kirkpatrick, 2006). The first level involves the reaction of the learners to the teaching or training they are experiencing. This can be gauged informally through observation and discussion or more formally via questionnaires. The second level focuses on what learning has taken place and this can be judged using assessment data such as comparing test results before and after training. The third level examines changes in behaviour: are learners able to apply their learning and transfer it to a different setting? The fourth level looks at results. Kirkpatrick's initial focus was on business settings, so the relevant indicators are measures of business performance. Gathering the information required to make valid judgements becomes increasingly difficult as we work up through the levels.

8.4.2 Evaluation and quality assurance

Organizations evaluate teaching, training, learning and assessment as part of their quality assurance processes. The approach they take is frequently influenced by external agencies which make judgements about their performance, such as Ofsted (Office for Standards in Education) for the further education and skills sector, the Quality Assurance Agency (QAA) for higher education (Ofsted, 2012; QAA, 2013) or the CIPD (Chartered Institute for Personnel and Development, 2010). Lesson observations are now a key aspect of quality assurance processes in many settings. Organizations vary in the approach they take to the frequency and style of such observations, for example whether the observations are carried out by peers or by managers and whether or not a formal grade is awarded. Lesson observations can be used to gather data to inform self-assessment, to identify good practice for sharing and to identify strengths and development needs of individual practitioners. Evidence of the learners' views is also gathered, using surveys and meetings.

Awarding bodies (for example, City and Guilds, CIPD, BTEC or a university) specify detailed processes required for any organization to be permitted to offer their qualifications. The terminology and processes used will vary but the objective is always to try to ensure that assessments are fair, accurate, reliable and valid and that standards remain consistent over time. Internal and external quality assurance (or verification) are about checking that the whole assessment process is properly carried out, looking at aspects such as assignment briefs, assessment records, assessors' qualifications and sampling assessments to make sure the standards are maintained. Moderation is a process by which practitioners reach a shared understanding of the standards, by discussion and by sampling each other's assessments.

As a practitioner, you may be involved with more than one of these regimes and it is essential to be clear about the processes and terminologies used. What is correct in one context does not always apply in another (see the learning activity at the end of this chapter).

8.5 Improving your session

8.5.1 Enjoy being a facilitator or leader

Most practitioners find that the time spent in the classroom or training room is the most enjoyable part of their job. Factors that help you to enjoy your sessions are your own attitude and approach to your role and the practical issues which can help a session run smoothly.

- Take an interest in your learners as people and cultivate a welcoming, inclusive learning environment. Think positively about your learners: this does not mean you always have to like them but that you value them as human beings (Rogers, 1995). The practitioner, as well as the learners, benefits from such an environment.
- Remind yourself of the value of your work: perhaps it is to develop useful skills and knowledge; to foster confidence or to provoke depth of thought and insight. Are you contributing to giving individuals a better chance in life? Helping a business provide a better service? Passing on skills and knowledge that will benefit the economy or the organization? By framing your work within a context that gives meaning and worth, you can inspire yourself and this will help you to inspire your learners.
- Be willing to experiment. Lack of variety can become boring; trying out new ideas can put energy and enthusiasm back into your sessions.
- Dress in a way that helps you to feel comfortable, confident and projects the image that you want to convey.

- Be well prepared, with a workable plan and organized resources.
- Look after your own health and well-being. There is a performance element to teaching and training and just like an actor or athlete, you cannot perform at your best without rest, exercise and a good diet. Preparation and marking are important but so is time to yourself and with your friends and family.

8.5.2 Enhancing your skills, attitude and knowledge

Many practitioners find assessment and evaluation the most difficult aspects of their role, whether in the classroom or in the workplace. Two factors will help you to feel more confident in making accurate assessment decisions. One is the level of your knowledge and expertise, and the second is the level of support from colleagues and the wider organization. Learners too face confidence issues of course, and lack of confidence can prevent them from evaluating their own work.

Knowledge and expertise

It is often the experienced learning and development practitioner, confident in his or her main subject matter, who is able to make good assessment decisions. This is because, according to Argyris and Schön (1974), they develop their own ways of working (mental maps) in an organization over many years. Inexperienced practitioners tend to rely upon recognized routines and strategies that are suggested by their colleagues and mentors, taking them for granted.

While assessment decisions based on pre-planned outcomes can be less risky, more open, shared and negotiated outcomes can be more enjoyable for both the practitioner and the learner, particularly where they encourage problem solving, creativity and critical thinking (see Argyris, 1982). Experienced practitioners are more often ready to cope with uncertainty, developing a 'prose' or narrative to display and develop their practice. The level and depth of subject knowledge, sometimes called pedagogic content knowledge or PCK (Shulman, 1986), often anchors confidence and enjoyment in the classroom. This has been linked to choice of assessment activities, where more knowledgeable teachers are more prepared to choose novel activities and to respond more positively to issues that arise (see Hashweh, 1987).

Levels of support

A confident practitioner, working in a safe and open environment, may feel able to consider assessment theories in the light of their existing practice. Those lacking in confidence and working in organizations where there is little support may prefer the reassurance of ready-made solutions. The conditions under which practice develops over time are crucial to being able to make confident assessment decisions, and additional support and the promotion of critical reflective practice are crucial if practitioners are to develop and improve.

8.5.3 Getting feedback on your performance

Feedback is one of the most powerful tools in promoting learning, and getting feedback on our teaching can be a very effective way to help us to improve. Organizations often have official systems for evaluation of teaching and learning and these can help to provide feedback. Questionnaires are frequently used as a tool for gathering feedback. You may find that your organization conducts regular learner surveys and these can provide useful insights. However, they may not provide sufficient detail to help you to improve, so you can supplement them with your own ways to get the views of learners and some ideas for this are discussed below. When you use a reaction survey, try to make sure your questions are focused on the learners' perspective rather than being practitioner centred. You are also likely to be observed in the class or training room: this may be from a mentor or advanced practitioner whose role it is to support your development, or a manager, or it may be as part of a quality assurance system where the main purpose is to generate a grade or give feedback on your work. The amount of feedback and developmental support may be variable: investigate the approach taken in your organization.

Learners can provide feedback both consciously and in more subtle ways. Develop the practice of reviewing the session with your learners. You can ask questions such as: What have I learned? What was the most difficult aspect of the session? What was the most enjoyable? What was the most useful? What were the best and worst moments? You can gather views in general discussion, in small group exercises, using sticky notes, feedback proformas or via electronic voting systems if available. Try to vary the questions and format that you use to provoke discussion, or the exercise can become stale.

It is not always necessary to question learners directly in order to get useful feedback. The results of tests, for example, can highlight to you that a particular topic did not work effectively and that you need to find a different way to help your learners understand a specific facet of the syllabus. Observing your learners during a session can also provide you with valuable feedback. Was there a 'buzz' of engagement during an activity? What did the questions they asked tell you about how well you had pitched the level of the work?

Peer observation and feedback can be a powerful tool. You can ask for feedback on a particular aspect of your teaching, for example how well you managed behaviour in a class that you find difficult. You could then reciprocate and are likely to gain interesting insights from the exercise. Delivery of learning is too often a closed-door activity and we often have few models beyond our own educational experiences. It is worthwhile to video-record some of your sessions, to enable you to observe yourself and your learners.

8.5.4 Getting creative

Section 8.2 above explores the importance of assessment as part of the learning process. There are many creative ways in which you can check on learning as a natural part of your session, without learners feeling the pressures traditionally associated with tests and examinations. It can be an enjoyable part of the role to develop your own methods to suit your situation and learners. Here are some approaches to consider; you can find more examples in Harvey and Harvey (2013).

Inexperienced practitioners often ask general questions such as 'does everyone understand?' and if no one is brave enough to reply, carry on assuming that everything is fine. You can give your learners more control of the learning process by providing ways in which they can signal how well they think they are doing. Flags, paper cups, paper hats, smiley, puzzled or sad faced icons, mini-whiteboards and marker pens can all be utilized in this way. Even if everyone in the room displays a green flag to signal that they fully understand, follow up with some questions to check this out.

Questioning gives opportunities to assess as well as extend learning and developing a variety of techniques can make this a more effective part of the learning process. If all learners know that they are likely to be questioned, it can aid attention and concentration. Lolly sticks or slips of card with learners' names can be used as a form of 'lucky dip' or learners can throw a ball to the next person they choose to answer: vary the methods you use.

Games and quizzes give opportunities for the creative teacher to show originality in recapping and checking learning. Quizzes, card games, matching games, board games, crosswords and puzzles can often be used make a session more fun and re-energize a group, although you will need to carefully judge the level and approach. Some learners enjoy a competitive element, especially if you provide small prizes. This can be particularly effective as part of the ending to a session.

Assignments and projects can give scope for creativity in the learners as well as the practitioner. For example, a Business Studies course included a summative assessment project, which required the learners to work in groups to plan and organize an event. The brief was open but the outcomes against which the learners were to be assessed were carefully specified and included aspects of budgeting, communication, teamwork and marketing. The process included an element of peer assessment and learners also wrote a business style report on their event. Over a period of time, the learners responded by organizing social and charity fund raising events including a summer ball, a cake stall, a fashion show, a fun run and a car boot sale. One group even took over a small restaurant (where one of the group had a part-time job) for an evening and produced a three course meal for themselves and guests, including their tutors. The learners responded so positively because they could see the relevance to skills that would be useful in employment and their project experiences provided them with real examples of things they had done, that they were able to draw on in job applications and interviews.

The format for presenting work for assessment can give further scope for creativity. Poster presentations, web-based pinboards (such as Pinterest), blogs and wikis can all provide scope for individuality and imagination.

8.6 Assessor and quality assurance qualifications

Assessment and evaluation are key aspects of the learning and development practitioners' role and you can enhance your skills and knowledge by undertaking relevant professional qualifications. For those practitioners who are not yet fully qualified and working in work-based learning (WBL), the first qualification often to be achieved is an Assessor Award. This provides the knowledge and skills specifically for assessment and typically, such practitioners will go on to take either a full teacher training qualification or CIPD qualification in learning and development practice (see Chapter 11). Such awards are part of the National Occupational Standards for Learning and Development, developed by LSIS (LSIS, 2013). Some FE and WBL organizations encourage their staff to undertake specific elements from this framework even if they are fully qualified as teachers, especially where vocational assessment and internal quality assurance of the assessment process form part of the job role. An example is City and Guilds Assessment and Quality Assurance (6317): the assessment units are at Level 3 while quality assurance units are at Level 4 (City and Guilds, 2013).

8.7 Summary, case study, discussion questions and learning activities

This chapter has reviewed the underpinning theories and principles of assessment and evaluation, identifying a range of assessment methods and evaluation tools. The focus has been on the learning session, in particular how practitioners can decide on the most appropriate strategy to suit the specific purpose of the topic and activities. We have included self-assessments, tasks and case studies to consider how assessment and evaluation theory can be used to understand the application of assessment and evaluation strategies. The final section has considered ways in which the practitioner can improve and develop their practice, in their own organizational context, by making use of feedback, developing their creativity in assessment practice and by undertaking specialist professional qualifications.

8.7.1 Case study 1 Using Kirkpatrick's model

Leena is responsible for running study skills sessions for learners on a range of Level 3 vocational and A level courses in a further education college. She covers topics such as time management, note taking, structuring an assignment or essay and referencing skills. She is interested in adapting Kirkpatrick's model of evaluation to her situation. This is her plan so far.

Table 8.2 Kirkpatrick's model

Kirkpatrick's model (Kirkpatrick and Kirkpatrick, 2006)		Leena's ideas
Level	Type of evaluation	
1	The **reaction** of the learners to the teaching/training	Produce a questionnaire to give to the learners
2	What **learning** has taken place? Has knowledge and understanding increased?	Test the learners at the start of the course and again at the end
3	Changes in **behaviour**. Can the learner apply their learning and transfer it to a different setting?	Ask the course tutors whether the learners' performance in their subjects has improved
4	Results	Do the learners who attend the study skills sessions have higher achievement rates in their main qualifications than those who do not? Do they feel more confident? Are they more likely to go on to higher education? Do they use any of the techniques and strategies learned in the study skills classes in their higher level studies?

Questions:

- Draft a questionnaire that Leena could use to gauge the reaction of the learners. What other ways could she use to gauge the learners' reactions?
- What are the advantages and disadvantages of setting a test at the start and end of the course? What other ways could Leena use to assess learning?
- Leena's ideas for judging results are ambitious. What does she need to consider if she is to carry out evaluation at this level?

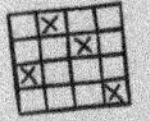

Activity 1 Create an assessment and evaluation document file

It is useful to gather all the documents relating to assessment and evaluation so that you can meet expectations, and so that you can choose the most appropriate methods of assessment for your session.

These documents might include the organization's policies and procedures, those of the awarding body, and sometimes those of organizations and regulatory bodies that have an interest in the quality of assessment. In particular you should try to find the following:

- If you are delivering a course designed by an external awarding organization they will provide a *course syllabus* or *specification*. This will have a section about assessment and it is important to read this carefully as it will help you to design sessions that fit with the purpose and ethos of the course.
- Larger organizations will have a *quality assurance* or *quality improvement* policy on assessment and evaluation. This will help you to ensure that you are assessing and evaluating learning in accordance with the requirements of the organization, particularly as they will be expected to report on the quality of your sessions. The staff intranet is a good place to begin to find policies and procedures.
- All awarding bodies have systems for evaluating the quality of assessment, and they use terms such as moderation, verification examination, and possibly standardization. Larger awarding bodies publish reports that help practitioners to resolve problems with externally set assessments.
- If you have designed your course from scratch or if it is an informal course then the best sources of support for ensuring the quality of assessment are networks of practitioners working in a similar area (also see references for further reading that will help you to design high quality assessments for your learners).

8.7.2 Case study 2 Using video recording

Amy works for a private training provider, supporting learners working in a range of businesses to gain qualifications in Business Administration. She holds taught classes, where the focus is on underpinning knowledge and she also visits candidates in their workplace, to assess competence in their work roles and to help them to assemble a portfolio of evidence for accreditation. Amy was undertaking her Certificate in Education and had agreed with her college tutor to video one of these one-to-one sessions. She sat down with her tutor to look at the video recording, with the intention of the tutor providing feedback. However, Amy did not need her tutor to tell her that there was a problem with this session. On watching the video she immediately became aware of her own body language and focus of attention. She was so concerned to have all the complex documents well organized, and to ensure that the maximum progress was made during the limited time available, that she did not make eye contact with the learner or engage with him as a person. Amy had not been keen to use video but now says that seeing herself was a transformative experience.

Questions:

- What ethical issues would Amy have had to consider before going ahead with recording the session? Whose permission would she have needed to gain?
- Why do you think watching the video had such a strong impact on Amy? Do you think that feedback from her tutor as an observer would have had a similar impact?
- How could this experience help Amy to improve her practice?

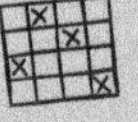

Activity 2 Self-assessment or peer observation checklist

Use the checklist below to give yourself an informal rating. Do this for a series of sessions and it will help you to pinpoint where you need to concentrate your efforts to improve. You could also use this for peer observations.

Table 8.3 Self-assessment and peer observation checklist

*** Excellent ** Good * Needs development x = Not applicable in this session

Date:
Time:
Group:
Location:

	***	**	*	x
Setting aims and objectives				
Making creative use of resources				
Using a variety of teaching and learning activities				
Giving explanations and instructions				
Asking questions				
Answering questions				
Giving feedback				
Creating a welcoming, purposeful learning atmosphere				
Making sure all the learners are fully included				
Making sure all the learners are able to make progress				
Assessing learning				
Making the session interesting and enjoyable				
Supporting the development in maths, English or other required skills				
Facilitating participation and debate				
Tracking learners' progress				
Managing behaviour				
Using specialist subject knowledge				
Using technology to aid learning				
Getting the level right for the learners				
Pace and timing				
Helping learners improve their study skills				
Promoting a confident presence				
Clarity of written communication, for example writing on boards or flipcharts				
Use of visual images				
Flexibility and adaptability in dealing with unexpected circumstances				

References

Argyris, C. (1982) *Reasoning, Learning, and Action: Individual and Organizational*. San Francisco, CA: Jossey Bass.

Argyris, M. and Schön, D. (1974) *Theory in Practice: Increasing Professional Effectiveness*. San Francisco, CA: Jossey-Bass.

Assessment Reform Group (1999) *Assessment for Learning: Beyond the Blackbox*. Cambridge: University of Cambridge School of Education.

Black, P., Harrison, C., Lee, C., Marshall, B. and Wiliam, D. (2003) *Assessment for Learning: Putting it into Practice*. Maidenhead: Open University Press.

Black, P. and Wiliam, D. (1998) 'Assessment and classroom learning', *Assessment in Education*, 5 (1): 7–71.

Chartered Institute for Personnel and Development (2010) *Centre Handbook*. London: CIPD.

City and Guilds (2013) *Assessment and Quality Assurance (6317)*. www.cityandguilds.com/Courses-and-Qualifications/learning/training-and-development/6317-assessment-and-quality-assurance (accessed 23 October 2013).

Eisner, E. W. (1985) *The Art of Educational Evaluation: A Personal View*. London: Falmer Press.

Harvey, B. and Harvey, J. (2013) *Creative Teaching Approaches in the Lifelong Learning Sector*. Maidenhead: Open University Press.

Hashweh, M. Z. (1987) 'Effects of subject-matter knowledge in the teaching of biology and physics', *Teaching and Teacher Education*, 3(2): 109–120.

Hattie, J. A. (1999) 'Influences on student learning', inaugural lecture, Professor of Education, University of Auckland. www.education.auckland.ac.nz/webdav/site/education/shared/hattie/docs/influences-on-student-learning.pdf (accessed 27 September 2013).

Kirkpatrick, D. and Kirkpatrick, J. (2006) *Evaluating Training Programmes: The Four Levels*. San Francisco: Berrett-Koehler.

LSIS (Learning and Skills Improvement Service) (2013) *Qualification Guidance for Awarding Organizations. Assessment and Quality Assurance Qualifications. Learning and Development Qualifications*. www.lsis.org.uk/publication-content/qualification-guidance-awarding-organisations-assessment-and-quality- assurance (accessed 23 August 2013).

Ofsted (2012) *The Common Inspection Framework for Further Education and Skills*. Manchester: The Office for Standards in Education, Children's Services and Skills.

QAA (2013) *The UK Quality Code for Higher Education*. www.qaa.ac.uk/assuringstandardsandquality/quality-code (accessed 3 November 2013).

Rogers, C. (1995) *On Becoming a Person: A Therapist's View of Psychotherapy*. Boston: Houghton Mifflin.

Sadler, D. R. (1989) 'Formative assessment and the design of instructional systems', *Instructional Science*, 18: 119–144.

Scriven, M. (1995) 'A unified theory approach to teacher evaluation', *Studies in Educational Evaluation*, 21: 111–129.

Scriven, M. (2001) *Evaluation Thesaurus* (4th edn). Newbury Park, CA: Sage Publications.

Shulman, L. S. (1986) 'Those who understand: knowledge growth in teaching', *Educational Researcher*, 15: 4–14.

Stufflebeam, D. L. (1983) 'The CIPP model for program evaluation', in G. F. Madaus, M. Striven, and D. L. Stufflebeam (eds), *Evaluation Models: Viewpoints on Educational and Human Services Evaluation*. Boston, MA: Kluwer-Nijhoff, pp. 117–141.

Tyler, R. (1949) *Basic Principles of Curriculum and Instruction*. Chicago, IL: Chicago University Press.

CHAPTER 9

USING TECHNOLOGY TO ENHANCE LEARNING

Cheryl Reynolds and Shailesh Appukuttan

Learning outcomes

After reading this chapter, the reader should be able to:

- Consider useful definitions of technology-enhanced learning.
- Understand digital literacy and the usefulness of this notion within learning contexts.
- Describe a range of TEL tools and their implications for pedagogical practices.
- Analyse a range of case studies for potential application within practitioners' own fields of practice.

Chapter outline

In section 9.1, we briefly outline the theory that underpins it, before offering a consideration of the context for and a definition of technology-enhanced learning (TEL). In section 9.2, we go on to consider practical applications of TEL and its potential for transformative teaching and learning through a series of illustrative examples, which seek to model approaches to TEL design in four key areas of the learning process: planning, delivering, evaluating and flourishing. We round this section off with a brief consideration of how the examples explored in this section help to develop digital literacy and relate to the learning theories that we outlined in section 9.1. In section 9.3, we share a selection of case studies, covering e-portfolios, assessment analytics, personal learning networks, massive open online courses (MOOCs) and social learning networks in blended learning models. In doing so, we aim to provide a broad range of TEL scenarios through which the benefits, challenges and drawbacks of working with technology are explored.

9.1 Underpinning theory

Technology-enhanced learning can be underpinned by any of the major theories of learning, ranging from behaviourist, short answer and rapid feedback quizzes to highly humanistic approaches that engage people in social learning experiences for personal growth and development. However, its particular properties mean that it often has at its heart a shared belief in a specific kind of learning that is based on both individual and collaborative enquiry. This emphasis arises out of three key affordances of technology: the enormous amounts of information to which it gives access; its capacity for building new content and resources; and its potential for collaborative learning between people separated by time and space. In consequence, technology-enhanced learning is often constructivist (Dewey, 1933; Kolb, 1984): building on what people already know and motivated by what they want to find out next. It is often situative (Brown et al., 1989) since it can be used to create and deliver interactive, authentic representations of real-life scenarios; furthermore, it is often collaborative, growing out of the interactions between participants (Sfard, 1998).

9.1.1 Digital literacies and knowledge workers

This constructivist, situative, collaborative bent of new technology colours the context of technology-enhanced learning and it is worth briefly exploring the significance of this context here before moving on to a more practical discussion. This is worthwhile because it gives us an opportunity to reflect on what is our purpose or goal when we pick up and utilize a technology-enhanced method. Historically, education has had a major role to play in providing learners with access to information. Lectures, presentations, handouts and textbooks were all largely concerned with delivering content to participants, who could not easily obtain that information in any other way. However, facts, knowledge and learning opportunities are increasingly accessible outside the class or training room, via the internet, and while there remain communities and individuals who have limited access to such resources, the availability of information globally is growing at an exponential rate. Google's strap line is 'Organizing the world's information' and the tens of thousands of results thrown up by any search make this seem not too ambitious a claim. If the role of trainers and educators is becoming less and less about delivering content, then we arguably need to reframe our purpose and adjust to the new, information-rich context in which we find ourselves. At the same time, the needs of the new global economy are increasingly not for people who can memorize facts, protocols and procedures but for flexible knowledge workers who are autonomous, resourceful and entrepreneurial; what Wesch (2009) calls 'knowledge-able' rather than knowledgeable. In other words, what the new global economy needs is workers who have the ability to find, filter, synthesize and apply rather than memorize and regurgitate knowledge.

'Knowledge-able' learners and workers in the twenty-first century need to be digitally literate. Drawn from the Web Literacy Standard (Belshaw and Casilli, 2013) digital literacy includes: navigation and search skills; discernment and filtering skills; online security and privacy awareness; designing, composing, remixing and coding for the web; sharing, collaborating and community participation; and, finally, copyright awareness and open practices. These broader aims feature in some of the case studies and examples given later in the chapter.

9.1.2 Defining technology-enhanced learning

The constantly evolving plethora of technologies available to teachers, trainers and learners and its enormous scale and diversity make it challenging to define. One way to address this challenge is to offer a definition that provides us with *a way of thinking* about technology rather than *a description of it.* Frequently defined as a set of tools with particular properties, affordances (possible functions) and applications, what we propose here instead is that we think of technology as a particular kind of *space* or *medium* within which learning can occur. Let us consider the video hosting website, YouTube, as an example. If we define this in terms of its properties, affordances and applications, we would say that it allows the uploading and sharing of video content, which viewers can watch and comment upon in order to be entertained or to find out and discuss new information and skills. If, on the other hand, we define it as a space or medium, we would say that it is an open, creative, collaborative, media-rich space that is both responding to and influencing how people interact with video content and through this, with one another. The second definition is richer, since it encompasses both the social consequences and the social drivers for YouTube as well as what it actually does. Similarly, an interactive whiteboard, rather than being defined as a tool with particular properties, can be defined as a change in the nature of the classroom as a space for learning, enabling different kinds of interactions between learners and teachers, between learners and content and between the learners themselves. The same applies to software packages such as word processors, spreadsheets and presentation applications, which can be conceived of as particular kinds of environments within and through which we create, share and consume learning. A definition of TEL along these lines, therefore, has the advantage of presenting us with a general conceptualization of diverse technologies, which includes platforms, devices, software packages and their consequences for users.

This way of thinking about technology is inspired by the seminal work of McLuhan (1994) and his notion that 'the medium is the message'. His argument was that the 'message' of a new technology such as television is not so much the daily news, or the thrice weekly soap opera, or the Saturday afternoon big match that is broadcast through it. Rather the 'message' of television is that families now routinely arrange their living rooms around a TV screen and spend time together as a family watching it, arguing about it, laughing at it or ignoring it. It is useful to think of technology in this way because it moves our focus away from the tool itself and towards its users; their motivations, their habits and their needs.

Our definition of TEL is, then, intentionally simple and broad, with no attempt to enumerate all of the different incarnations of technology that can be found within a learning context: TEL is learning that occurs within a novel space or medium that has been enabled by technology, growing out of social imperatives and resulting in social change.

This social change encompasses, of course, educational developments: changes to the ways that learning is routinely designed, delivered and evaluated; and the broad pedagogical consequences of using technology for learning and development. The next section illustrates how some technology-enhanced learning tools, although vulnerable to rapid obsolescence, can be used in practice and their educational development implications in various contexts.

9.2 Practical applications of technology for learning

In section 9.1 we offered a definition of technology as a kind of space in which participants can operate. In this next section, we break this down into different categories of space and then organize different technologies into those categories. In arriving at these categories, we have drawn on the research of Garrison and Vaughan (2008) whose work on blended learning stipulated three essential types of presence required for effective online teaching and learning: *teaching* presence, *cognitive* presence and *social* presence. They suggest that much online provision pays an inordinate amount of attention to teaching presence, focusing on the didactic delivery of content and failing to encourage enough cognitive or reflective presence from the learner. The need for learners to make social links and engage in interactions with peers is, they suggest, also frequently neglected. What we suggest here is that the notion of 'presence', while of some use and value, is somewhat confusing and becomes more useful and accessible if we reconceptualize it as spaces in which these three types of presence might be played out or performed. We therefore arrive at the proposition that we need *teaching* spaces in which to deliver content, *cognitive* spaces in which to create, think and reflect, and *social* spaces in which to build links and converse with others. In addition to this list of three, we also propose a fourth type of space that allows for the *capture and storage* of information. In Figure 9.1 we propose different kinds of technologies that might fall into each of these four categories.

The arrows shown in Figure 9.1 represent likely workflows of participants. Learners could enter this workflow at various different points and in designing TEL solutions, you might use this diagram to decide on the process you would like them to follow. For example, learners could be given the task of capturing parts of a lesson on camera, editing it in a video editing tool, uploading it to a virtual learning environment and then projecting it to the rest of the group at a future session for discussion. You will note that Figure 9.1 includes some traditional spaces such as libraries, classrooms and study rooms. These are offered as a reminder that technology is always utilized in a physical context and is often best used as part of a blend or mix of online and real-world scenarios. They also serve as a foil for or comparison with their technological counterparts.

You will note that there is an overlap between the cognitive and creative and the teaching and social categories because a number of technologies are multi-functional and can be used in a number of different ways. Blogs are an example that can serve as teaching and social spaces as well as cognitive and creative spaces. Also, you may feel that you would like to move some items around or to add them to another box. For example,

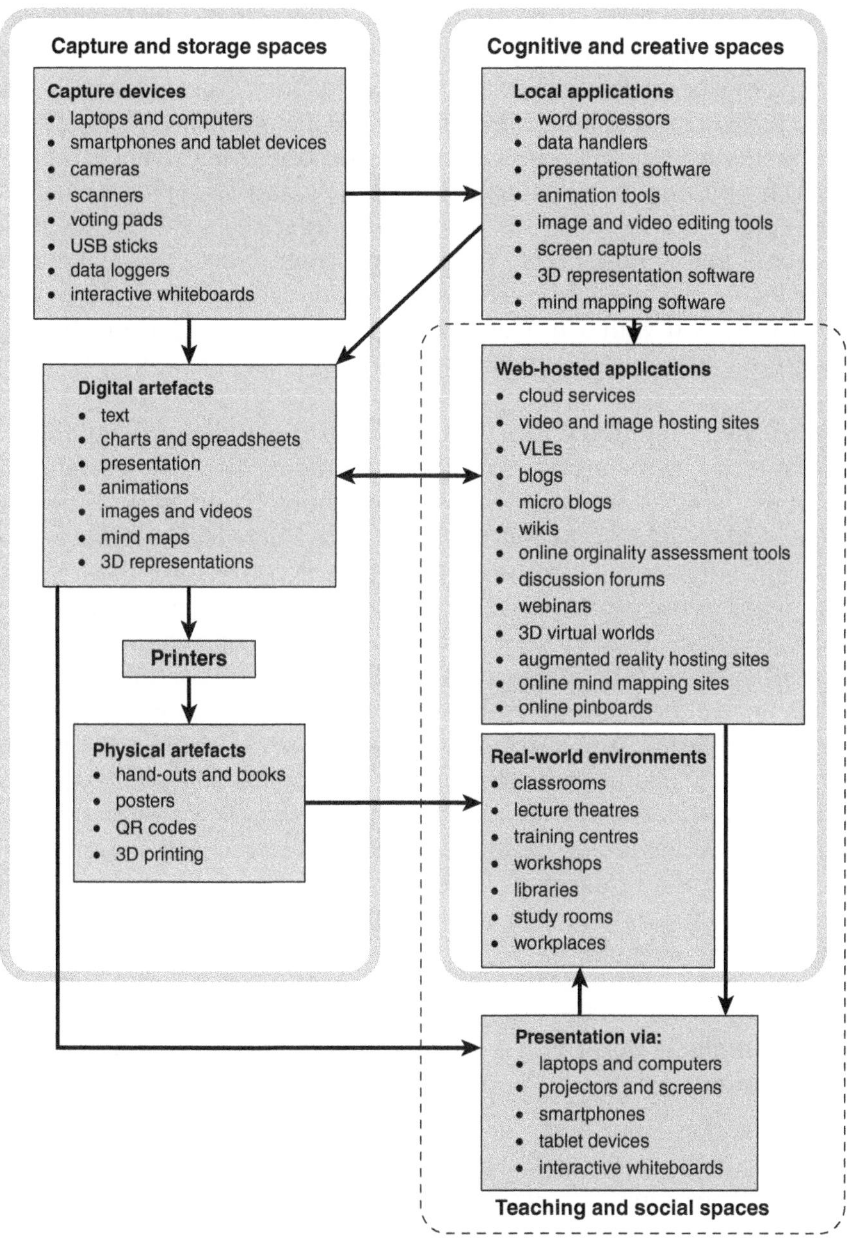

Figure 9.1 Using technology-enhanced learning

many of the web-hosted services listed in Figure 9.1, though often primarily used as cognitive, teaching and social spaces, also act as storage spaces where content can be retrieved at a future date. In particular, cloud storage is similar to data storage on your own computer except that the data is stored on remote servers and is accessible from, and can be synchronized between, various devices and shared with other individuals. Examples of this type of storage include Dropbox, Google Drive and Sky Drive. Editing Figure 9.1 is, in and of itself, a useful exercise that we invite you to attempt, arriving at your own representation of technologies that reflects the ways in which you and your learners typically use and understand them. We have represented them in this way as a starting point for the discussion which will follow in the rest of this chapter, which seeks to make use of Figure 9.1 in a series of worked examples and case studies. This, we hope, will provide you with a model that you could use to devise technology-enhanced solutions to a teaching or learning challenge within your own practice.

How, then, might you use Figure 9.1 to meet such a challenge? In general terms, we suggest that, after identifying the key learning outcomes that you want to achieve, you ask yourself which kinds of space are needed to achieve those outcomes and whereabouts on the figure you want your learners to be operating. Are you setting them solitary tasks where you want them to create or reflect as individuals or do you want them to work together in peer support networks? Do you want to be able to deliver a substantial amount of content to them in a didactic, teacher-centred fashion, or do you want them to be able to capture and record some data? You can then review Figure 9.1 to identify potentially useful technologies that might best suit your objectives. To illustrate this general approach in more detail, we offer here four examples. We have chosen them in order to cover four key phases in the teaching and learning process: designing learning, delivering learning, evaluating learning and flourishing through the further application of that learning.

9.2.1 Example 1: Designing a technology-enhanced approach to the training of nurses

One of the key challenges in subjects like nursing that have a strong practical component is ensuring that techniques demonstrated by tutors in practical sessions are adequately retained by the learners for application in their own, real-world working environments. The trainer cannot be with the learner on every occasion that the technique is employed and cannot therefore correct misconceptions or poor habits as frequently as might be desired in an ideal world. Similarly, a learner who has forgotten how to use a particular piece of equipment or carry out a particular procedure during their working practice may not have immediate recourse to help and support from busy colleagues. In this example, we explore how a technology-enhanced solution can be designed to overcome this problem. Our aim here is to provide a list of steps that could be used to design any number of different solutions that use technology to improve the teaching, training or learning experience. The chosen example is intended to illustrate how this might be done with a view to helping the tutor to identify the conceptual and practical affordances of the idea even before starting the work. This, it is hoped, will help you to make decisions and necessary arrangements or adjust the design of the learning activity if necessary.

Worked example of designing for learning using TEL

1. Identify the intended learning outcomes

Trainee nurses will be able to accurately and safely carry out an intravenous cannulation. This is the insertion of a hollow tube into a vein, usually in the arm, to allow either drainage or installation of substances for a short period of time.

2. Identify the kinds of space needed to attain this outcome

Since this outcome requires a reminder of a technique previously demonstrated by the tutor, what is required on this occasion is:

- a *capture and storage space* to lodge a video reminder of the technique
- a *teaching space* where the learners can view the video.

3. Select the most appropriate technologies from Figure 9.1

Tutors should consider the following points when selecting technologies:

- A widely available hosting site such as YouTube or Vimeo provides a good capture and storage space for video content.
- Since the aim is to provide taught input within the learners' own working environment, a mobile device or smartphone (a mobile phone with additional productivity applications, camera and multimedia functions) provides the most accessible and unobtrusive *teaching space* for this kind of intervention.
- As learners need a quick and easy way to retrieve the specific video on their mobile device, a Quick Response (QR) code (see Figure 9.2) helps to facilitate easy access to this teaching space.

Figure 9.2 QR code that links to a training video on intravenous cannulation

A QR code is an array of black and white squares as shown in Figure 9.2. It is used for storing a web address or other information for reading by the camera on a smartphone or tablet device. QR codes can be attached to the equipment or in accessible places within the workplace so that learners can quickly read the QR code and access the taught content.

4. Does the tutor need to develop new skills to facilitate this approach?

Tutors will need to have knowledge of some or all of the following:

- video capture and editing, or help from a technician with these skills
- a good, working understanding of data protection and copyright issues and ethics to ensure that any video content produced meets requirements
- uploading of video content to YouTube or another video hosting site (it is good practice to keep the original files as a backup, local copy)
- generation of a QR code that links to this video (this can be done easily by copying and pasting the web address of your video into a QR generator such as www.qrstuff.com)
- installation of a QR code reader onto a smartphone or tablet device for testing purposes.

5. Do learners need to develop new skills to facilitate this approach?

Learners will also need to install a QR code reader on a smartphone or tablet device and will need to be shown how to read the QR code by opening this software application (or 'app' as called in mobile and tablet devices) and then holding their camera steady over the code until it is read. They can then click to navigate to the video content and view it on their mobile device. There are a number of free QR code readers available for smartphone and tablet devices.

6. Do you and the learners have the necessary devices and support?

A video camera and preferably a tripod are required for this intervention. At this planning and designing stage, and having identified the preferred approach and requisite skills and equipment, it is important to check whether you and your learners have access to the necessary devices and support, before you invest time in a solution that could turn out not to be feasible.

7. Do you and your learners have the necessary access to these spaces?

Some institutions block access to popular video hosting sites like YouTube as a matter of policy. Check your organization's policy and if blocked, explore whether alternative platforms are allowed. Also, mobile usage is often banned in certain environments, particularly clinical ones, so check whether they are allowed in staff rooms or other areas that are close enough to the clinical environment to make retrieval on site feasible. Even if the internet connection is available, check if it is reliable, and has the required speed and capacity. Otherwise it may result in users unable to access the learning activity or resource and defeat all the work and thought that went into developing it.

8. Do you and your learners have the institution's permission or support to use this kind of approach?

Further to checking whether or not the sites you wish to use are blocked, it is also advisable to check the institution's policy with regard to internet access and mobile usage and even to specifically request permission to employ a novel approach of this kind before embarking on the intervention.

9. Are there ways in which you can make the content more interactive, engaging and motivating?

Clarity of video and audio content as well as lucidity and conciseness of presentation are important in making material of this kind engaging and productive. In addition, you may want to exploit the social affordances of video hosting sites. Videos on sites like YouTube and Vimeo can be commented upon and this may provide engaging opportunities for a *social space* for learners, where they can ask and answer questions of you and of one another.

10. Do you intend to assess the learning?

Opportunities for assessment may arise in a number of spaces for this intervention:

- Follow up practical sessions where learners demonstrate their cannulation technique offer opportunities to provide learners with feedback.
- The nature of any comments on the video hosting site can be used to give the tutor an indication of whether or not learners are developing a working understanding of cannulation.
- Learners could be provided with a *reflective space* such as a blog or e-portfolio where they could record their reflections on their developing skills with this procedure. This could be shared with you and others such as peers and mentors to provide learners with feedback on their reflections.
- Learners could be encouraged to capture video of their own cannulation technique to aid with this reflection. This would require that you provide opportunities for them to acquire the skills or access the help outlined in point (3) above.

11. Is the approach to learning design reusable and/or revisable in the same or different environment and is it sustainable?

- Video content of this nature is reusable but will need regular updating in response to changes to clinical guidelines. A monitoring and deletion policy is needed to make sure that outdated materials do not persist.
- Colleagues and learners could collaborate to produce content that can be shared across provision for a more sustainable and efficient approach.
- This kind of approach may transfer well to other practical subjects where learners need workplace reminders of specific tasks. These include scenarios within catering, hair and beauty, uniformed services, construction, engineering, and sport and exercise science.

9.2.2 Example 2: Delivery of a session on learning theory to trainee teachers through the use of a 'flipped classroom'

The example above focused on the challenge of delivering and supporting the development of practical skills. This second example considers instead the challenges of delivering theory. We highlighted earlier in the chapter the point that information is now much easier to come by than at any other point in human history: sites like iTunes U host videos and podcasts from Harvard professors; among the trivia and frivolity that makes up the bulk of YouTube lurks an enormous amount of serious academic and detailed professional information; Google Scholar gives access to an unprecedented library of journal articles and books, many of which have excerpts or the full text of the original; the list of available resources is endless. Our point in the introduction to this chapter was that where such information is accessible, classes or training sessions that are made up entirely of content delivery are out of place. Learners need to be given some other reason to turn up than simply being told things that they could easily learn elsewhere. One response to this dilemma is to 'flip' the classroom (EDUCAUSE, 2012). This means that participants are provided with content before the session rather than during it, so that when they arrive at the session itself, they are ready to ask questions about, and to discuss, apply, synthesize or evaluate that content. This kind of approach is often conceptualized as flipping the delivery with the 'homework' so that unlike traditional approaches, the delivery is done at home beforehand and the 'homework' is done in the classroom.

In the example that follows, we explore how technology can be used with a 'flipped' classroom approach to deliver learning theory within teacher education programmes. Trainee teachers require an understanding of a range of learning theories that they can use to identify their current approaches and to develop alternative ones that are congruent with the type and level of learner and their intended learning outcomes. Developing a confident grasp of the language of learning theory helps them to engage in analytical and evaluative discussions about their own practice and that of colleagues and this in turn means that they are able to contribute to broader discussions about education, what it is and what it ought to be. It is therefore an extremely important area of teacher education but one which, since it is one step removed from the day-to-day routines of teaching, is often a challenge to deliver in ways that foreground and develop the usefulness of the ideas covered. This example explores how a flipped approach can help to meet this and similar theoretical challenges. It assumes that the design stage explored in the first example has already been completed for this example and considers instead the detail of the next phase, which is the delivery itself. However, important considerations adopted in the design phase in order to arrive at this model included:

- What kind of spaces were required to facilitate the outcomes, including the development of a confident voice for learners when talking about theory?

- How much face-to-face time was available and what were the optimum uses of this time together in the classroom, in order to capitalize on the need for learners to develop confidence in discussing theory?
- What was the duration of the pre- and post-session online activity?
- What would be the delivery style adopted by the tutor, presenter or facilitator in the different phases of delivery?
- How could the face-to-face session and online activities be made interactive, engaging and motivating?
- Could the various sites of delivery cope with issues such as seeking support for any technology issues?

Worked example of the 'flipped classroom' approach to delivery

1. What were the learning outcomes being pursued?

Trainee teachers were developing their knowledge of learning theory so that they could use it to analyse and evaluate their own practice and to confidently discuss appropriate approaches to their own teaching.

2. How were technology-enabled spaces used during the delivery?

The capture, storage and teaching spaces used on this occasion were all provided by Google Sites at http://sites.google.com, which styles itself as 'the easiest way to make information accessible to people who need quick, up-to-date access' (Google, 2013). This platform enables a team-oriented approach for the sharing of resources and files, with comment functionality for readers' responses. Using this application, an introductory homepage was created with a left-hand menu linking to separate web pages on each of four key theories of learning: behaviourism, cognitivism, constructivism and humanism. These pages included a mixture of text, file attachments, images and video. The videos and file attachments were hosted on Google Drive, which gives privacy control. The homepage outlined the purpose and structure of the website and explained the approach and timescale for delivery.

- Before the face-to-face session:

Learners were sent a link to the Google Site on learning theory two weeks before the session and informed of the need to prepare for their taught session by studying the instructions and explanations on the homepage carefully. They were also allocated to one of four groups, each group concentrating on a particular theory. They were set the task of studying their theory in detail, asking questions about it or responding to the questions of others using the comment function on the website. It was impressed upon the learners that they would each be required to explain the theory which they had studied to members of the group who had been looking at alternative theories and so they needed to come to the session equipped with some knowledge and understanding of that theory in order to be able to take part.

- During the face-to-face session:

This was a three-hour session and occurred in a traditional classroom setting with tables arranged in four islands. The approach adopted was a 'jigsaw' method and followed three main phases (Petty, 2006: 144). In phase one, learners were grouped into 'home teams' with others who had studied the same theory as them in the pre-session online phase. On this occasion, then, the home teams were the behaviourists, the cognitivists, the constructivists and the humanists. These teams were given half an hour to devise a participative, engaging and collaborative 20-minute session that introduced their theory to learners from the other home teams. It was made clear to the learners at this point that they would be split up in the next phase so that each team member would be responsible for delivering their theory to a group unfamiliar with it. This fostered a shared sense of responsibility and ensured that every member made an important contribution. In this way, the classroom was being used simultaneously as a teaching, a cognitive and a social space.

In phase two, the teams were rearranged so that each contained members from every home team, and at least one behaviourist, one cognitivist, one constructivist and one humanist. They then took turns to deliver their prepared 20-minute session within these new groups. This fostered a lively, discursive and collaborative exchange, informed by the knowledge and understanding developed prior to the session through the website and through the planning that had occurred in the home teams during the first half hour. The tutor's role during this phase was to move around the groups, listening carefully, intervening where they could hear misconceptions or puzzlement and recording feedback for the whole group on the quality of the exchanges heard.

In phase three, the home teams reconvened for the final half hour and reflected on how their input had gone, adjusting their 20-minute plans accordingly and refining their session into a final, agreed format. They were also asked to discuss the application of the different theories that they had learnt about to their own practice as teachers and to record their ideas on this for an online follow-up activity. The tutor closed the session by providing feedback to the whole group on the overall quality of shared sessions and a perspective on the theories that underpinned the jigsaw approach adopted.

- After the face-to-face session:

The learners were instructed to check and reinforce their learning from the shared face-to-face session through studying all of the original theory pages on the website. Each home team was also provided with a new web page that they could collaboratively edit. A 'Help' menu item was set up with video demos showing learners how to edit these web pages and an email address to contact if they hit any technical difficulties. They were asked to post their finalized session plans there and given one week to feed back via this web page to the rest of the group on their discussion about the application of theory to their own working practice. This feedback included text, images and video and provided four new web pages which learners could use to explore how others used and applied theory as teachers in a range of contexts. As before, comments were used to ask and clarify questions. The tutor then fed back on these web pages, correcting any misconceptions and recognizing constructive and insightful contributions. The Google Site was therefore, like the classroom, being used as a teaching, a cognitive and a social space as well as a site for the capture and storage of ideas for later consumption.

9.2.3 Example 3: Evaluation of learning in a construction apprenticeship

In the first two examples, we considered the design and delivery of technology-enhanced learning. In this section, we turn to a more detailed consideration of how technology can help us to evaluate the impact of our teaching on our learners, finding out what we have taught well and what we might need to alter to teach more effectively in the future (Hattie, 2013: 9). In a traditional classroom, insight into what each and every learner is thinking can be time-consuming and difficult to obtain, with the danger that the session loses its sense of pace and purpose and becomes mired in evaluation of learning rather than the learning itself. Technology can offer an answer here through its scope to provide quick and efficient capture, storage and sharing of data for evaluation purposes. There are a number of ways in which this can be done, including through the use of classroom voting systems. However, since not all institutions or organizations possess such systems, this example exploits instead the affordances of the web application Padlet at http://padlet.com. The Padlet application provides a shared online space to allow the learners to 'pin' their ideas and questions to a shared, online 'pinboard' or 'wall'. While recognizing that in choosing Padlet we have focused on a particular tool that may evolve or become obsolete with time, we offer it here as illustrative of a set of affordances that are of use and value in the evaluation of learning and that might be sought in similar applications or solutions. Our aim, as with the previous examples, is to provide you with a list of questions that you could work through in order to design any number of different evaluative strategies using different technologies. The chosen example here is used for illustrative purposes and to help you to arrive at good, technology-enhanced evaluative strategies. The context through which we will explore this example is the teaching of tiling skills to a group of young adults as part of a construction apprenticeship.

Worked example of using Padlet for evaluation of learning

1. What are you evaluating?

The tutor and peer group will be able to gain insights into and evaluate the degree and type of learning that has occurred during a series of practical sessions on applying wall and floor tiling.

2. What kinds of space are needed to support this evaluation?

- a capture and storage space for learners' contributions
- an informal, responsive and flexible social space to allow peers and the tutor to evaluate one another's work and ideas.

3. Which are the most appropriate technologies from Figure 9.1?

An online pinboard was selected on this occasion. What was required was an informal and flexible environment where learners could 'pin up' photographs of their most recent projects and comment on one another's work (Figure 9.3). Both the pictures and the comments that learners made on the pinboard allowed the tutor to gain an insight into the level at which they were working and what they might be ready to do next in order to develop their skills further.

4. What are the affordances of the space that make it a good evaluative environment?

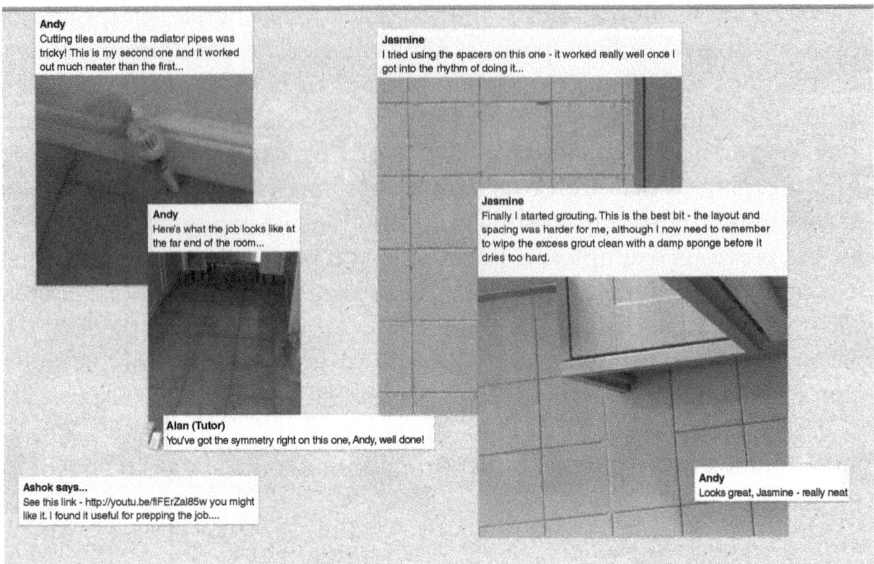

Figure 9.3 Padlet pinboard used by construction apprentices to report on their projects

http://padlet.com/wall/tve6vzxqn6

Through this kind of application, tutors and learners gain insight into the range of responses across the whole group. Learners can pin their contributions anywhere on the board and the board grows to accommodate contributions as they are posted. Learners can pin a comment or reply to anywhere on the board and this means that it is less hierarchical and structured than a standard discussion board. It is also highly visual, encouraging the learners to contribute images and videos. This suits the type and level of learner whose entry behaviour includes a preference for the visual rather than the written word. However, it also encourages the development of literacy and digital literacy through allowing written comments. The learners can also see their own performance or viewpoints much more clearly in relation to the rest of the group, giving them an additional perspective from which to evaluate their own learning. It is therefore potentially a very valuable tool for self-assessment and reflection as part of a developmental assessment cycle (Tummons, 2005).

5. How is the evaluation carried out?

The data generated can be used to measure the impact of the teaching on the learners' skills, knowledge and understandings. This data can be used as part of joint review activities in the classroom. As an example, a project from a learner, shared via Padlet, can be used as the prompt for a burst of 'assertive questioning' (Petty, 2006: 104) where the teacher asks for the responses of others in the group to the project, its merits and what they could suggest to their peer for future projects. This helps to stimulate different perspectives, comparing, contrasting and valuing different perspectives before the tutor offers a summing up of the discussion. In this way, the session becomes much more responsive to the learners' own work, making it more inclusive and engaging. In addition, the data can be explored in more detail after the event and the tutor can use it to inform their curriculum design for subsequent sessions as well as to identify learners who need more help or more challenge.

9.2.4 Example 4: Flourishing using a Twitter hashtag to discuss a topic, live or asynchronously

The cyclic stages of design, delivery and evaluation are discussed above through various worked examples. The learning development tends to stay within the context and space in which it is featured. This section considers the 'spinning-out' of those cycles and expanding learners' and practitioners' space to flourish further by engaging and networking with people outside the context and even from other disciplines.

Trying to arrange forums for discussion with relevant people can pose lots of practical and logistical problems. Technology can address some of those issues of time, space and gathering people with a shared interest. One way to do this would be joining a professional forum that is relevant in terms of discipline, subject or level and facilitating discussions. However, not all people might join the same forum or network. Another way would be to start one of your own which can be challenging and time-consuming, especially in terms of reaching the relevant audience and getting enough participants. Moreover, if everyone starts their own forum, it can soon lose the value of meaningful participation and networking. In addition managing registration and access to such networks could be another level to pass through before the actual engagement can happen.

Worked example of using hashtags

The example here focuses on using Twitter which is a micro-blogging site where people send short comments or information (tweets) about personal or professional issues, or share (retweet) similar updates from others. It brings some of the affordances of joining an existing network as well as starting your own discussion as you would in an online forum but with the openness and access to a wider audience, bringing the economies of scale which could increase the chances of having a useful dialogue. Many social networking sites use keywords or tags to group the threads or topics, making it easy for accessing. In Twitter, this is known as hashtags and 'can be seen as metadata, describing the content of a tweet; it enables users to search the subject of a tweet, rather than the specific content' (Minocha and Petre, 2012: 106).

The example we use here considers developing your professional identity through networking and engaging in professional discussions online through micro-blogging. This example would require participants to register a Twitter account and update their profile with relevant interests and expertise. In this scenario, a staff development trainer who is new to social media is trying to develop a Personal Learning Network (PLN) online. The trainer then searches Twitter for 'staff training design' and picks some discussion around how staff themselves need to feel part of the design and delivery of their training. Practicalities and tips are being both contributed and discovered by participants. The trainer notices a hashtag *#stafftraining* that appears in many relevant tweets and uses it in their own tweets to join the discussion. They then add some people who seem to tweet useful things to a new list 'trainers'. Sometimes the responses they get are immediate, as in a live chat, and sometimes, they come after a few days as they would in an asynchronous discussion forum. Over a few weeks, the trainer notices some people seem to respond more to queries and contributions; and then adds those people to a new list called 'mypln' (as in 'my personal learning network'). Thus, the trainer now only has to keep a close watch on the tweets from the list 'mypln' and to keep adding appropriate people to that list.

1. What are the opportunities and threats micro-blogging offers or poses for professional development?

The huge international spread of Twitter users and its increased use for learning activities and conferences offers great opportunities for personal and professional development. It is very useful for sharing concepts or news and getting feedback or comment. You could use a popular hashtag such as #loveLD (for enthusiasts about learning development) or follow up the conversation after an event using specific hashtags of your own. For example, the trainer above could suggest and agree particular discussion times with a specific #hashtag (e.g. '#staffdev') and interested parties could participate in a live chat, focusing within that topic area.

A point of caution to note in all online activity is that things you share publicly live longer or permanently. Care should therefore be taken when you are using such networks in a professional capacity. While initially the abundance of resources and information appears useful, if one does not have a strategy to filter them, they can soon accumulate and overwhelm with content which may not be of use and become a waste of time.

2. Could micro-blogging contribute to your evidence of development?

Specialist individuals or bodies you follow from your field, or the news and discussion you appear to be interested in or share, can show your understanding of your specialism and the currency of your awareness of the field. Such conversations could lead to collaborative projects or initiatives, which will show the direct impact of networking.

3. Does micro-blogging offer the affordance of sharing, collaborating, coaching, mentoring and networking?

As above, if managed well, micro-blogging offers great opportunities for working with others by sharing and receiving support and advice, and in turn, supporting others. It can lead to the development of an online or even face-to-face PLN.

4. How does micro-blogging contribute to the development of knowledge workers?

It enables networking and promotes currency of information. It develops the important skills of making decisions, especially in terms of filtering content, for example just by using or following particular hashtags or people. Through contextual topics, it develops participants' fluency in standard, international, subject-specific lexicons for everyday conversations about your work. For knowledge workers, it highlights the concept of, and provides opportunities for accessing, filtering and managing data as well as synthesizing it and disseminating new information.

9.3 Summary, case studies, discussion questions and learning activities

In this chapter, we have discussed the theory and application of TEL in a range of different contexts in order to provide some illustrative examples and ways of working with technology. Relating these scenarios to the potential digital literacy outcomes described in the opening section of the chapter, all of the examples and case studies, to varying degrees, provide some potential for development in this regard. For example, there are opportunities for learners to develop their navigation and search skills and their digital literacy in the use of QR codes, flipped classrooms, online pinboards and micro-blogging, personal network and professional identity formation, MOOC participation and blended learning. In particular, if they take part in online discussions or exchanges, they can develop their skills in community participation. If they create online reflections about their learning, there are opportunities to explore online security and privacy and any image, video creation and sharing that they engage in is a chance to develop their ability to compose, remix and code for the web, while observing copyright and data protection issues. Thus, these kinds of intervention are an excellent vehicle for developing applicable digital literacy among participants, which can transfer to other contexts in the future.

It is also possible to relate these examples to the learning theories outlined at the start of the chapter. The use of QR codes, for example, leads to highly situative learning opportunities, where the learning content is both temporally and spatially close to the site of use of that content. This, arguably, helps learners to more effectively transfer and apply learning within their own realistic working environments, than if they have had to retain that information over a period of time and to transfer it from one physical context to another. The potential for collaborative learning is also inherent in the examples chosen through the scope to make comments on and converse on video hosting sites, micro-blogs, blogs and online pinboards and through sharing online reflective journals. Finally, all of the approaches described above are fundamentally constructivist since they seek to build on the learners' existing understanding of their working environments and to help them relate their learning to the task in hand by accessing new information which is just beyond their current capabilities or knowledge.

9.3.1 Introduction to the case studies

The following case studies include scenarios, issues, solutions and questions around the use of technology-enhanced learning. They are inspired by the viewpoint of the French sociologist Michel Foucault. When considering the challenges of dealing with contemporary culture and social change he said, 'my point is not that everything is bad, but that everything is dangerous, which is not exactly the same as bad. If everything is dangerous then we always have something to do. So my position leads not to apathy but to a hyper- and pessimistic activism' (Foucault, 1997: 256). If we mimic this position, our response to technology ought to be as critical readers, wary of the dangers inherent in its use but poised to exploit its power to transform learning. To this end, we present here a series of cases that explain the nature of particular technological interventions, followed by questions to prompt a discussion that looks both for problems and opportunities inherent in the technologies suggested.

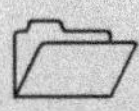

9.3.2 Case study Professional identity (incorporating e-portfolios)

The scenario:

In common with many vocational courses, the Apprenticeship in Agriculture, Horticulture or Animal Care requires learners to build a portfolio of evidence, through which they can show how they have fulfilled the requirements of the course. There are key benefits to the institution and to the individual of doing this through an e-portfolio, including retrievability of data for assessment and inspection purposes, and development of digital literacy. For the individual, it provides a space for the capture and storage of evidence as well as a cognitive and reflective workspace for the exploration and development of ideas and plans. This can then be shared with tutors, mentors and current or potential employers. In this case study, an e-portfolio tool was used by apprentices, which prompted them to create a home or profile page as an initial task.

The issue:

As part of this profile creation, as well as adding details about their current role and place of work, learners were prompted to upload a photograph or video of themselves. This appears on the 'homepage' of their portfolio. The issue that arose when this solution was deployed across a large cohort was that some learners made puzzling choices of image that were incongruent with the professional identity which they were seeking to establish in the rest of their portfolio.

Outcomes and solutions:

This proved to be a productive stimulus for debate around professional online identity through which apprentices were prompted to consider the importance of digital literacy and an awareness of their audience when making these kinds of choices in the future.

(Continued)

(Continued)

Question:

- Is it important for those training for professional roles to engage in the creation of an online identity as part of their course in order to allow them the scope to develop their digital literacy?

9.3.3 Case study Assessment analytics

The scenario:

Email was the main method being used for the submission of work at a large further education college in the UK. Tutors would routinely annotate this work in a word processing application or print it out and handwrite their feedback on the learners' scripts.

The issue:

An Ofsted college inspection of this provision identified the limited use of assessment data as a weakness. While it was clear that the progression of individual learners was being carefully monitored and used as part of a developmental dialogue on a one-to-one basis, the institution was criticized for not tracking cohort-wide data and was prompted to look for ways to more closely monitor patterns of achievement across large provision.

Outcomes and solutions:

Electronic assessment was introduced to resolve this issue. The GradeMark application, which is part of the Turnitin suite of tools from iParadigms, was used. Tutors could use this to correct common grammatical and spelling errors, by dragging and dropping pre-written comments onto the learners' work from what is called a QuickMark palette. This freed up marking time for tutors to engage with more complex and challenging aspects of the learners' work, such as the content, composition or style of the work. A GradeMark report could then be generated showing the overall frequency of the use of particular QuickMark comments across the whole cohort.

Questions:

- What are the potential benefits and drawbacks of the use of this kind of system?
- In what ways could the data generated by the GradeMark report be used by the institution and by tutors?

9.3.4 Case study Personal development networking

The scenario:

Conferences and professional conventions are an important developmental opportunity for many professionals, both in terms of the sessions, presentations and keynotes that they hear and the networks that they develop with other people.

The issue:

The percentage of people with whom you come into contact at such events tends to be limited by the time available and by chance meetings, based on proximity in sessions or at social or break out events.

Outcomes and solutions:

Increasingly, conferences publish a Twitter hashtag for the event. For example, the hashtag for the Association for Learning Technologies Conference in 2013 was #altc2013. Delegates at that event were invited to include the characters #altc2013 in their tweets about the event. Clicking on the hashtag in any of these tweets brings up a stream of all the tweets that contain that same string of characters. Tweeting tends to occur in the run up to the event, during keynotes and sessions and for a short period after the event. This increases the potential to gain insight into the responses of a wider group of people and to identify those with a shared interest or with whom one would like to network. Twitter also provides a way for delegates to contact one another by using an '@ reply.'

Questions:

- Are there ways in which hashtags and @ replies could be used for an event or session that you are planning?
- What are the potential benefits and drawbacks?

9.3.5 Case study MOOCs

The scenario:

MOOCs are 'massive open online courses'. They are a relatively new phenomenon, whereby educational institutions publish materials and activities on the internet and allow anybody from anywhere in the world to sign up and participate in an online course around those

(Continued)

(Continued)

materials. Participation generally takes the form of reading materials, watching videos, listening to podcasts, taking part in discussion forums, completing online quizzes and creating blogs that respond to the content of the course.

The issue:

MOOCs, particularly those run by large and powerful organizations such as Harvard and Stanford, can attract tens of thousands of participants. MOOCs, however, tend to have a very high dropout rate, and while the attrition is high, the accreditation of those who do make it through to the end of the course is problematic, since they are difficult for institutions to assess because of the number of people taking part. The exchange value in the job market of qualifications gained in this way is, therefore, questionable.

Outcomes and solutions:

The benefits of MOOCs are that they allow people who might otherwise not have access to this kind of content to participate and develop as professionals.

Questions:

- Can completion of MOOCs form a useful part of a continuing professional development programme:
  - in terms of the content covered by participants?
  - in terms of the participant's CV and employability?

9.3.6 Case study Blended learning

The scenario:

A part-time degree course at a UK University was asked to alter its mode of delivery from weekly attendance at a 3-hour evening class to a blended approach whereby learners attended for only 5 Saturday day-schools, spaced throughout the year, with online support between day-schools.

The issue:

The course team felt that much of the learning on the degree was achieved through the discussions that happened in the classroom and that the social elements of the course were also important for retention, achievement and as part of an overall positive experience of education. To make up for the decrease in social contact inherent in the new, blended learning model, Facebook was considered as a platform for fostering relatively informal, though still somewhat academic exchanges between learners. However, it was felt that the adverts and the 'noise' of the wider social world on Facebook would be too much of a distraction from the course and would not provide learners with a sense of focus and privacy that was important for some in their studies.

Outcomes and solutions:

An alternative platform called Yammer was identified that had many of the social affordance of Facebook but was advert-free and could be set up as a 'walled garden' where only tutors and students of the degree course could participate.

Question:

- Was this a satisfactory solution to foster social presence among tutors and learners? Were there benefits and drawbacks to doing this in an online environment rather than face-to-face?

References

Belshaw, D. and Casilli, C. (2013) *Web Literacy Standard* https://wiki.mozilla.org/Learning/WebLiteracyStandard (accessed 1 November 2013).

Brown, J. S., Collins, A. and Duguid, P. (1989) 'Situated cognition and the culture of learning', *Educational Researcher*, 18 (1): 32–42.

Dewey, J. (1933) *How We Think: A Restatement of the Relation of Reflective Thinking to the Educative Process* (2nd edn). London: D. C. Heath.

EDUCAUSE (2012) *7 Things You Should Know about Flipped Classrooms*. http://net.educause.edu/ir/library/pdf/eli7081.pdf (accessed 1 November 2013).

Foucault, M. (1997) 'On the genealogy of ethics: an overview of work in progress', in P. Rabinow (ed.), *Michel Foucault – Ethics: Subjectivity and Truth, the Essential Works of Michel Foucault 1954–1984, Vol. 1*. New York: The New Press, pp. 253–280.

Garrison, D. R. and Vaughan, N. D. (2008) *Blended Learning in Higher Education: Framework, Principles, and Guidelines*. San Francisco, CA: Jossey-Bass.

Google (2013) *Google Sites Overview*. www.google.com/sites/overview.html (accessed 19 November 2013).

Hattie, J. (2013) 'Know thy impact: teaching, learning and leading', *In Conversation*, 4 (2): 18. www.edu.gov.on.ca/eng/policyfunding/leadership/spring2013.pdf (accessed 19 November 2013).

Kolb, D. (1984) *Experiential Learning: Experience as the Source of Learning and Development*. Englewood Cliffs, NJ: Prentice-Hall.

McLuhan, M. (1994) *Understanding Media: The Extensions of Man*. Cambridge: First MIT Press.

Minocha, S. and Petre, M. (2012) *Handbook of Social Media for Researchers and Supervisors: Digital Technologies for Research Dialogues*. www.vitae.ac.uk/policy-practice/567271/Handbook-of-social-media-for-researchers-and-supervisors.html (accessed 19 November 2013).

Petty, G. (2006) *Evidence-based Teaching: A Practical Approach*. Cheltenham: Nelson Thornes.

Sfard, A. (1998) 'On two metaphors for learning and the dangers of choosing just one', *Educational Researcher*, 27 (2): 4–13.

Tummons, J. (2005) *Assessing Learning in Further Education: Meeting the National Occupational Standards*. Exeter: Learning Matters.

Wesch, M. (2009) 'From knowledgeable to knowledge-able: learning in new media environments', *Academic Commons*, 7 January.

CHAPTER 10

REFLECTIVE PRACTICE AND CPD

Kevin Orr, Jane Wormald and Kate Lavender

Learning outcomes

After reading this chapter, the reader should be able to:

- Understand the relevance of reflection to continuing professional development (CPD).
- Identify the tensions around effective engagement with reflective practice.
- Explore ideas to implement models of reflection in day-to-day practice.
- Identify strategies for enhancing personal and career aims through CPD and reflective practice.

Chapter outline

This chapter examines continuing professional development and what this might mean for practitioners in education and training. How CPD is understood affects the choices that practitioners make as well as the opportunities that are available to them. We will identify how practitioners might decide what CPD they want or need. Reflective practice is included here as an aspect of professional development. This chapter discusses what is meant by reflection and the way it is perceived and used, drawing on some key influential writers in this area. There follows some useful reflective models that are outward looking, while also challenging a superficial or merely introspective engagement with 'reflection' that dilutes its value. This chapter will be applicable to those new to reflective practice and to support more experienced practitioners with suggestions of how to embed reflective practice into education or training. Further reading and more in-depth analyses of the ideas explored in this chapter can be found in the references at the end.

10.1 Underpinning theory

This chapter discusses some definitions of CPD in relation to the disputed concept of professionalism. The examination of reflective practice centres on ideas that were initially introduced by Dewey and subsequently developed by theorists such as Schön. His ideas of *reflection-on-action* and *reflection-in-action* are introduced. These concepts have informed various models of reflective practice; this chapter, however, focuses particularly on models developed by Kolb (1984), Gibbs (1988), Johns (2000) and Brookfield (1995).

10.2 Developing CPD: theory and practice

Ongoing professional development subsequent to initial training is a requirement for very many professions. School teachers in the United Kingdom have had five compulsory in-service training (INSET) days per annum since 1988; solicitors must complete 16 hours of continuing professional development each year; CPD is a requirement of the Chartered Society of Physiotherapy; and the Chartered Institute for Personnel and Development (CIPD) stipulate 35 hours per annum for members. But what is CPD and who is it for? For the CIPD (2013), it 'is a combination of approaches, ideas and techniques that will help you manage your own learning and growth'. This certainly implies that CPD is 'a good thing' but such a nebulous description is characteristic of many definitions of CPD. This is unfortunate because CPD may be laudable and wholesome but it can also be all things to all people regardless of its quality or impact. While for Beevers and Rea (2010: 18)

CPD 'is the action we take to maintain, update and grow the knowledge and skills required for our professional role', the Institute for Learning's (IfL) (2009) definition of CPD is rather more useful because it involves the effect of the development:

> CPD means maintaining, improving and broadening relevant knowledge and skills in your subject specialism and your teaching and training, so that it has a positive impact on practice and the learner experience.

It is still, however, a very broad description. That may be inevitable, however. There are three main reasons why understandings of CPD are so often rather vague: no one is against CPD as such (though they may understand the concept in very diverse ways) so the concept is rarely critically examined or discussed; CPD is often individually organized and so necessarily is defined according to the needs of the individual; and finally CPD relates directly to professionalism, which is itself a slippery and controversial term. Stronach et al. (2004) are justified in arguing that professionalism is an overused and imprecise word. This section attempts to unpick what CPD might mean as well as what it might involve for those working in education and training. The intention is to get you to think critically about the decisions you make for your own professional development so that it might bring about the meaningful 'learning and growth' to which the CIPD refer.

Let's start by unpicking the idea of professionalism to help you decide what it means for you and your development. It is argued that, 'Few professionals talk as much about being professional as those whose professional stature is in doubt' (Katz, 1969: 71) and although this was written about nurses the same might be said of practitioners involved in education and training. Professionalism is a term that once applied to a limited range of roles such as lawyers and doctors but has in modern times been extended to cover almost any group of employed workers. Its meaning can be as bland as describing someone who does their job well or it can refer to membership of a closed group, such as the bar for barristers. Reflection is at the heart of much CPD and it is examined closely elsewhere in the chapter. For the purposes of this discussion of CPD, however, there are three elements of professionalism that will be highlighted. These are: responsibility to the public (in our case that will normally mean our learners); responsibility to the rest of the profession (our colleagues in and beyond our organization); and the autonomy of decision-making that is integral to being a professional. This understanding of the professional as an individual within a social setting, and especially the professional practitioner in education and training, can help to identify appropriate CPD activities. Importantly, it can help to demonstrate how those activities have affected the individual professional's understanding and practice by looking at professional relationships. Just as importantly, seeing the professional within a social, economic and political context also helps to expose just what the individual practitioner can and cannot control or influence.

Let's first of all examine responsibility to the public, which is behind the notion of CPD maintaining a professional's 'licence to practise'. This implies that regular professional development maintains currency of knowledge and techniques, which in turn maintains competence to engage with the public as a practitioner. This obligation, as noted above, is central to many professions including accountants and nurses and until recently was a statutory requirement for those teaching and training in the publicly funded learning and skills sector in Britain. The removal of this statutory obligation, following the Final Report of the Independent Review Panel on Professionalism in Further Education (often referred to as the Lingfield Review), which had been set up by the Minister of State for Further Education, Skills and Lifelong Learning (DBIS, 2012), is certainly controversial. It also coincides with the removal of public funding and statutory obligations from the IfL, the professional body for learning and skills in the UK. Nevertheless, there is the clear intention from this influential review that CPD for education and training practitioners should be encouraged, albeit not required by law. They recommend that a 'duty [be] placed on employers to support continuing professional development in both the occupational and pedagogic realms through an appropriate allowance of study opportunities and time (at least 30 hours each year)' (DBIS, 2012: 25). The review also recommends a similar duty on practitioners 'to participate in activities intended continuously to enhance their performance' (DBIS, 2012: 25).

Such an obligation to maintain competence underpins the important role of the education and training practitioner within society and recognizes the duty to update in order to continue to play that role. For practitioners in education, training and organizational development, that means developing both subject and pedagogical knowledge, as we explore below in the section on dual professionalism.

The Lingfield review (DBIS, 2012: 21) was even clearer about the second element we are highlighting here: the collegiate nature of professionalism, in this case specifically for practitioners in the further education (FE) sector:

> The Review panel is convinced that the essence of professionalism lies in the applicability of the word 'colleague'. Is there a sufficient sense of shared identity, of solidarity, among those who teach across the wide variety of organizations in FE to justify their regarding one another as colleagues? Our answer to that question is an emphatic 'Yes'.

The emphasis on the word 'colleague' rather than what that entails conceptually or practically may strike some as peculiar. It may even seem like a rather loose foundation on which to build professionalism. Nonetheless, professionals have a responsibility to each other, not least to uphold the values of their profession. Moreover, many would say that CPD organized and carried out collectively, among groups of colleagues, is particularly developmental because professional knowledge is produced and applied collectively. People work in teams so they should develop in teams. This might mean peer observations of sessions, or critical friendship groups to review initiatives or resources.

The final element, professional autonomy, is especially significant with regard to CPD. It is useful to make the distinction between staff development, promoted by the organization in pursuit of organizational goals, and professional development, which is identified by the professionals themselves. This is not to say that one is more valuable than the other; both have their place and their value. There may, furthermore, be considerable overlap between the two. For this discussion, however, we are concerned more with development that has been selected and pursued by the professional, often alongside colleagues, rather than development that is required by their employer. We are, therefore, concerned with development that has been identified as a result of professional autonomy. This distinction between staff and professional development has become important in the sector. As long ago as 1997 Randle and Brady (1997: 232) recognized a rift between practitioners and certain managers in what was understood by common values:

> Traditionally, staff and managers aspired to a common set of educational values, encompassing the notion of professional expertise and some discretion in design, delivery and assessment of provision … [which is] being replaced by a new type of manager primarily concerned with resource management, particularly financial resources.

This recollection of a shared aspiration is rather overstated and in any case Randle and Brady's research only related to colleges. Nevertheless, what they observed about the management culture may be discernible elsewhere in the sector. In a similar vein Grundy and Robison (2004: 147) identified two incentives for professional development, which they refer to as 'systemic and personal'. In the English further education and skills sector the systemic has been the major impetus for development since the first introduction of professional standards by the government in 1999. These were at first voluntary, then they had statutory force, and now once again they are nominally voluntary. That matters, but the broader point that arises from the dichotomy described above is this: to what extent should professionalism, and therefore CPD, be constructed around compliance with institutional and national policies, and to what extent should professionalism and CPD be under the control of the individual practitioner? Cullingford (2002) suggests that institutions need to embrace the creative tension of the interdependence between professional development and their own institutional needs. This may be commendable but finding an appropriate balance or symbiosis is not straightforward because it is affected by funding at least as much as it is affected by any individual's sensibilities. The social, economic and political context matters, as highlighted above. At the heart of this issue, however, is what constitutes ethical behaviour. If CPD is to mean more than just learning about a new online register or a new course curriculum (though both may be useful), then we should be able to recognize and articulate our professional values. Those values need to be articulated in order for them to be challenged: 'Trust me, I'm a professional', does not suffice. Those values, that is what the professional believes is right and wrong, should underpin and direct CPD. So, as a start to undertaking CPD you might consider what type of professional you are and what type of professional you aspire to be. Once you have thought about that and reached some conclusions, then you can decide what that means for your own ongoing development. You can turn theory about professional development into practice.

10.2.1 Should all CPD be documented?

Many training organizations and professional bodies require professional development to be logged and audited, which in some cases is simply a matter of adding up the hours to reach the required number. It is certainly worth checking any requirements to which you are subject. But apart from demonstrating what you have done so others can measure it, is documenting CPD inherently useful? Whether documented or not, learning takes place even if we are not immediately conscious of it. Sometimes this can be discerned as becoming used to a situation (often expressed as a growth in confidence) or as absorbing the work practices and language of those with whom we work. What we learn in this way, however, is not necessarily good or useful. Negative or cynical attitudes to learners are learnt in the same manner as more positive attitudes, for example. So, documenting professional learning for one's own use may help to recognize and evaluate professional development, especially in relation to an individual's articulated values. This may be particularly important for informal learning beyond training courses and qualifications, because recognizing that learning may help us to better harness and direct it.

A record of your CPD may also simply remind you about what you have learnt and so provide a synopsis of your professional development. This might also enable you to consciously plan your career so that you develop and attain what you require to move on. It may also be helpful to regularly update your curriculum vitae (CV) so that you can show future employers what you have done. Keeping a learning journal or log may be a good place to begin all of this. A learning log is a personal document that records not just the courses you have done but also what you gained from them and how you might apply what you have learned. You may also record informal learning from critical incidents or discussions with colleagues.

10.2.2 Dual professionalism

The term dual professionalism has been used to describe how practitioners in the further education and skills sector need to have expertise in their subject or vocational area as well as in the pedagogy related to teaching or training in that area. The idea of dual professionalism rests on there being two sets of knowledge and skills for practitioners and each of those sets needs to be addressed through CPD. The dichotomy between the two may not always be clear (can you teach something well if you do not fully understand it?) but planning CPD, including reflection, to involve both aspects of your practice may be helpful.

10.2.3 How should I organize my CPD?

Elsewhere in this chapter we discuss models of reflection and how reflective learning may be incorporated into your practice. The structured examination of your practice that reflection implies may expose or highlight areas of knowledge that you wish to enhance, which will help you to plan CPD. Remember that you should primarily direct the professional development you require. Although CPD is necessarily a consciously planned process it does not just involve formal courses or training events. It might also include discussions with peers or mentors, reading relevant literature, or observing a colleague, for example. Responding to these questions might help you decide the CPD that you want to pursue. Many of the questions below will take careful consideration as well as research to find out what is available, but what is important is to be as precise as you can be. Be aware that not all that you have learnt and not all the changes you have made may be positive.

10.2.4 The kind of practitioner you are

What philosophy or ethical stance supports your practice? One way to think about this is to describe what you consider a good practitioner to be like.

- What does that mean for your practice? You might think about the ways that you were taught or trained and whether you wish to act differently or not.
- How would you like learners to experience your practice during your sessions? This is about seeing how you practise from the perspective of your learners to judge if there is congruence between how you would like to practise and what you currently do.

In the light of the answers to these questions, what do you wish to change or improve in your knowledge or practice? Be as specific as you can be. This is when writing a plan is particularly useful as the process of writing may itself help to inform and clarify your thoughts.

10.2.5 Your previous professional development

- How have you changed as a professional since you started practising?

You may conclude that you are more confident, but what does that mean and is it necessarily a good thing? You might also want to examine your motivation and enthusiasm, too.

- What have you learned from your formal CPD in the last six months or two years?

This is about the courses or events you have attended. Describe how what you have learned has informed and changed your practice.

- What have you learned informally?

Here you should think about what you have observed from colleagues or what you have taken away from discussions in your office or staffroom.

It might also be what you have learned about new legislation or institutional policy in your area. Again, describe how what you have learned has informed and changed your practice.

10.2.6 Your career aims

- Where do you want to be and what do you want to be doing in (for instance) six months, five years and ten years? Again, be specific.
- In the short and longer term what do you need to do to help achieve these aims? You may need to re-train if the courses to which you currently contribute are about to lose funding or have reached saturation, for example. There may be a need for you to start a long course such as a part-time degree to gain a different job, perhaps.

Reflection can become a useful practice to begin to understand and explain new learning. The following section discusses what is meant by reflective learning.

10.3 Reflective learning: theory and practice

Reflection has a multitude of meanings depending on its purpose and its depth of analysis when reviewing past events. It ranges from levels of descriptive accounts of incidents that have happened, to an astute awareness of self and others in the context of multiple perspectives including the cultural, social, political and historical.

Practitioners often teach in the way they see and wish to portray themselves. Most draw on and relate to ways in which they have previously absorbed experiences, whether conscious or not, or in purposeful strategies to meet a particular end, for instance a business model or behavioural intervention. We often replicate, sometimes unconsciously, techniques and ways of teaching or training that we have ourselves experienced. As most of us are aware, these can range from brilliant to dubious! Reflective learning offers an opportunity to continually and purposefully consider how, why and what we do. It allows us to capture and examine experiences in order to negotiate a growing understanding of what has occurred or been understood. In turn, this lets us consider how we may react in future practice. This applies for learners at any level or stage of education or training. Learning through reflection is essentially a considered audit of the known, the new and the potential of knowledge and understandings. It may include how the learner and others recognize the impact or significance of their actions or thoughts.

The models and examples that follow are just some ways to develop reflective learning and practice. They ask you, the practitioner, to think beyond describing 'what happened' to consider the context, how and why something happened the way it did, and then to consider how that can inform future activity.

10.3.1 Importance and relevance of reflection

Reflective learning has become widely accepted in educational and business environments as essential to good practice. However, it can also be ineffective or even negatively effective if it is trivialized, diluted or superficially engaged with. The business world needs snappy yet astute and effective responses to survive; yet learners need to absorb, understand, build and project new ideas.

How practitioners conceptualize their own teaching and learning often links to how this is made effective in their professional role. We live in an ever-busy and competitive work world and our use for 'reflection' and reflective models can tend to become too focused on rapid communication of the key ideas and needing fast, effective techniques to do this. Many reflective theories have been adapted and simplified and the business world has picked up on some effective, easy access models that make 'reflection' quicker. Some models are detailed and prescriptive, so easy to checklist. These models allow access to a larger audience and may step a little way along the road to reflective practice, but this light touch engagement can also be criticized as being reductive and likely to miss crucial inferences. Too often active reflective practice, while acknowledged as important, is either skimmed or sidelined, criticized as introspective musings, or learners are asked to complete written reflections in isolation, as an additional rather than a central task. Many busy professionals find it hard to find time to capture written reflections that appear to be solely for the purpose of assessment. Frequently, individual reflections are encouraged through an increasing necessity to track and prove competence, rather than engaging with collaborative discussion and co-constructing knowledge and understandings. Developments in technology may change the way we can capture and display our own and co-constructed reflections. Some innovative use of electronic blogs is used in some educational institutions, providing opportunities to evidence reflections in various interactive formats. This type of creative collection comes closer to the forms of reflective learning fore-fronted by some of key writers discussed below and also more closely reflects the skills and attributes that we are told are necessary for employability in the twenty-first century, for instance, creative, holistic and diverse thinking, collaborative knowledge construction, flexible cognitive and practical application to roles and research. This type of process for learning also enables individuals to be flexible to change and to be able to transfer these reflective skills to be effective in any context, being of crucial benefit to the lifelong learner in any field.

10.3.2 So what is reflective learning: navel-gazing or conscious dialogue?

In its simplest form reflection can be defined as how we consider experiences, how and why they occur and then what can be instigated in order to change or improve that experience in the future.

Educational pioneer Dewey (1933) first identified reflective thinking as having a primary purpose to address and then importantly enable challenge to one's own preconceived and assumed understandings. He suggested that reflective practitioners need three characteristics: those of being open-minded, responsible and wholehearted in order to be able to think something through and to effectively action change. Subsequent models devised to develop reflection rarely forefront the latter as a central attribute and it is perhaps why reflection can sometimes be experienced or criticized as ineffectual and lightweight pondering.

In the world of education, Kincheloe (2008) shares a view of most critical educators by suggesting that practitioners are very rarely encouraged to identify and challenge the way they think and act, particularly in their relationship to the social, cultural, political, economic and historical world around them. Given time to reflect in this meaningful manner acknowledges the wider influences on us as practitioners and on that of our learners. It reduces an inward looking and self-absorbed reflection, often described as 'navel-gazing', and becomes more outward looking, considering your individual impact on the wider world and its influence on you, those around you and your practice. Crucial to this perspective is engagement with others in the use of these understandings to enable individual and community-based change. This is not a superficial exercise, but demands a responsibility to the task, to be open-minded, critical, analytical, honest and enthusiastic in order to effect positive change.

These features form what could be identified as a conscious practitioner, where reflection is not self-orientated, yet has an awareness of how one's own identity is constructed and how it is constantly changing. It could include aspects of autobiography that is conscious of elements identified by Kincheloe (2008) that shape identity and consciousness, but also contextualizes self in the experience and locale of others, and towards a common good. With the more intense depth of this type of reflection, there is also a developing awareness of the diversity of the world and of the factors that shape the distribution of power. With new understandings of differing perspectives and experiences, there can be considerable internal disorientation as we challenge our previously absorbed values and perceptions. This can, however, develop understandings and the vocabulary to enable positive change in ourselves and in the world around us.

To find a way into this reflective interrogation, there are many models to explore, some of which are given as suggestions of practical application later in the chapter. An effective introduction might be through Kolb's (1984) integration of Dewey's ideas in his useful 'learning cycle' including: experiencing something, reflectively observing it, learning from the experience, planning and then trying out a new approach, which in turn is reflected upon. It is an accessible example of one type of reflection. A similar 'reflective cycle' by Gibbs (1988) is popular in healthcare professions and in education. While being an accessible model, it can be criticized for its focus on bettering the same outcome, maybe useful for a business or in some professions, but lacking questioning and alternative practice that may bring about a more creative solution or approach (Zeichner and Liston, 1996). Reflective learning can be experienced and adopted at many levels. A broad view of regularly thinking about and considering your practice is generally regarded as a positive attribute, you think about what you do and aim to do better. The depth of reflection will then depend on the quality of interaction with the problem or in understanding the experience noted.

Schön (1987) was central to what is defined as 'reflective practice' that is, a focus on positive practical outcomes from thinking about what we do and subsequently, or concurrently, acting on that observed understanding. He called these 'reflection-on-action' and 'reflection-in-action'. Schön's ideas have been developed in many forms and found great prominence in healthcare and educational practice and teaching.

As teaching or training practitioners, an ability to examine views, judgements and assumptions also means examining personal and professional values. Repeated examining and testing of experiences and thinking allow a practitioner to develop a 'knowing-in-action' (Schön, 2000: 59), an increasingly intuitive response based on experience. This can be very useful, though it could also be limiting in its unfaltering reaction, rather than in a continually developing response to the experience. Lack of experience of understanding of your own or others' reactions can lead to unconsidered patterns of response that may not be helpful and may even be damaging.

Many of us recognize the notion that we simply 'know' things, we intuitively know how to react in situations or are able to do things without thinking, but also find it hard to put this into words. Polanyi's (1967) term *tacit knowledge* is where we become immediately skilful in reaction, or we understand or recognize something directly without going through a reasoning process. Schön (1987: 29) links this tacit knowledge to a situation that he describes as 'knowing-in-action' but draws a subtle distinction between that and reflection. As Polanyi talks about making the implicit explicit, so Schön encourages practitioners to reflectively analyse the components that enable you to 'reflect-in-action' (Schön, 1987: 31) and make subtle, seemingly intuitive changes but at the same time to be aware of these changes so the action becomes 'knowledge-in-action' (Schön, 2000: 49).

Brookfield, a leading adult educator, offers a useful response to viewing the practitioner's own practice by challenging assumptions of how you see, respond to and understand the world. He identifies four 'critical lenses' (1995: 29) to critically reflect the perspective of others as well as your own. Importantly, he includes not only the perspective of those directly engaged in learning:

1. the practitioner
2. the learner
3. colleagues
4. the specialist literature in the subject field.

More recently 'critical' reflection has also required a consciousness of the impact that we make on the wider world and its influence on us. A 'critically reflective' approach requires consideration of socially just responses to, and understandings of, our behaviours following reflection, where the depth of critical engagement in learning allows a panoramic understanding. This is sometimes noted as a social rather than individual perspective and approach to reflection. As an educational practitioner, a critical reflection would consider all the influences and relationships impacting on a situation (a 360 degree or all-round view), rather than respond automatically on the basis of prior experiences; this approach may require considered experimentation. Some (for example, Valli, 1992) also will include the importance of understanding moral and ethical aspects in a definition of effective reflection and most identify the importance of dialogue to weigh up different viewpoints and to explore different solutions.

A further expansion of critically reflective practice includes 'reflexivity' which features all the characteristics of critical reflection with an increased self-analysis and a politically charged dynamic requiring action for social, political or emancipatory adaptation or change.

10.3.3 So, can reflective learning be taught?

The work of Rogers (1995), in his humanist approach for education, has parallels with many current educators' thoughts and practice when he identified that he could not teach another person how to teach, but rather could act as a facilitator or enabler for learning. He argued that central to success in all interactions in learning contexts was the trust, respect and understanding of the practitioner to each learner in order to effectively engage learning. The practitioner can offer ways to the learner of expanding thinking, supported by existing models to open possibilities to engage in learning through a reflective process. These signposts to understanding and exploration indicated by the practitioner allow a way in for the learner to acknowledge new perspectives and to allow ownership of purposeful change. The consideration of perspectives of human, social, scientific, historical, ethical, cultural and political contexts allows the learner to have a deeper engagement with the broader influences that shape both individuals and whole communities.

As we have seen there are numerous models from simplistic to holistic. A surface or half-hearted approach is ineffectual, as the reflective learner needs deep engagement for the process to have purpose or reason. Reflective learners are inquisitive and open-minded, share and learn from collaborative engagement, take responsibility and then look forward with the wholeheartedness that Dewey identified. These attributes and skills enable ownership; learners have to take responsibility for truly engaging in their own reflections in order to learn expansively.

10.4 Embedding learning

Practitioners are increasingly required to undertake reflection and self-evaluation in order to facilitate effective personal and professional development. Structured reflective practice is used in a number of professions such as teaching and social care, but is rarely used in other, more technical forms of learning and training. While many practitioners would consider that they actively engage in reflection on a day-to-day basis, rarely do they engage actively in a conscious way. Schön (2000) considers this type of subconscious reflection as 'reflection-in-action' or 'thinking while doing' and while practitioners need to be able to think on their feet they also need to engage in another form of reflection – 'reflection-on-action'. For Schön, practitioners become more expert in their profession when they move away from relying on convention and procedures within a particular practice and start to take time to reflect on situations in order to refine their practice. The reason for this is that professional practice is increasingly complex and messy and conventions and procedures will not always provide the best solutions, therefore being able to adapt practice in unpredictable situations is essential. The idea of taking time to step back and analyse practice after the event is therefore what Schön considers reflection-on-action.

Often the idea of reflecting on practice after the event can seem mystifying or even pointless to learners especially when it is conceived as a constraint on their time. Lack of understanding about the relevance of reflecting-on-action is a barrier to most learners and stops them from getting the most out of reflective practice. Learners will often write reflective logs as required for their formal learning but without a structured approach to reflection, those logs are rarely more than a diary account of what happened and how they felt. A structured approach to reflection allows learners to complete a reflective cycle and see the benefits of reflective practice more clearly.

The benefits of developing a structured approach to reflective practice are many. Models and theories of reflective practice allow learners to see their practice from a different perspective, which limits the use of a purely emotional response to professional situations. This develops a sense of self-awareness that helps to make better informed responses to everyday work as it aids reflection-in-action. As reflection can often be seen as a very personal and insular prospect, a structured approach helps to put learners' experiences into context allowing learners to see beyond themselves and their feeling to the bigger picture. The contextualization of learning is also useful in the classroom as learners can see the relevance of their learning to their chosen profession which can aid motivation.

This section will discuss four models that are commonly used to aid reflective practice: Kolb's learning cycle (1984); Gibbs' reflective cycle (1988); Johns' model of structured reflection (2000) and Brookfield's critical lenses (1995). All of these models aim to take reflection beyond the descriptive and emotional and towards analysis and evaluation in order develop greater understandings and action. The practical application of these models will be discussed along with the benefits and limitations of them.

10.4.1 Kolb's learning cycle (1984)

Kolb (1984) offers a model for structured reflection based on four stages of learning. The four stages are: concrete experience, reflective observation, abstract conceptualization and active experimentation. The stages are constructed so that a learner can enter the cycle at any stage; it is an ongoing cyclical process. Learners often find it difficult when reflecting to know just what to reflect on ('nothing significant happened'). However, because this model allows the learner to enter the cycle at any stage, they do not necessarily have to start with the 'concrete experience' stage. The learner may want to start with the 'active experimentation' stage whereby they may plan to make some sort of change to their ordinary practice. They would then implement the change (concrete experience), reflect (reflective observation) and then move on to reading up about related theory (abstract conceptualization) and the cycle continues.

The main essence of the model is that it allows learners to take responsibility for their learning. By allowing learners to enter at any stage of the cycle they do not have to wait for a critical incident or an experience of significance to occur. It encourages the learner to repeat the cycle and actively engage in reflection as an ongoing part of their professional practice. The model is relatively practical and allows learners to apply their reflection; however, the 'reflective observation' stage of the

Table 10.1 Kolb's learning cycle (1984) (adapted)

Stage in cycle	Examples for teaching and learning
Concrete experience	Classroom experience Field work Work-based or professional experience Critical incidents
Reflective observation	Reflective journals Blogs Portfolios Group discussions Brain storming
Abstract conceptualization	Theory Analogies Empirical studies Case studies
Active experimentation	Simulations Action research Project groups Action planning and target setting

model is non-prescriptive. For learners that are new to reflective practice this can be a barrier to reflecting effectively as the model doesn't give guidance on *how* to reflect. However, Kolb's (1984) four-stage model of learning was developed further by Gibbs in 1988 to incorporate some more prescriptive guidance on how to reflect.

10.4.2 Gibbs' reflective cycle (1988)

Gibbs' reflective cycle (1988) breaks down reflection into six specific stages. These are description, feelings, evaluation, analysis, conclusion and action planning. The model also offers a series of questions to aid progression from one stage of the cycle to the next. Although it can be argued that the prescriptive nature of such a model limits learners to the six stages only, the questions may prompt a deeper level of reflection by allowing learners to consider different aspects of a situation. The prompts also allow the learner to move through the stages in order to develop a holistic reflective account. For example, see Table 10.2.

Unlike Kolb's learning cycle, it would prove difficult to enter Gibbs' reflective cycle at any stage. It is essential the cycle is started with the description, as each stage is a precursor to the next. Furthermore, while the model is termed a 'cycle' it would appear that it is probably more linear than other cycles. However, the advantage of this style of model is that

Table 10.2 Gibbs' reflective cycle (1988) (adapted)

Stage in the cycle	How?
Description	Describe the event, including its context and circumstances
Feelings	What are your thoughts about the experience or event? What were your assumptions?
Evaluation	What was positive or negative about the experience or event? Can you identify underlying themes or wider issues?
Analysis	How can you make sense of the experience or event? Can your assumptions be challenged?
Conclusion	What can be done differently now? What can be developed further?
Action plan	Moving forward, this may be in the form of target setting (particularly useful for learners), identify areas for personal or continuing professional development, and areas for action research

is provides a clear structure for *reflective writing*. The action plan stage of the cycle can also provide a base from which the cycle can be repeated.

There are a range of forms that reflective writing can take. Usually, reflective writing is used in education and training for learners to demonstrate their reflective practice. Learners may be asked to keep reflective journals, diaries or other logs, usually on a weekly basis. However, often learners find it difficult to know what to write about in these logs. By using a model such as Gibbs' reflective cycle, learners can use the stages as subheadings to structure these pieces of writing in a logical manner.

10.4.3 Johns' model for structured reflection (2000)

Another model that provides cue questions to help facilitate reflection is Johns' model for structured reflection in nursing (2000). These cue questions are especially useful for structuring reflective writing, as the answers to the questions posed can form the template for a reflective diary. The questions, as in Gibbs' model, are grouped into subheadings under particular stages of the reflection. Johns' model focuses on the process and outcomes of experiences as a base for developing professional practice.

Table 10.3 Model of reflection (adapted from Johns, 2000)

Looking in	Find a space to focus on self Pay attention to your thoughts and emotions Write down these thoughts and emotions
Looking out	Write a description of the situation What issues seem significant?
Aesthetics	What was I trying to achieve? Why did I respond as I did? What were the consequences for myself and others? How were others feeling? How did I know this?
Personal	Why did I feel the way I did within this situation?
Ethics	Did I act for the best? What factors were influencing me? What knowledge did or could have informed me?
Reflexivity	How does this situation relate to previous experiences? How could I have handled this better? What would have been the consequences of alternative actions? How do I feel now about the experience? How can I support myself and others better in the future?

Although his model was developed to be used in the nursing profession, it can be easily adapted to be applied to professional practice more generally. Johns suggests that the model for structured reflection is a technique that is especially useful in the early stages of learning how to reflect. 'Looking in' and 'looking out' enables learners to think of reflection as not just an insular process based on feelings but to challenge assumptions in the workplace and to give context to experiences.

The act of written reflection is an important part of reflective practice. Writing about practice enables learners and professionals to clarify thoughts and make connections between thinking, learning and doing. However, the notion of a reflective diary or journal alone does lend itself to the descriptive; therefore using a model in written reflection prompts learners to go beyond the descriptive and into the analytical, thus feeling the full benefits of engaging in deeper reflective practice.

> It is not sufficient simply to have an experience in order to learn. Without reflecting upon this experience it may quickly be forgotten, or its learning potential lost. It is from the feelings and thoughts emerging from this reflection that generalisations or concepts can be generated. And it is generalisations that allow new situations to be tackled effectively. (Gibbs, 1988: 9)

The idea of writing in a reflective diary or journal portrays reflective practice as a personal and insular activity. And while reflective practice does involve elements of the personal (such as writing about feelings) it can also involve others. Johns' model helps learners to think beyond experiences as 'what they felt' and 'what they did' and to challenge other forces at work in professional practice. The idea of challenging commonly taken-for-granted assumptions in everyday practice is a move towards what is known as critical reflection.

10.4.4 Critical reflection

Stephen Brookfield (1995) identified the importance of a practitioner's ability to reflect upon their practice critically, by challenging the very assumptions that underpin teaching practice. This differs from other forms of reflective practice as it goes beyond the experience or incident upon which is being reflected, by taking into account the ways in which political and social forces impact professional practice. Critical reflection also differs from the other forms of reflection as it requires the professional or learner to consider other parties in that reflection. Brookfield (1995: 31) identifies these other considerations and 'critical lenses' and suggests four critical lenses that practitioners should take into account, as shown in Figure 10.1:

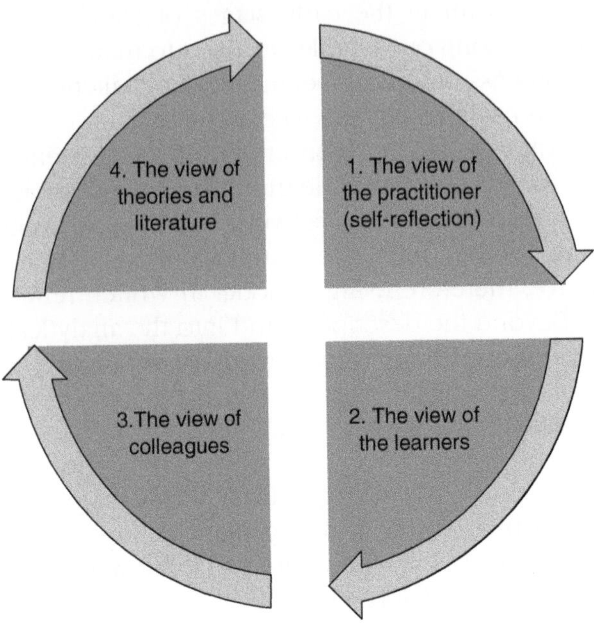

Figure 10.1 Critical lenses

By engaging in reflection using the four lenses, practitioners are taking a collaborative approach to reflection. The use of a wide variety of sources (or lenses) allows for a much deeper reflection by taking into account those whom the practice effects. It also lays bare the practitioner's assumptions to be challenged by them and their peers. Like Kolb's learning cycle, a critical approach to reflection requires the practitioner to engage with the literature around their practice to inform their development.

In order to reflect critically practitioners must be open to considering their practice from a range of perspectives, in doing this they are able to engage in more critical conversations around the nature of practice. It is during these conversations that practitioners are often made aware of issues they hadn't considered and share good practice. Case study 2 below shows an example of how critical reflection can be used to effectively support teaching and learning.

It is also while engaging in critical reflective practice that practitioners are able to identify and question social and political issues that may affect their practice. It is through greater awareness of these issues that action can be brought about for change (Brookfield, 1995). However, in practice, engaging in this type of reflective practice has its issues. Brookfield (1995) refers to a range of dilemmas that can occur when questioning social and political issues within an organization. First, many practitioners find it difficult to engage for fear of rejection by other members of the organization; this is coupled with a sense of having no right to think critically of such issues. Second, he suggests that this fear of rejection can be a reality in what he refers to as 'cultural suicide'; this is whereby practitioners are alienated for expressing their views within an organizational context. It is important therefore for practitioners engaged in critical reflection to find mutually supportive groups or bodies. Professional bodies can often provide collaborative environments and networks that can support and promote critical reflection.

The benefits of collaborative reflection with groups of learners can be more easily facilitated with the use of technology. Blogs are often used in order to promote collaborative reflection. For those who find it difficult to engage with critical reflection for the aforementioned reasons, blogs provide a certain amount of anonymity for users. That isn't to say they are completely anonymous, but that it can be less overwhelming to reflect behind a computer screen than face-to-face in a group. As long as ground rules are set for appropriate conduct in an online forum they can be a really useful step for learners towards critical reflection.

Learners and practitioners often find it difficult to write about themselves. They can either be overly critical of themselves and their practice or blame others for their experiences. In order to enable learners to identify with reflective practice and to realize its benefits, case studies and scenarios can be used to practise using the models. This allows learners to consider the stages of a model and its uses by applying it to a scenario that they can identify with in a 'mock reflection'. Conducting this activity in groups also allows different learners to contribute different perspectives to the 'mock reflection' and discuss their own experiences that may be related. Furthermore, case studies or scenarios can be a good way to engage learners in reflecting upon aspects of professional practice such as ethics and moral dilemmas. Through practising reflection in these ways, learners can ease themselves into the daunting proposition of reflective practice and find out what really works for them.

10.5 Summary, case studies, discussion questions and learning activities

This chapter has outlined key features of CPD and reflective learning, identifying what is meaningful to individuals' learning and growth and its potential impact on their profession. Above all, we have argued that CPD and reflection is purposeful when the practitioners actively engage with maintaining and improving practice within their professional context. This recognizes both the limitations of the context and the opportunities it provides as well as understanding the important role of practitioners themselves.

Below are two scenarios that practitioners may face followed by some questions to help you reflect on the issues and to prompt discussion.

10.5.1 Case study 1 Taking a part-time degree as CPD

Joe, a construction trainer in a large further education college, had recently been awarded his certificate in education (Cert. Ed.) having completed a two-year in-service part-time course at the college where he is now employed. Prior to joining the college he had worked 'on the tools' as a bricklayer in various organizations for 15 years. Joe went straight into the construction industry from school and though he has some GCSEs and a BTEC, before the Cert. Ed. he had not studied for a long time.

Joe feels confident about the currency of his vocational knowledge because he has only recently left the industry. He also works for a firm some weekends and so he keeps his practical skills and knowledge up to date. Joe was less confident about the academic aspects of his new role. Despite having his Cert. Ed. he still felt anxious about working in a further education college. When Joe considered his own professionalism, he identified his wish to broaden the range of methods he used with his learners and also wanted to develop his confidence in dealing with academic matters in the college. Above all, Joe wanted a recognized qualification that would hold status in his college and beyond so that he could develop his career.

The college offered a part-time degree in education and training as a top-up from the certificate in education. This degree course included modules that focused on education policy, improving teaching and learning, as well as reflective practice. Having first discussed this course and the commitment it would involve with his family he approached his manager who supported his application. The college agreed to pay half the fees. Two years and a lot of hard work later Joe passed his degree with a 2.1 classification, the first person in his family to gain a degree. Joe is now looking for promotion in the college.

Discussion questions:

- How can Joe's experience help him in getting promotion and improve his practice?

- Why do you think CPD is regarded as highly pragmatic and relevant? Does Joe need to continue undertaking 35 hours CPD each year in order to get promoted?
- Can you identify what might be useful CPD for you in your professional contexts or to forward your career aims?
- What are the benefits and tensions of making autonomous choices in CPD?

10.5.2 Case study 2 Using critical reflection in practice

Anna is a health and safety trainer at a training provider. While she has always been good at engaging her learners on short courses, she seems to be having a problem with two learners taking the course. Anna has told these learners on numerous occasions to put their smartphones away; however, they still seem to be using them during delivery. This is having a knock-on effect and other learners on the course are now using their smartphones more. Anna thinks this must be something to do with her ability to engage learners and her practice as a trainer. She is aware of Brookfield's four critical lenses, and decides to try and reflect critically using them.

Anna consults her learners about the use of smartphones during delivery. Most agree that they are a distraction in the session; the two learners in question, however, have another explanation. They explain that English is not their first language and they are using a translation facility so when they come across a term or phrase they don't understand in the session they can quickly look it up for their own understanding. Anna then consults her colleagues, most were surprised by this use of smartphones as their experiences were that when they caught learners using them they were texting or emailing from them. Anna then consulted the literature and theory about learners for whom English is not their first language in a UK educational context and found that there were many cultural differences and barriers that impacted on their learning. Furthermore, without knowledge of these issues she realized other trainers may be labelling these learners as deviant or with behavioural problems. Anna adapted her practice by introducing the key health and safety terms and definitions that she would be using throughout the course and thoroughly explained them to all learners. From using the lenses, Anna realized that her training provider didn't offer any CPD on training learners for whom English is not their first language. She took

(*Continued*)

(*Continued*)

this reflection to her manager and the learning and development officer who then arranged a series of development sessions on this subject. Her critical reflection had effected change by challenging her own, her colleagues' and the providers' assumptions about the nature of certain behaviours in training sessions.

Discussion questions:

- Brookfield (1995) interprets the first lens (view) as your autobiography. Discuss how your autobiographies are the most important sources of insight into your practice.
- How would you use one of these models of reflection to improve your practice?
- Discuss how each model of reflection above could be effective in writing a reflective journal. What might the challenges be?

References

Beevers, K. and Rea, A. (2010) *Learning and Development Practice*. London: CIPD.

Brookfield, S. (1995) *Becoming a Critically Reflective Teacher*. San Francisco, CA: Jossey-Bass.

CIPD (2013) *CPD and Personal Effectiveness*. www.cipd.co.uk/hr-topics/cpd-personal-effectiveness.aspx (accessed 30 November 2013).

Cullingford, C. (2002) 'Institutional development and professional needs: some reflections', in G. Trorey and C. Cullingford (eds), *Professional Development and Institutional Needs*. Aldershot: Ashgate, pp. 223–235.

DBIS (Department for Business, Innovation and Skills) (2012) *Professionalism in Further Education: Final Report of the Independent Review Panel* (Lingfield Review). London: DBIS.

Dewey, J. (1933) *How We Think: A Restatement of the Relation of Reflective Thinking to the Educative Process*. Chicago, IL: Henry Regnery Co.

Gibbs, G (1988) *Learning by Doing: A Guide to Teaching and Learning Methods*. Oxford: Further Education Unit, Oxford Polytechnic.

Grundy, S. and Robison, J. (2004) 'Teacher professional development: themes and trends in the recent Australian experience', in C. Day and J. Sachs (eds), *International Handbook on the CPD of Teachers*. Maidenhead: Open University Press, pp. 146–166.

Institute for Learning (IfL) (2009) *Guidelines for Your Continuing Professional Development (CPD)*. London: IfL.

Johns, C. (2000) *Becoming a Reflective Practitioner: A Reflective and Holistic Approach to Clinical Nursing, Practice Development and Clinical Supervision*. Oxford: Blackwell Science.

Katz, F. (1969) 'Nurses', in A. Estioni (ed.), *The Semi Professions and Their Organization: Teachers, Nurses, Social Workers*. New York, Free Press, pp. 54–81.

Kincheloe, J. (2008) *Critical Pedagogy* (4th edn). New York: Peter Lang.

Kolb, D. A. (1984) *Experiential Learning: Experience as the Source of Learning and Development*. Upper Saddle River: Prentice-Hall.

Polanyi, M. (1967) *The Tacit Dimension*. New York: Doubleday.

Randle, K. and Brady, N. (1997) 'Managerialism and professionalism in the Cinderella service', *Journal of Vocational Education and Training*, 49 (1): 121–139.

Rogers, C. (1995) *A Way of Being*. New York: Houghton Mifflin Company.

Schön, D. (1987) *Educating the Reflective Practitioner*. San Francisco, CA: Jossey-Bass.

Schön, D. (2000) *The Reflective Practitioner: How Professionals Think in Action*. Aldershot: Ashgate Publishing Limited.

Stronach, I., Corbin, B., McNamara, O., Stark, S. and Warne, T. (2004) 'Towards an uncertain politics of professionalism: teacher and nurse identities in flux', *Journal of Education Policy*, 17(1): 109–138.

Valli, L. (ed.) (1992) *Reflective Teacher Education: Cases and Critiques*. Albany, NY: SUNY Press.

Zeichner, K. M. and Liston, D. P. (1996) *Reflective Teaching: An Introduction*. Mahwah, NJ: Lawrence Erlbaum Associates.

CHAPTER 11

WORKFORCE DEVELOPMENT AND POLICY ISSUES

Denise Robinson and Lyn Ashmore

Learning outcomes

After reading this chapter, the reader should be able to:

- Identify the issues surrounding the professionalism versus craft debate.
- Understand the range of qualifications and standards for the sector.
- Identify the key stakeholders in learning and development.
- Consider the future of learning and development in the sector.

Chapter outline

This last chapter is both a follow-on from the previous chapter on continuing professional development (CPD) and a compilation of some of the threads across the book on what it is to be a learning and development professional, but in particular in the further education and skills sector. However, it must be noted that the nomenclature of the sector itself has been subject to various changes over the last 15 years or so.

Initially, the term further education was regarded as too limited and the term lifelong learning was used to reflect the incorporation of other elements of vocational, work-based and adult education and training. More recently, the term further education and skills has been used to reflect the growing emphasis on the education and training of skills, as well as other aspects of lifelong learning, and includes private as well as public sector organizations.

The chapter starts by examining our understanding of the term 'professional' in relationship to initial teacher education and training. The term professional is, in itself, contentious and has been debated particularly since the 'professionalisation agenda' (DfES, 2004) was placed on government policy-drives. Furthermore, the position of professionals in the public sector (where government policy guides, if not directs, workforce development), can put professionals in an ambiguous position (Evans, 2010). The different approaches to professionalism are examined and how they relate to the role of teachers and trainers in the sector. We also identify the professional bodies across the sector, including further education (FE), work-based learning (WBL), adult and community learning (ACL), higher education (HE) in FE, Chartered Institute for Personnel and Development (CIPD) (for those aligned to learning and development in organizations), along with their concomitant standards and guidelines. The chapter also examines the key stakeholders that are involved in the sector and how these impact on learning. Such stakeholders are numerous and tend to change frequently, according to different government strategies. Some, such as the learners themselves, have a much more prominent and central position.

Last, we consider how learning and development is likely to change in the future and how this might impact on practitioners. The chapter ends with questions for you to consider either as an individual or in groups.

11.1 Identifying professionalism in the sector

11.1.1 What is a professional?

The term professional can be regarded as a wide-ranging term which is sometimes symbolic rather than one which is specific to a certain set of occupations or a profile of certain characteristics. The previous chapter identified three main features of the professional and related them to CPD: responsibility to the public (in our case that will normally mean our learners); responsibility to the rest of the profession (our colleagues in and beyond our organization); and the autonomy of decision-making that is integral to being a professional. Here we will relate professionalism to initial teacher education and the qualifications and standards debate. In particular, the following approaches to professionalism are pertinent to this chapter:

- the trait or functionalist approach to professionalism with attributes such as the acquisition of an expert base of knowledge and skill obtained through specific training and qualifications (Gleeson and James, 2007)
- the construction and application of a code of practice (drawn up by the professional organization).

For example, the Institute for Learning has a code of professional conduct with seven behaviours that should be upheld by members (IfL, 2008); the CIPD has eight behaviours with an additional ten professional areas setting out what the practitioner needs to do (activities) and know (knowledge) (People Management, 2010). Essentially the notion of what it means to be a professional tends to emphasize three core issues: knowledge, autonomy and responsibility (Hoyle and John, 1995). While teacher autonomy is cited as having a central feature in their working lives, it has been asserted that teachers find it increasingly difficult to exercise autonomy as government (and their agencies) extend greater detailed control over their work (Gleeson and James, 2007). Yet work undertaken by Robson et al. (2004) with vocational teachers revealed that, despite the restrictions of the introduction of, for example, a competence-based curriculum which requires teachers and trainers to enact the curriculum as specified, the teachers regarded themselves as autonomous. They pride themselves in providing expert specialist knowledge and maintaining the standards of their particular subject, going beyond the curriculum as specified, rather than merely relating to a prescribed and potentially limiting competence-base of the course (Robson et al., 2004: 192).

11.1.2 Are teachers professionals?

How far can we assert that teachers and trainers are professionals? In 2010, Michael Gove, the then Secretary of State for Education, delivered a speech at the National College Annual Conference in which he purports that teaching is a craft 'and it is best learnt as an apprentice observing a master craftsman or woman' (Gove, 2010). This reveals his philosophy, which underpins the government policy of shifting teacher education (for schoolteachers) into schools and away from universities

(DfE, 2013a). The present direction of government is to align teacher education as a craft approach by reducing the university element of their education and developing training schools which will undertake the vast majority of teacher education, if not all of it (see School Direct details via DfE, 2013b).

This has been underwritten by an open hostility to theory and its supposed relationship to a political stance. For example, a Department for Education spokesperson has been quoted as saying:

> For too long left-wing training colleges have imbued teachers with useless teaching theories that don't work and actively damage children's education. (Noble-Rogers, 2013)

Yet, a report by the Organization for Economic Cooperation and Development (OECD) in 2011 on the teaching profession states that professional formation requires an appropriate balance between theory and practice. However, the implementation of this policy in the schools sector is moving the education of such schoolteachers towards a craft-based approach, reducing opportunities to engage in reflection on theory and practice. The elimination of the requirement for a teaching qualification (or alternative qualifications) for those teaching in academies, free schools, university technical colleges and studio schools (DfE, 2013c) has been promoted as placing the responsibility for teacher standards firmly with the employer rather than a professional body. This philosophy has been extended to the further education and skills sector with the ending of the regulation (Cabinet Office, 2013) that required FE teachers in England to be teacher qualified and those trainers and tutors in the wider sector to be qualified if the employer received public funds (DIUS, 2007).

11.1.3 Teacher education and the FE and skills sector

The vast majority of those undertaking teacher education in the further education and skills sector are already employed in the workplace, with around 90 per cent of trainee teachers enrolled and studying a teaching qualification on an in-service basis (Orr and Simmons, 2010). Despite the moves to professionalize the teachers in the sector, research reveals how some consider that they have become de-professionalized through the implementation of managerialist practices (Wahlberg and Gleeson, 2003). This concurs with the notion of the teacher as a service provider, subject to the extended market philosophy and controlled through the 'managers' right to manage'

(Ball, 2003). According to Evetts professionalism is being used to 'promote and facilitate occupational change and as a disciplinary mechanism' (2012: 6). By this means, the understanding and practice of teacher professionalism is politicized within a managerialist framework rather than one of a collegiate nature.

Much has been written about the compulsory schools sector in relationship to teacher education and policies. Typically, this is not the case for the further education and skills sector; often we have to extrapolate from what has been researched and written about the schools sector with regard to professional status and roles. However, the further education and skills sector is very different to the schools sector. With the demise of the LLUK (2011), we no longer have an overarching agency that can provide access to workforce data. The data we have is accessed by the following: the SIR (Staff Individual Records) data sets of the 357 FE colleges in England: the reports from surveys undertaken by the Association of Employment and Learning Providers (AELP) for the WBL sector with the support of LSIS for 2010–11 and 2011–12: and the reports from HOLEX (for the ACL sector) for the same years, again with support of LSIS (HOLEX/LSIS, 2013). Both the latter two surveys were based on voluntary responses from the relevant members of the representative organizations. Of the AELP 496 provider members, 22 per cent responded, and for HOLEX a response rate of fewer than 66 per cent is given. The SIRs are collected by all FE colleges and, therefore, the data reflects all those employed by such colleges. The last year data was collected and analysed for English FE colleges was for 2009–10 (LLUK, 2011). It is not clear whether the AELP or the HOLEX surveys will continue in the future but it may be that the Education and Training Foundation will facilitate this particular undertaking.

Yet, knowledge of the workforce across the sector based on a coherent, robust and all-encompassing system of data collection and analysis is essential for planning and development on a national and regional basis. The latest figures from the LLUK data analysis reveal that less than half of the FE college workforce is comprised of teachers or trainers and that the female to male ratio of full-time teachers was approximately 50:50 (LLUK, 2011: 6). The average age of teachers was 45. In terms of qualifications the number of teachers with a teaching qualification of the Certificate in Education or the Postgraduate Certificate in Education was 47.6 per cent, with 46.1 per cent enrolled on these courses. This compares to the AELP (2013) report where we find that 'teaching staff holding or enrolled on a relevant teaching qualification, rising by ten per cent to 83 per cent' (AELP/LSIS, 2013: 3). The number of ACL staff who now hold, or who are working towards, a recognized teaching qualification, has risen to 83.6 per cent of all teaching staff (HOLEX/LSIS, 2013: 2).

11.1.4 Professional standards

This section examines the position across the sector in relation to professional standards for teachers. However, it starts with schools as the overlap across the 14–19 age range between the schools sector and the further education and skills sector is considerable. The General Teaching Council (GTC) has now been abolished and the Teaching and Development Agency (TDA) has become the National College for Teaching and Leadership (NCTL). This determines the criteria for teacher training courses in the schools sector and was established in April 2013; its aim is to enable and support the development of a self-improving, school-led system. There are two key aims: improving the quality of the education workforce; and helping schools to help each other to improve. It will continue to oversee the induction process for teachers and award Qualified Teacher Status (QTS). It will also uphold high standards of professional conduct through its regulatory role, taking appropriate action in cases of the most serious allegations of professional misconduct.

For the further education and skills sector, LLUK (a Sector Skills Council (SSC)) established the professional standards for all teachers, trainers and tutors in the sector (LLUK, 2007) and these include a reference to professional values that are said to underpin practice. These were reviewed in 2011, while the qualifications framework itself was amended by LSIS in 2013. The standards themselves have been reviewed by the Education and Training Foundation in 2014; the number of statements has been significantly reduced. The Institute for Learning, (which is to transfer the stewardship of its legacy to the ETF as of Autumn 2014), as the professional body for the sector, has developed a code of conduct (IfL, 2008). IfL has a clear focus on the positive impact on the learner experience, as well as subject specialism and pedagogy (IfL, 2008). From 1 April 2012, IfL members with Qualified Teacher Learning and Skills (QTLS) status are also recognized as qualified to teach in schools as recommended in the Wolf Report (2011). Despite the attempts to improve the professional standing of teachers in the sector, there have been continued criticisms and some of these aligned to fundamental and structural differences compared to the schools and university sectors. For example, Lucas and Nasta (2010) have commented that the training of FE college teachers has been one that is locked into an industrial and occupational model, thus making comparisons and bridges across the sectors difficult.

For those involved in organizational learning and development, the CIPD is the preferred human resource (HR) professional organization to join and it exists to:

Its professional standards cover ten professional areas and eight behaviours, set out in four bands of competence and these are detailed via its map, which covers every level of the HR profession, from Band 1 at the start of an HR career through to Band 4 for the most senior leaders. As a professional organization, it achieved its royal chartered status in 2000. A chartered status is an objective which the Education and Training Foundation may wish to seek.

In universities and other higher education institutions, and including HE in FE, the UK Professional Standards Framework written by the Higher Education Academy (HEA) provides a general description of the main dimensions of the roles of teaching and supporting learning within the higher education environment. It is written from the perspective of the practitioner and outlines a national framework for comprehensively recognizing and benchmarking teaching and learning support roles within higher education, 'a flexible framework which uses a descriptor-based approach to professional standards' (HEA, 2006). The Framework identifies four Descriptors – ranging from those who are new to teaching (Descriptor 1) to those who are highly experienced and leaders of teaching and learning (Descriptor 4) – and through these formulates the areas of activities, the core knowledge and the professional values.

The position of part-time teachers and trainers has typically been regarded as problematic in terms of their availability and willingness to undertake initial teacher training qualifications or to continue their professional development. For example, HOLEX – the national network of local adult learning providers, and the sector membership body for local authority adult and community learning services, independent 'former external institutions' and 'specialist designated institutions' – has indicated that a full teaching qualification may not be necessary and may place a barrier to employment. However, Jameson and Hillier, in their work on part-time ACL and FE teachers, found that despite the limits of their employment position, they 'make creative use of professional autonomy and agency to mitigate problematic "casual employment" conditions' (2008: 39).

In addition to what we would normally regard as the parameters of professional development, the role of research is increasingly becoming an important role for teachers in the sector (Hillier and Morris, 2010). Hence in the amendments to the qualification framework by LSIS in 2013, reference is made to the significance of action research.

11.2 Key stakeholders in the learning and skills sector involved in shaping the learning process

11.2.1 The main institutions in the sector

The further education and skills sector is large and is typically referred to in terms of its 'constituents'. The largest is the FE colleges sector with 357 colleges but including specialist colleges and sixth-form colleges. In addition to the WBL and ACL providers (of which there are 142 local authority sole and partner providers) and 25 independent ACL or third sector providers comprised of: the Third Sector National Learning Alliance (TSNLA), the National Institute of Adult Continuing Education (NIACE), Fairtrain and HOLEX. The Department for Business, Innovation and Skills (DBIS) has underlined the role of the third sector in a report (DBIS, 2013b) which identifies how the sector can access difficult-to-reach learners and sections of society and how they can help to both deliver learning opportunities themselves but, in co-operation with other providers, can ensure that this element of the sector is incorporated into learning activity.

As identified in Chapter 1, there is also a range of new institutions which bridge the compulsory schools sector and the learning and skills sector. University Technical Colleges (UTCs) provide technical education which is based on the National Curriculum but focuses on a vocational curriculum, particularly engineering and sciences, for 14–19 year olds. The first UTC, the JCB UTC, opened in 2010 and is sponsored by Harper Adams University and JC Bamford (Excavators Limited). Presently, there are a total of five UTCs with 28 more from September 2013 (see DfE, 2013d). In a similar vein, Studio Schools are aimed at young people (14–19 year olds) who learn in more practical ways and which includes experience in the workplace. There are 16 Studio Schools and 16 more from September 2013 (DfE, 2013e).

In addition to these, there are the countless companies and organizations that are involved in learning, training and development, whether it be to induct new employees, support and deliver some of the training for apprentices or to support further learning and development opportunities through CPD.

11.2.2 Employers and agencies

The position of employers has been a key feature of debate across the further education and skills sector and it can be argued that they should and do have a significant role to play in influencing the learning process. The discussion on vocational education and training has focused on concerns expressed both by employer bodies (for example, the Confederation of British Industry (CBI, 2011) and Institute of Directors (IoD, 2004)) and government agencies (Wolf, 2011) that education and training have not met employer or employment requirements. At the same time, a study undertaken for the Construction Industry Training Board, one of the oldest training boards founded in 1964, has highlighted that:

> Not all employers recognize the return on investment of training, and this is often where short term strategies are evident. (CITB, 2013: 4)

The main agencies involved in the development activities in the learning and skills sector over the last 20 years or so has included the Training and Enterprise Councils (TECs) (1990–2001), Learning and Skills Council (LSC) (2001–2010), Further Education Development Agency (FEDA) (1995–2000), Learning and Skills Development Agency (LSDA) (2000–2006), Quality Improvement Agency (QIA) (2006–2008), Learning and Skills Improvement Service (LSIS) (2008–2013 – a merger between the Centre for Excellence in Leadership and the QIA), and the latest is the formation of the Education and Training Foundation (ETF) (initially referred to as the FE Guild), established on 1 August 2013. This, according to its website, has been set up 'to improve professionalism and standards in the further education and skills sectors' (ETF, 2013).

All these agencies (and others not necessarily mentioned here) had to a greater or lesser extent, some responsibility for representing sector interests (particularly employer interests) and in influencing government policy as well as (in some cases) contracting with institutions (public and private) to deliver courses.

11.2.3 Teachers, tutors and trainers

Teachers have a role through their unions and professional associations such as the University and College Union (UCU) and the Association of Teachers and Lecturers (ATL). The Institute for Learning, as the professional body for all teachers, trainers and tutors across the further education and skills sector, promotes debate and issues position papers on government policy, which relate to teacher professionalism in the sector. It emphasises the need to lobby government on related matters and identifies that 'the voice of the individual teacher and trainer is rarely the loudest in the further education and skills landscape' (IfL, 2013: 12).

11.2.4 The learner voice

Last but not least, are the learners themselves. How may they influence the learning process? It is suggested that learners have had relatively little say for a long time, but that over the years a call has been made for an improvement in 'learner voice' and that this should represent a 'deeper cultural change towards genuine on-going participation and engagement with learners' (Rudd et al., 2006: 11). Rudd and colleagues refer to the ladder of participation with eight levels of participation from 'manipulation', where learners are directed, to 'learner control' (2006: 11) where learners themselves are empowered to initiate and design their own education. While this latter may seem a step too far for some other stakeholders (including perhaps, teachers and trainers) there are various examples of progressive moves towards this. Improvements are evidenced in the requirement to include course and session learner evaluations as part of the quality assurance procedures across all constituents of the sector. Learners' views are typically incorporated into amendments to course design, learner support, and the design of the learning activities and methods. In 1998, a FEDA report identified attrition in FE colleges and recommended that one way to improve retention was to listen more carefully to the learners and provide regular evaluation opportunities, which was something that did not necessarily happen on a regular or meaningful basis (Martinez and Munday, 1998: 115). There may be an element of paying lip-service to engagement with learners through the required learner evaluations; rather the core issue may be one of power relationships and control. As Fielding and Ruddock say, 'the important point is that consultation processes can sometimes reflect rather than challenge the existing dividing practices in the [learning institution] and the systems for valuing some [learners] above others' (2002: 2). This is a controversial issue and one which may never be totally resolved, reflecting, as it does, fundamental differences in approaches to learner control.

11.3 The future of learning and development in the sector

There are a range of factors which may affect the future of learning and development. Some are organizational, structural or political and some are related to the development of technology.

11.3.1 Vocational education and training

One major influence has been government white papers (DfES, 2005 and DfES, 2006) on vocational education and training and reports, the most recent of which has been the Wolf Report (2011) and the Commission on Adult Vocational Teaching and Learning (CAVTL, 2013). Previously, the Tomlinson Report (2004) and the Leitch Review of Skills (Leitch, 2006) argued that Britain needed to improve its economic competitiveness and one element of this was to improve the curriculum by making it more diversified and vocationally relevant:

> our future prosperity will depend on building a Britain where people are given the opportunity and encouragement to develop their skills and abilities to the maximum; and then given the support to rise as far as their talents will take them. (DIUS, 2007: 3)

Such reports, alongside government policy movements, have led to a shifting of emphasis towards vocational education and training and away from general education that has been available in FE colleges and ACL. Such policies and reports have also revealed the tensions and contradictions in government philosophy on vocational education and training. The Tomlinson report and its implementation with the introduction of a new specialized diploma route (DfES, 2005), reveals some of these tensions and contradictions. The first five diplomas were introduced in 2008 and were intended to offer an equivalent route to that of GCSEs and GCE Advanced level qualifications. This initiative was regarded as heralding in a new era of qualifications that would combine both academic and vocational curricula and which would be attractive to all young people, although the original intention to eliminate GCEs at Advanced level was not accepted by the government (DfES, 2005) and revealed the portend of what was to come. Yet, in leaving A levels outside the diplomas and as an alternative to diplomas, the opportunity to make radical changes seemed to be lost (Melville, 2005). Criticisms of the diplomas revealed low take-up and achievement rates (TES, 2011), and it was announced that they were not to continue (TES, 2010). A further blow to the status of vocational qualifications came when the coalition government (DfE, 2012a) decided to eliminate 90 per cent of vocational qualifications from school league tables. So, while GCSE and A Level qualifications have been maintained (admittedly with some changes) since their introduction in the 1950s, the landscape of vocational qualifications has been turbulent. The tendency has been to attempt to bring parity of esteem between the academic and vocational routes (Vickers and Bekhradnia, 2007) and to offer more employer friendly vocational qualifications, but the outcome has usually resulted in a reversion to the perceived 'gold standard' of GCE A levels (Baird et al., 2000). As Wallace has commented, the various attempts over the years to synergize the vocational and academic curricula have failed and: 'FE remains focused on the instrumental and the functional' (Wallace, 2013: 83).

11.3.2 Apprenticeships

The history of apprenticeships has been one of decline from the 1960s up to 2001 when the number was as low as one-ninth of the share of employment (Fuller and Unwin, 2003: 6). Modern apprenticeships were introduced in 1994 with the objective of increasing the number of the workforce who operated at the intermediate or technician level (Fuller and Unwin, 2003: 6). However, the New Labour government tried to align the apprenticeships with their social inclusion policy. Since then, the Wolf Report (2011: 7) has identified that, of the 2.5 million young people aged 14–19, 'the majority follow courses which are largely or entirely vocational'. Furthermore, she asserts that vocational education has suffered from micro-management and is in a worse state today than it was 30–40 years ago (Wolf, 2011: 9) and that in order to rectify the problem of the lack of employer commitment, the recommendation is given that subsidies are provided for employers when apprentices are involved in general education as well as specific skill training (Wolf, 2011: 12).

11.3.3 Raising of the participation age

Since September 2013, learners have been required to stay in some form of education or training until the end of the academic year when they turn 17, and from 2014 they will have to continue until the end of the academic year when they become 18. However, this does not have to mean staying in school, but can be:

- full-time education, for example, at a school or college
- an apprenticeship
- full-time employment (over 20 hours a week) combined with part-time education or training.

However, according to Simmons (2012: 1) this will make relatively little difference as 'the vast majority of young people continue to take part in education after they reach the minimum school-leaving age, and most are still participating at the age of 18', and those in employment are required to do only 280 hours per annum. Where it will make a difference, is to those NEETs (Not in Education, Employment or Training), individuals who presently are not engaged in any form of development or working. This group of 16–19 year olds had risen to one in seven by the end of 2011 (Woodin et al., 2013: 642) and has become a focus of government policy that underpins the skills and training agenda as:

> A pervasive discourse has presented education as crucial to both economic growth and social justice, for instance, by fostering personal well-being, a thriving civil society and a reduction in anti-social behaviour. (Woodin et al., 2013: 636)

The implications for the further education and skills sector are considerable. It was envisaged at the instigation of this policy in the Education and Skills Act (2008) that the majority of the additional learners who will be included as learners will be those individuals who have not been pre-disposed towards remaining in education or training beyond 16 and who may, on this basis alone, become 'reluctant' learners. The organizations and agencies involved in the implementation of this legislation will extend beyond schools and FE colleges; it is likely that the third sector as well as work-based learning organizations and private companies will become involved in delivering courses designed to re-engage and support previously low-achieving learners. Employers are encouraged to participate with the provision of support for accredited training and no requirement to pay for the release of learners to attend college (where the courses will be free).

At the same time as the raising of the participation age (RPA) was introduced, announcements were made that all young people would be required to achieve a grade C in maths and English at GCSE. The argument was that employers expected grade Cs as an indication of a satisfactory level in these core subjects and that this would also improve job prospects for the individual learners concerned (DfE, 2013f). In order to support this development, DBIS announced that bursaries were to be available for pre-service trainee teachers in the sector (full-time and part-time) who were undertaking associated specialist courses in teacher education for maths, English and special educational needs (SEN) or, using the term more frequently used in the sector, learners with disabilities and difficulties (LDD), and intended to teach to at least GCSE level (DBIS, 2013a). Furthermore, the Centres for Excellence in Teacher Training (CETTs) are facilitating maths and English enhancement courses across England for those teachers and trainers in the sector who will now be expected to teach maths and English to GCSE level. The ETF, working alongside the National Centre for Excellence in the Teaching of Mathematics (NCETM) and the Association of Centres for Excellence in Teacher Training (ACETT) are delivering these enhancement courses, along with strategic hubs to support CPD for practitioners (see the NCETM website for details). In addition, FE colleges have been able to enroll 14–16 years olds from September 2013 (DfE, 2013g); this further extends the age-range taught in colleges and has implications for those teaching such learners.

A further element to the RPA is the requirement for all learners at 16–19 years of age to participate in a study programme as from September 2013 (DfE, 2012b). To address the recommendations from the Wolf Report (2011), the study programme must include English and maths to GSCE if the learner has not already achieved this to a C grade; should include work experience; and, last but most importantly, should include at least one qualification of substantial size. This is to ensure that learners (particularly those who previously have undertaken various courses at low level with no or little expectation of progression), do progress onto a higher level course.

11.3.4 Vocational HE in FE

The focus of such debates has tended to equate higher qualifications with maintaining and improving the position of the UK economy. Such was this belief that the New Labour government in 2003 (DfES, 2003) raised the spectre of a target of 50 per cent of young people to be in HE by 2010. Although this target was dropped by the 2010 coalition government, student enrolments have overtaken the target and the latest numbers reveal that some 446,000 students have enrolled for 2013–14, 9 per cent above the enrolments for 2012–13 (*Guardian*, 2013). The profile of HE has been increased in FE colleges and more tutors are now involved in the delivery of HE courses. This is likely to continue, particularly given the tendency for FE colleges to charge lower fees and to offer local, vocational provision that offers a ladder of success to some learners who might not otherwise be able to access HE. This may be perceived by teachers themselves to be yet another strain for those teaching in FE, where teaching can now extend from 14 year olds to degree-level courses, or as an opportunity to extend their subject or vocational teaching to a wider audience. This raises the issue of further demands on the teacher in terms of the expectation of scholarly activity and the notion of a new 'extended' professional covering both FE and HE sectors (Wilson and Wilson, 2010).

11.3.5 Impact of technology

The learning and development landscape is being transformed by the use and incorporation of information technology (IT) with its expectation of the development of new skills for practitioners. It is possibly an understatement to say that the introduction of affordable, accessible electronic technology has brought substantial and fundamental change to teaching and learning and that this will continue into the future. While learning and teaching technology has changed over the years, it is the pervasiveness of electronic technology into the workplace, teaching and training spaces as well as our personal lives that has caused fundamental changes to the way we deliver some courses. In addition to the skills needed to use emails for operational purposes and an organization's virtual learning environment (VLE) platform (for example, Moodle or Blackboard) where learning resources and course details can be accessed by tutors, learners and administrators, teachers and trainers are increasingly expected to participate in social networking and interaction with learners on an almost 24-hour, seven-days-a-week basis. This has caused some challenges for practitioners (McCarroll and Curran, 2013) and, while some teachers have welcomed this, others have been wary of the potential of further incursions into their private time and the impact of work intensification (Avis, 2005). However, the trend in delivery and pedagogy is towards the inclusion of electronic resources as a minimum with a greater or lesser use of blended learning (see Chapter 9 for further discussion). The implications for future professional development are clear; all teachers and trainers are expected to interact with learners to some extent on an electronic basis and more electronic systems are being used to record assessments and learner progress, including software tools to facilitate electronic marking.

11.4 Summary and discussion questions

This chapter has considered the role of the professional in relationship to initial teacher education and whether teaching can be regarded as a profession or as a craft. The position of professional standards and the latest developments with the Education and Training Foundation and comparisons with other teachers and trainers across the sector are discussed. The key stakeholders, including the institutions, are identified along with the individual groups which make up the sector. Lastly, the immediate policies that have introduced considerable change are highlighted with their implications for the future of the sector.

11.4.1 Questions

Professionalism

1. How would you describe your position as a teacher or trainer in the sector or organization in which you work?
2. If you consider yourself to be a professional, how is this manifested?

3. Are you a member of a professional organization? Is this based on your present or previous vocation or first occupation?
4. Should teachers and trainers in the further education and skills sector be required to join a professional organization as a teacher or trainer rather than that of their first vocation or occupation?

Stakeholders

1. Who are the stakeholders in your provision? What role do they have? How do they participate? Is this valued by your organization?
2. What are the pros and cons of stakeholder participation?
3. Should learners influence the learning process? Give examples of how you have involved learners in the process and how you have justified this.

The future of learning and development

1. Have you engaged with blended learning? What have been the implications and effects on teaching and learning strategies in your organization? What additional skills will you need to develop?
2. How will the raising of the participation age affect disaffected teenagers who are forced into courses that they do not wish to take?
3. What might be the benefits to such learners, as individuals and to the economy?
4. Will you be affected by the raising of the participation age? If so, how and what teaching and learning strategies will you use (or have you used)?

References

AELP/LSIS (2013) *Work Based Learning Workforce Survey 2011/12*. London: LSIS.

Avis, J. (2005) 'Beyond performativity: reflections on activist professionalism and the labour process in further education', *Journal of Education Policy*, 20 (2): 209–222.

Baird, J.-A., Cresswell, M. and Newton, P. (2000) 'Would the real gold standard please step forward?', *Research Papers in Education*, 15 (2): 213–229.

Ball, S. (2003) 'The teacher's soul and the terrors of performativity', *Journal of Education Policy*, 18 (2): 215–228.

Cabinet Office (2013) *Draft Deregulation Bill*. London: Cabinet Office. www.gov.uk/government/uploads/system/uploads/attachment_data/file/210035/130701_CM_8642_Draft_Deregulation_Bill.pdf (accessed 14 April 2014).

CAVTL (2013) *It's about Work … Excellent Adult Vocational Teaching and Learning*. www.excellencegateway.org.uk/cavtl (accessed 6 December 2013).

CBI (Confederation of British Industry) (2011) *CBI Responds to Vocational Education Report*. www.cbi.org.uk/media-centre/press-releases/2011/03/cbi-responds-to-vocational-education-report/ (accessed 9 October 2013).

CIPD (2013) *CIPD and Public Policy*. www.cipd.co.uk/publicpolicy/default.aspx (accessed 6 December 2013).

CITB (Construction Industry Training Board) (2013) *Skills Utilisation in the Construction Sector*. London: IFF Research. www.citb.co.uk/documents/research/skills%20utilisation%20in%20the%20construction%20sector%20%20final.pdf (accessed 14 April 2014).

DBIS (Department for Business, Innovation and Skills) (2013a) *Bursaries of Up To £20,000 Offered to Teach Maths, English or Special Educational Needs (SEN)*. http://news.bis.gov.uk/Press-Releases/Bursaries-of-up-to-20-000-offered-to-teach-maths-English-or-Special-Educational-Needs-SEN-690cc.aspx (accessed 6 December 2013).

DBIS (Department for Business, Innovation and Skills) (2013b) *Third Sector Engagement and Participation in the Learning and Skills Sector: Executive Summary*. London: BIS. www.gov.uk/government/uploads/system/uploads/attachment_data/file/185724/bis-13-586-third-sector-engagement-and-participation-in-the-learning-and-skills-sector-executive-summary.pdf (accessed 14 April 2014).

DfE (Department for Education) (2012a) *14–16 Qualifications: 2014 Performance Tables* www.education.gov.uk/childrenandyoungpeople/youngpeople/qandlearning/a00202523/14-16-qualifications-2014-performance-tables (accessed 6 December 2013).

DfE (Department for Education) (2012b) *Study Programmes for 16- to 19-Year-Olds*. Crown Copyright. http://webarchive.nationalarchives.gov.uk/20130401151715/https://www.education.gov.uk/publications/eOrderingDownload/government%20response%20to%20consultation%20on%20study%20programmes%2016-19.pdf.

DfE (Department for Education) (2013a) *School Direct: The New Way into Teaching*. www.education.gov.uk/get-into-teaching/teacher-training-options/school-based-training/school-direct.aspx?sc_lang=en-GB (accessed 6 December 2013).

DfE (Department for Education) (2013b) *School Direct*. www.education.gov.uk/schools/careers/traininganddevelopment/initial/b00205704/school-direct (accessed 6 December 2013).

DfE (Department for Education) (2013c) *Teachers from the European Economic Community*. www.education.gov.uk/schools/careers/careeropportunities/overseas-trainedteachers/a00199246/teachers-from-the-european-economic-area-eea (accessed 6 December 2013).

DfE (Department for Education) (2013d) *What Are University Technical Colleges (UTCs)?* www.education.gov.uk/schools/leadership/typesofschools/technical/a00198954/utcs (accessed 6 December 2013).

DfE (Department for Education) (2013e) *What Are Studio Schools?* www.education.gov.uk/schools/leadership/typesofschools/technical/a0077819/about (accessed 6 December 2013).

DfE (Department for Education) (2013f) *Major Reform Will Help Hundreds of Thousands of Young People Get Good Jobs*. Press release 3 September. www.gov.uk/government/news/major-reform-will-help-hundreds-of-thousands-of-young-people-get-good-jobs (accessed 6 December 2013).

DfE (Department for Education) (2013g) *Information about the New 14–16 Provision*. www.education.gov.uk/schools/teachingandlearning/qualifications/a00218341/wolf-review-recommendation-19 (accessed 6 December 2013).

DfES (Department for Education and Skills) (2003) *The Future of Higher Education* (Cm5735). London: Department for Education and Skills.

DfES (Department for Education and Skills) (2004) *Equipping Our Teachers for the Future: Reforming Initial Teacher Training for the Learning and Skills Sector*. Crown Copyright. www.bis.gov.uk/assets/biscore/corporate/migratedD/publications/E/equippingourteachersforthefuture-115-61 (accessed 14 April 2014).

DfES (Department for Education and Skills) (2005) *14–19 Education and Skills White Paper*. Norwich: Stationery Office.

DfES (Department for Education and Skills) (2006) *Further Education: Raising Skills, Improving Life Chances*. Norwich: Stationery Office.

DIUS (Department of Innovation, Universities and Skills) (2007) *The Further Education Teachers' (England) Regulations*. http://dera.ioe.ac.uk/6717/1/guide2007no2264.pdf (accessed 6 December 2013).

ETF (Education and Training Foundation) (2013) *Welcome to the Education and Training Foundation*. www.et-foundation.co.uk/ (accessed 6 December 2013).

Evans, L. (2010) 'Professionalism, professionality and the development of education professionals', *British Journal of Educational Studies*, 56 (1): 20–38.

Evetts, J. (2012) 'Professionalism in turbulent times: changes, challenges and opportunities', paper presented at the Propel International Conference, 9–11 May, Stirling.

Fielding, M. and Ruddock, J. (2002) 'The transformative potential of student voice: confronting the power issues', paper presented at the Annual Conference of the British Educational Research Association, University of Exeter, England, 12–14 September. www.learningtolearn.sa.edu.au/tfel/files/links/The_Transformative_Potent_1.pdf (accessed 10 December 2013).

Fuller, A. and Unwin, L. (2003) 'Creating a "modern apprenticeship": a critique of the UK's multi-sector, social inclusion approach', *Journal of Education and Work*, 16 (a): 5–25.

Gleeson, D. and James, D. (2007) 'The paradox of professionalism in English further education: a TLC project perspective', *Educational Review*, 59 (4): 451–467.

Gove, M. (2010) Speech to the National College Annual Conference, June 16, Birmingham.

Guardian (2013) 'Number of students starting university back to levels before tuition fees raised'. www.theguardian.com/education/2013/sep/24/uk-student-numbers-recover-tuition-fees (accessed 14 December 2013).

HEA (Higher Education Academy) (2012) *UK Professional Framework*. www.heacademy.ac.uk/ukpsf (accessed 6 December 2013).

Hillier, Y. and Morris, A. (2010) 'Critical practitioners, developing researchers: the story of practitioner research in the learning and skills sector', *Journal of Vocational Education and Training*, 62 (1): 89–101

HOLEX/LSIS (2013) *Adult and Community Learning Workforce Survey, 2011/12*. www.lsis.org.uk/sites/www.lsis.org.uk/files/Adultper cent20andper cent-20communityper cent20learningper cent20workforceper cent20surveyper cent202011-12.pdf (accessed 6 December 2013).

Hoyle, E. and John, P. (1995) *Professional Knowledge and Professional Practice*. London: Cassell.

IfL (Institute for Learning) (2008) *Code of Professional Practice*. www.ifl.ac.uk/membership/professional-standards/code-of-professional-practice (accessed 6 December 2013).

IfL (Institute for Learning) (2013) *IfL Strategy Update*. London: IfL.

IoD (Institute of Directors) (2004) *Developing Skills, Delivering Success? An Assessment of the Learning and Skills Council*. www.iod.com/influencing/policy-papers/education-and-skills/developing-skills-delivering-success-an-assessment-of-the-learning-and-skills-council (accessed 6 December 2013).

Jameson, J. and Hillier, Y. (2008) '"Nothing will prevent me from doing a good job": the professionalisation of part-time teaching staff in further and adult education', *Research in Post-Compulsory Education*, 13 (1): 39–53.

Leitch, S. (2006) *Prosperity for All in the Global Economy: World Class Skills, the Final Report* (Leitch Review of Skills). London: Stationery Office.

LLUK (Lifelong Learning UK) (2007) *New Overarching Professional Standards for Teachers, Tutors and Trainers in the Lifelong Learning Sector*. London: LLUK.

LLUK (Lifelong Learning UK) (2011) *Further Education College Workforce Data for England: An Analysis of the Staff Individualised Record Data, 2003/2004–2009/2010*. http://dera.ioe.ac.uk/2979/1/SIR_Report_200910_FINAL.pdf (accessed 6 December 2013).

LSIS (Learning and Skills Improvement Service) (2013) *Further Education and Skills in England. 2013 Qualifications for Teachers and Trainers. Guidance-for-Employers-and-Practitioners*. http://webarchive.nationalarchives.gov.uk/20130802100617/http:/lsis.org.uk/sites/www.lsis.org.uk/files/Guidance-for-Employers-and-Practitioners-2013-April.pdf (accessed 6 December 2013).

Lucas, N. and Nasta, T. (2010) 'State regulation and the professionalisation of further education teachers: a comparison with schools and HE', *Journal of Vocational Education and Training*, 62 (4): 441–454.

Martinez, P. and Munday, F. (1998) *9,000 Voices: Student Persistence and Drop-out in Further Education*. London: FEDA.

McCarroll, N. and Curran, K. (2013) 'Social networking in education', *International Journal of Innovation in the Digital Economy*, 4 (1): 1–15.

Melville, D. (2005) 'Did A-level reforms fall victim to election fever?', *Times Educational Supplement*, 25 February.

National Centre for the Excellence in Teaching Mathematics (2013) www.ncetm.org.uk/NCETM (accessed 14 December 2013).

National College for Teaching and Leadership (2013) www.education.gov.uk/aboutdfe/executiveagencies/a00223538/nat-college-teach-leader (accessed 6 December 2013).

Noble-Rogers, J. (2013) 'School Direct puts university teacher training routes under increasing pressure', SecEd. www.sec-ed.co.uk/blog/school-direct-puts-university-teacher-training-routes-under-increasing-pressure (accessed 6 December 2013).

OECD (2011) *Building a High Quality Teaching Profession: Lessons from Around the World*. Paris: OECD Publishing.

Orr, K. and Simmons, R. (2010) 'Dual identities: the in-service teacher trainee experience in the English further education sector', *Journal of Vocational Education and Training*, 62 (1): 75–88.

People Management (February 2010) CIPD *HR Profession Map*. www.people-management.co.uk (accessed 14 December 2013).

Robson, J., Bailey, B. and Larkin, S. (2004) 'Adding value: investigating the discourse of professionalism adopted by vocational teachers in further education colleges', *Journal of Education and Work*, 17 (2): 183–195.

Rudd, T., Colligan, F. and Naik, R. (2006) *Learner Voice*. Bristol: Futurelab.

Simmons, R. (2012) 'Raising the participation age to 18: 100 years on', *Post-16 Educator* (68).

TES (2010) 'Diploma rule lifted', *TES*, 25 June.

TES (2011) '"Nobody really wanted it": the Diploma meets its doom', *TES*, 13 November.

Tomlinson, M. (2004) *14–19 Curriculum and Qualifications Reform: Final Report of the Working Group on 14–19 Reform*. London: DfEs Publications. Crown Copyright.

Vickers, P. and Bekhradnia, B. (2007) *Vocational A levels and University Entry: Is there Parity of Esteem?* Oxford: Higher Education Policy Institute. www.hepi.ac.uk/files/29VocationalAlevelsandparityofesteem-full.pdf (accessed 6 December 2013).

Wahlberg, M. and Gleeson, D. (2003) '"Doing the business": paradox and irony in vocational education – GNVQ business studies as a case in point', *Journal of Vocational Education and Training*, 55 (4): 423–446.

Wallace, S. (2013) *Understanding the Further Education Sector: A Critical Guide to Policies and Practices*. Northwich: Critical Publishing.

Wilson, A. and Wilson, B. (2011) 'Pedagogy of the repressed: research and professionality within HE in FE', *Research in Post-Compulsory Education*, 16 (4): 465–478.

Wolf, A. (2011) *Review of Vocational Education: The Wolf Report*. London: DfE, Crown Copyright.

Woodin, T., McCulloch, G. and Cowan, S. (2013) 'Raising the participation age in historical perspective: policy learning from the past?', *British Educational Research Journal*, 39 (4): 635–653.

Further reading

Avis, J., Fisher, R. and Ollin, R. (2009) 'Professionalism', in J. Avis, R. Fisher and R. Thompson (eds), *Teaching in Lifelong Learning: A Guide to Theory and Practice* (2nd edn). Maidenhead: Open University Press, pp. 40–47.

Bolton, G. (2010) *Reflective Practice: Writing and Professional Development* (3rd edn). London: Sage.

Bossche, P. V. D., Dochy, F., Gijbels, D. and Segers, M. (2012) *Psychological Theories of Learning in the Workplace*. Maidenhead: Routledge.

Bradbury, H. (2010) *Beyond Reflective Practice: New Approaches to Professional Lifelong Learning*. London: Routledge.

Cole, D. (2008) 'Deleuze and the narrative forms of educational otherness', in I. Semetsky (ed.), *Nomadic Education: Variations on a Theme by Deleuze and Guattari*. Rotterdam: Sense Publishers, pp. 17–34.

Couros, A. (2009) 'Open, connected, social: implications for educational design', *Campus-Wide Information Systems*, 26 (3): 232–239.

Cunliffe, A. (2004) 'On becoming a critically reflexive practitioner', *Journal of Management Education*, 28 (4): 407–426.

Department for Business, Innovation and Skills (2012b) *Professionalism in Further Education: Final Report of the Independent Review Panel*. www.gov.uk/government/publications/professionalism-in-further-education-final-report-of-the-independent-review-panel (accessed 23 August 2013).

Emejulu, A. (2008) *Reclaiming Social Purpose in Community Education*. http://criticalychatting.files.wordpress.com/2008/11/theedinburghpapers-pdf.pdf (accessed 10 November 2013).

Fisher, R., Fulford, A., McNicholas, B. and Thompson, R. (2009) 'The curriculum in the lifelong learning sector', in J. Avis, R. Fisher and R. Thompson (eds), *Teaching in Lifelong Learning*. Maidenhead: McGraw-Hill, pp. 103–117.

Gagné, R. M., Wager, W. W., Golas, K. G. and Keller, J. M. (2005) *Principles of Instructional Design*. Toronto, ON: Thomson Wadsworth.

Gibbs, G. (1995) *Assessing Group Work*. Oxford: Oxford Centre for Staff Development.

Gronlund, N. E. and Brookhart, S. M. (2009) *Writing Instructional Objectives* (8th edn). Upper Saddle River, NJ: Pearson Education, Inc.

Harrow, A. J. (1972) *A Taxonomy of the Psychomotor Domain: A Guide for Developing Behavioural Objectives*. New York: David McKay.

Hillier, Y. (2012) *Reflective Teaching in Further and Adult Education* (3rd edn). London: Continuum.

Hobley, J. (2008) 'Responsive reflection', in F. Fawbert (ed.), *Teaching in Post-Compulsory Education: Skills, Standards and Learning and Skills* (2nd edn). London: Continuum, pp. 21–35.

Krathwohl, D. R. (2002) 'A revision of Bloom's Taxonomy: an overview', *Theory into Practice*, 41 (4): 212–218.

Lave, J. and Wenger, E. (1991) *Situated Learning: Legitimate Peripheral Participation*. Cambridge: Cambridge University Press.

Lawrence-Wilkes, L. and Ashmore, L. (2014) *The Reflective Practitioner in Professional Education*. London: Palgrave Macmillan.

McGregor, D. and Cartwright, L. (2011) *Developing Reflective Practice: A Guide for Beginning Teachers*. Maidenhead: McGraw-Hill Education.

Pollner, M. (1991) 'Left of ethnomethodology: the rise and decline of radical reflexivity', *American Sociological Review*, 56: 370–380.

Ranson, S. (2003) 'Public accountability in the age of neo-liberal governance', *Journal of Education Policy*, 18 (5): 459–480.

Roberts, J. (2006) 'Limits to communities of practice', *Journal of Management Studies*, 43 (May): 3.

Robinson, K. and Aronica, L. (2013) *Finding Your Element: How to Discover Your Talents and Passions and Transform Your Life*. London: Allen Lane.

Rushton, I. and Suter, M. (2012) *Reflective Practice for Teaching in Lifelong Learning*. Maidenhead: Open University Press/McGraw-Hill Education.

Simmons, R. (2008) 'Raising the age of compulsory education in England: A NEET solution?', *British Journal of Educational Studies*, 56 (4): 420–439.

Stufflebeam, D. L. and Shinkfield, A. (2007) *Evaluation Theory, Models, and Applications*. San Francisco, CA: Jossey-Bass.

Williams, B. (2001) *Truth and Truthfulness*. Princeton: Princeton University Press.

Wormeli, R. (2001) *Meet Me in the Middle: Becoming an Accomplished Middle Level Teacher*. Portland, ME: Stenhouse.

Zwozdiak-Myers, P. (2012) *The Teacher's Reflective Practice Handbook*. Abingdon: Routledge.

INDEX